WRITING IN THE CONTEMPORARY WORLD

s Editor: Sander L. Gilman, University of Illinois

Contemporary
Jewish Writing
in Switzerland

An Anthology

Edited by Rafaël Newman

University of Nebraska Press : Lincoln & London

Acknowledgments for the use of copy-
righted material appear on pp. 263–64,
which constitute an extension of the
copyright page. Publication of this volume was assisted by a grant from Pro
Helvetia, the Arts Council of Switzerland, and the National Endowment for
the Arts. �*/
© 2002 by the University of Nebraska
Press. All rights reserved. ⊗ Manufac-
tured in the United States of America

Library of Congress Cataloging-in-Publication Data
Contemporary Jewish writing in Switzerland:
an anthology / edited by Rafaël Newman.
p. cm. – (Jewish writing in the contemporary world)
Includes bibliographical references.
ISBN 0-8032-3342-6 (cloth: alkaline paper)
1. Swiss literature – Jewish authors – Translations into
English. 2. Swiss literature – 20th century –
Translations into English. 3. Jews – Switzerland –
Literary collections. I. Newman, Rafaël Francis David
Amadeus, 1964– II. Series.
PT3876.J48 C66 2002   830.8'089240494–dc21
2002018115

For Caroline, Hella, and Mahalia:
My Swiss-Jewish Family

Contents

Preface

My fond thanks go to all of the authors collected here, whose readiness to contribute and whose attentive and thoughtful collaboration were the *sine qua non* for this book and for my pleasure in preparing it. To Sander Gilman, for his confidence and enthusiasm on both sides of the Atlantic, I owe a particularly pleasant debt of gratitude. I am also grateful to the staff of the UNP for their friendly and reliable assistance. The following people provided me with advice, information, and invaluable support, both material and intellectual, in the course of my research (the alphabetical list also includes those who read and commented upon the translations and my introductory essay, and thus improved them): the UNP's two anonymous reviewers; Barbara Basting; Fred Bild; Elio Bollag; François Bondy; Lil Bondy; Georg Brunold; Iso Camartin; Mario Camelo; Jacqueline Clément-Tanner; Bella Cohen; Stanley Corngold; Arthur Denner; Yvonne Domhardt; Philipp Dreyer; Birgit Erdle; Sigmund Feigel; Roger Francillon; Thomas Fries; Thérèse Galperin; Daniel Ganzfried; Uriel Gast; Heiko Haumann; Julia Hell; Tanja Hetzer; Peter Hughes; Batya Kaplan; Zalman Kossowsky; Tim Krohn; Aline Kundig; Benjamin Dove Landau; Eva Lezzi; Hugo Loetscher; Gabriele Markus; Shoshana Merkle; Beatrice Michel; Lize Mifflin; Franziska Selma Muheim; Melinda Nadj Abonji; Peter Neumann; Jerry Newman; Jacques Picard; Bojana Ristich; Gabi Rosenstein; Anne Rothschild; Romey Sabalius; Alex Schlesinger; Peter A. Schmid; Philippe Schwed; Andreas Simmen; Bettina Spoerri; Marianne Weinberg; Marianne Weissberg; Stina Werenfels; Maja Wicki; Carol Wiedmer-Homan; Daniel Wildmann; Nina Zafran; Daniel Zahno; and Kathy Zarnegin. An award from the UBS Cultural Foundation and a grant from Pro Helvetia, the Arts Council of Switzerland, brought much-needed assistance at crucial points in the work.

As ever and above all, I am grateful to Caroline Wiedmer, of the courageous head and capital heart. Her will and wisdom are indispensable to my every venture.

Introduction

The modern Jewish affinity for the Swiss view of the world has been noted in various contexts. Switzerland, and in particular its army, served as one of the models for the Jewish state that arose out of the Holocaust: a model for an opting-out, defensive but prickly state—what the Swiss themselves often refer to as their 'hedgehog' attitude.[1] The roots of this connection are various. Pierre Heumann, in *Israel entstand in Basel* (Israel was born in Basel), reminds us that Theodor Herzl, who held his first International Zionist Congress in Basel in 1897, had favored a generally Germanic system of orderly bureaucracy for his fledgling national project;[2] and John McPhee, in *La Place de la Concorde Suisse*, has detailed how the Israelis sent agents to Switzerland in the early days to learn how the citizen militia functioned and to fashion the Israeli army on those homely precepts.[3] There is thus a significant and already venerable history of modern Jewish sensitivity to Switzerland as the very type of the small, modern, democratic state with its roots in an ancient and independent history.

That the affinity should operate the other way, too—that non-Jewish Swiss should feel themselves drawn to the Jewish culture and to an identification with things Jewish—has seemed less obvious. Serguei Hazanov, a Russian Jew who now lives and writes in Geneva, makes of this apparently unrequited regard a piece of high comedy:

Well then, are Schwyzerdütsch and Yiddish cognate tongues? That is the question. It's nothing but a linguistic hypothesis, a parlor game, but imagine that it's true, and that the German Swiss turn out to be a lost Jewish tribe! Do you think they would immediately rush off to Israel to fight against Yasser Arafat? I rather fear the opposite: the noble descendants of Abraham, Isaac, and Jacob would invade the hills and dales of the land of William Tell.[4]

That is, even if the German-speaking Swiss did turn out secretly to be members of the Jewish family, this would hardly be enough to tempt them to exchange the security of their peaceful, prosperous homeland for the violence and instability of Israel. Nor, by extension, could it persuade them to trade their internationally respected image as neutral brokers of peace and prosperity for an association with the fractious, controversial, and often highly partisan 'Chosen People' of myth and history.

Or could it? With the publication of his *Bruchstücke: Aus einer Kindheit 1939–1948* in 1995, the Zurich-based Swiss clarinetist Binjamin Wilkomirski won international renown and praise for his spare and brutal account of survival as a Jewish child in the Nazi death camps, an autobiographical accomplishment likened in its stark grandeur to the works of such survivors as Primo Levi and Ruth Klüger.[5] Wilkomirski's rendering of the dreary life of a changeling in bourgeois postwar Switzerland, meanwhile, and his suggestion that Swiss immigration authorities had conspired with local cantonal officials to obscure his past as a Jewish orphan and camp inmate, gave Switzerland its own version of *Vaterliteratur*, that genre of writing in which, during the 1970s and 1980s, postwar Germany had reckoned with the role its parents and grandparents had played in the Holocaust. *Bruchstücke* (Fragments) represented an implicit unveiling of the symbols of the Nazi death camps in the idealized Swiss landscape and of a coldness and a will to repression, discovered in the attitudes of Swiss foster-parents and teachers, that were in many ways equivalent to those of postwar Germany. That the whole was framed in Wilkomirski's book by the account of a discovery of a Jewish otherness under the surface of wealthy uniformity (his foster family had resided in a well-to-do Zurich neighborhood) lent the work the force of an intervention into the drab face of Swiss normality. *Bruchstücke* shattered the ostensibly placid milieu of homogeneous Switzerland and was said by some to reveal there not only an unsuspected difference, but also the vile and intolerant efforts of the Swiss elite to repress that difference and, indeed, to repress even the traces of this repression.[6] As the Swiss political agenda was taken over, in the late 1990s, by the World Jewish Congress (WJC) campaign to reclaim funds deposited in Swiss banks by Jewish Holocaust victims, as well as by the attempts

of would-be Jewish refugees turned away at the Swiss border to
sue Switzerland for damages, Wilkomirski hovered over the proceedings like an ambiguous ghost, the sign both of Switzerland's
past rejection of otherness and of its potential for integration and
acceptance.[7]

The revelations that followed at the end of the decade, however,
which should have laid this disturbing ghost to rest, seemed, on the
contrary, only to have given it fresh blood. In the late summer of
1998, the Swiss-Jewish writer Daniel Ganzfried published a series
of articles in the central-left Swiss weekly Die Weltwoche, in which he
made a case that Wilkomirski's 'history' as a Latvian-born Jewish
survivor and emigrant had been invented. Ganzfried claimed to
have seen files that proved that the author was in fact the illegiti-
mate son of a non-Jewish woman from the western part of Switzerland, one Berthe Grosjean, who had put him up for adoption in the
early 1940s, and that he had subsequently been taken in by the
Doessekker family of Zurich.[8] There followed a series of articles,
letters, and public exchanges in which the case was debated and
charges and countercharges were made, including (at either extreme) indictments of the Swiss Germanist academy for its role
in the promotion of the work as a worthy contribution to the genre
of Holocaust memoir and the suggestion that Ganzfried and those
who believed him were carrying on a campaign of character as-
sassination.[9]

The affair continued with DNA tests proposed and declined, legal
claims made, and suicide threats uttered and culminated in the
publication, in June 2000, of a historical report commissioned by
the literary agency that had represented Bruchstücke, in which 'Wilkomirski' was definitively found to be a fiction.[10] But as it became
more and more obvious to all parties that Doessekker was either a
deliberate con artist or a seriously disturbed person, but in any
event not a Jewish survivor of the Holocaust, the discussion about
his person and his writings continued to focus on the specific role
that the Holocaust had played in his identity construction, as well
as in its willing reception by the reading public. Surely, however, it
would have been equally important to set Bruchstücke against the
background of hoaxes practiced on the publics of other countries
by authors posing as members of minority groups other than Jew-

ish, cases that have been noted in academic discussions of ethnicity and literature and that would have broadened the field of discussion to include the various forms of ethnic stereotyping available to the Swiss audience.[11] Only Daniel Ganzfried, however, took up the case from that critical perspective by suggesting that Doessekker's performance as a Holocaust survivor was to be read as the strategic and calculated deployment of a whole host of ethnic clichés and para-anti-Semitic stereotypes. He pointed out that Doessekker had made use of such hackneyed gestures as inconsolable weeping, hand wringing, and fractured German in a bid to ingratiate himself with his larger society, one in which Jews were at best tolerated and at worst mistrusted. Ganzfried maintained that Doessekker could count as well for the positive reception of this performance on the European Jewish community, which had itself grown dependent upon such cartoon book images as part of a misguided public relations campaign.[12]

Ganzfried, whose own experience as the author of a fictionalized account of Holocaust survival had made him especially sensitive to the complex ramifications of memory and historical documentation, was thus alone in identifying Doessekker's ethnic role playing as one of the central problematics of the affair. But it was precisely this role playing that had taken the affair beyond the issue of borrowed history, or, indeed, of the commercializing of the 'Holocaust Industry,' and into the contested realm of what Homi K. Bhabha has called 'hybridity.' The term denotes the performance by immigrants (or their descendants) of their inherited ancient foreign cultural, religious, and ethnic traditions against the backdrop of contemporary sociopolitical conditions in their host country, so as to create something new, something perhaps ironic, something 'hybrid'—the invention, indeed, of a brand-new tradition.[13] For what Doessekker had done, after all, although himself neither a Jew, nor, indeed, an immigrant or the descendant of one, was to create a synthesis, however questionable in its authenticity and quality and however unintended as fiction, of Jewish and Swiss material. Doessekker had thereby created an elaborate figure of speech: he had masqueraded as a Jew—specifically, as the very type of the 'innocent' Jewish Holocaust sufferer, the child survivor—in order to embody something of his own that otherwise defeated his powers of representation. Doessekker's subject position is in this sense a nuanced reprise of the posture of the medieval minstrel Süsskind of Trimberg, a Frankish poet whose works were collected in Zurich.[14] Because Süsskind had, in one celebrated poem, used the readily apprehensible figure of the Jewish exile as a means of making vividly public his professional disenfranchisement, he stands, for good or ill, at the head of the Swiss-Jewish literary tradition, a tradition that was now faced by this new and peculiarly literary hybrid.

The problem that such a case poses for contemporary Swiss-Jewish writers is clear: if the stylized vocabulary of gestures, of cadences and turns of phrase, indeed, if the very history of 'the Jews' is available to anyone who chooses to adopt it in the course of creation and thus make of that performance a kind of literature, a kind of fiction, a Swiss-Jewish hybrid, then what can it be that sets 'authentic' Swiss-Jewish literature apart? What entitles descendants of Jews from the Argovian 'Jewish' villages, or from Alsace, or Budapest, or Warsaw, or Ljubljana to write as Swiss Jews in the very likely absence of actually practiced confessional identity? What entitles them, if not the spurious and suspect appeal to 'blood,' to 'race,' to genetics? How is one to insist upon one's own entitlement to the subject position taken up by 'Wilkomirski' without becoming merely strident, without losing the irony so crucial for fiction, for poetry, and for drama? And yet how could one leave unanswered this challenge to one's very identity in a country in which a law prohibiting Jewish ritual slaughter remains on the law books to this day?[15]

There is no one answer, of course, to these questions, which have been articulated more sharply than ever before by the case of Wilkomirski. Indeed, the texts by contemporary Swiss-Jewish writers assembled here all date, with two or three exceptions, from the period prior to the revelations about 'Wilkomirski.' And yet the questions are implicitly asked and answered, according to the specific subject position of each of the writers as they take up issues of Jewish or Swiss (or international) interest, as a Jew, as a Swiss, as a European—but also, as the case may be, as a woman, as a left winger, as the descendant of Holocaust survivors or refugees to Switzerland, as a Zionist, as a critic of Israel, as a visitor to America, as an expatriate Swiss, as a Jew who lives among non-Jews, as a 'half Jew.'[16] The topics broached by these texts are, then, as varied as are their authors, but there are some common themes to be discerned nonetheless: Switzerland as a kind of utopia, for instance, as in the extract from Jean-Luc Benoziglio's meditation on Swiss-French relations after Vichy; Luc Bondy's recollection of his childhood with refugee grandparents in Zurich; Rose Choron's lyrical evocation of her posh—and very sheltered—Swiss youth; Sergueï Hazanov's discovery of the Land of Milk and Honey among the Alps, and not by the Sea of Galilee; or Yvonne Léger's memory of a successful flight across the Swiss border in wartime. But Switzerland is equally available to the literary imagination as a dystopia: in Roman Buxbaum's nightmares of a Helvetian concentration camp (the very spareness of whose evocation acts as a corrective for the pathos of Doessekker's similar accounts); in Sergueï Hazanov's lurid, Walker Percyesque scenes of sectarian fragmentation and syncretism; in Shelley Kästner's collage of actual Swiss letters to the editor from the period of the WJC campaign, growing in a crescendo of anti-Semitic rage; in Charles Lewinsky's uncannily authentic alternative history of a Switzerland under Nazi occupation; in Regine Mehmann Schafer's queasy reversal of the polarities of *kashrut*, or Jewish dietary law, to explain the hostility of some members of the Swiss petty bourgeoisie to their Jewish in-laws; in Marianne Weissberg's vision of a Swiss metropolis, readily recognizable as Zurich, in the hands of conservative fundamentalists, parochial hypocrites, and fascist misogynists; and in Stina Werenfels's bitter chocolate—box Switzerland, in which polite German tourists praise Israel while Swiss physicians comment crudely on their Jewish patients.

The gaze of these particular Swiss writers is, as often as not, turned outward, as is that of so many of their colleagues generally in such a small yet internationally central country. There are encounters with Israel, both ancient Biblical and recent Zionist, as in the Jerusalem evoked in Gabriele Markus's poems, or the dangerous road between Jerusalem and Tel Aviv in Marta Rubinstein's 'The Schneyder,' a fable of *aliyah*, or Zionist 'return' to Israel. There is Ganzfried's New York, cast as the staging ground for a meeting between Swiss-Jewish father and son, as well as the site of the

various confused radicalisms that grew out of the advent of the
'New World Order' in the early 1990s. There is Paris, the scene of
Sylviane Roche's reckoning with the history of progressive politics
in the twentieth century as it unfolded there but also, crucially, in
Prague, in Budapest, and in Moscow; and there is Sarajevo, the
constant doppelganger for Miriam Cahn's uneasily privileged life in
the Basel Bohème.

There are also the signal places of the Holocaust—the Auschwitz-
Buna and Bergen-Belsen of Ganzfried's novel, the Majdanek and
Birkenau of Buxbaum's dreams, the Buchenwald of Roche's mem-
oirist hero—as well as the birthplaces, and graveyards, of East
European Jewry—Markus's Czernowitz, Roche's Ruda Pabianicka,
Ganzfried's Nyír.[17] And everywhere, in places named and nameless,
there are the intersections of Jews and non-Jews in the Diaspora:
erotically charged, as in Amsel's 'In the Tower'; cramped and stiff,
as in Guggenheimer's 'Adler'; or fraught with unresolved tensions
arising from a shared, adversarial past, as in Werenfels's Pastry, Pain
&. Politics, Weissberg's Manhunt, or Mehmann Schafer's 'Trayf and
Kosher.'

What is it about any of these texts, however, beyond the Jewish
origins and Swiss passports of their authors, that makes them
'Swiss-Jewish'? It cannot be simply their subject matter, for Switzerland, or at least a town possibly identifiable as Zurich, appears,
for instance, in the writings of Gottfried Keller as a utopia, or at
least as a paradise of holy fools; and, as symbolized by the Güllen of
Friedrich Dürrenmatt's 'The Visit,' Switzerland figures, famously,
as a dystopia—and neither of these authors was Jewish. The world
beyond Switzerland has been a constant theme for Swiss writers of
various backgrounds and degrees of affinity to the national project,
from Madame de Staël to Max Frisch, and the period of the Holocaust is being increasingly treated by non-Jewish Swiss writers, as
in Daniel Zahno's powerful account of Sinti and Roma persecution,
'Mein Herr,' or Yvette Z'Graggen's Les Années silencieuses, an early
account of the attempt to come to terms with Swiss involvement.[18]

Is there, perhaps, some formal characteristic that might help to
identify the texts collected here as Swiss-Jewish? Their very generic
multiplicity, however—novel, memoir, short story, poem, and performance piece—defies this attempt at classification. Or might one

discern a tissue of intertextual allusions, of anxieties of influence even, to connect the present generation of Swiss-Jewish writers to the past? Their role models, however, come more often than not from beyond the Swiss borders. Benoziglio, for instance, claims to have been more influenced by the French-Jewish postmodernist Georges Perec than by Albert Cohen, although, like Cohen, Benoziglio's family origins are partly in the eastern Mediterranean. Markus, meanwhile, a singer of classic German art songs, pays tribute in her poems and short prose pieces to the poets Paul Celan and Rose Ausländer, both of the vanished region of Galicia, as well as to the Belgian surrealist painter René Magritte, rather than to Margarete Susman, her predecessor in the Swiss-German-Jewish lyrical mode.[19] Hazanov, who admits to having been influenced by the Bible and Sholom Aleichem, among others, clearly borrows his form, as well as his title, from the French classicist de Montesquieu's *Lettres persanes*, although André Kaminski's *Nächstes Jahr in Jerusalem* is itself part epistolary, as well as being similarly concerned with Slavo-Swiss relations. And Werenfels, who studied in New York, owes her feisty Fritz Weintraub in equal measure to Neil Simon and Woody Allen, rather than to the inventions of her countryman Kaminski, or indeed to those of Kurt Guggenheim, both of whom had a way with a *shlemiel*.[20] Of the writers assembled here, few express open indebtedness to Swiss literature at all, and then, as often as not, it is to non-Jewish writers that they refer; Ganzfried, for example, has often invoked the name of Dürrenmatt, while Roche counsels the reading of Yvette Z'Graggen, among other writers of the Romandie.[21]

One further theoretical model, in addition to the notion of hybridity, that might elucidate the character of Swiss-Jewish literature within the larger cultural context of Switzerland is the concept of a 'minor literature,' as proposed by Gilles Deleuze and Félix Guattari in their celebrated study of Kafka. In a 1993 essay on postwar developments in Germany, Jack Zipes updated the model by using it to explain the uncanny power of Jewish culture in the land of the Holocaust.[22] Within the special context of Germany, Deleuze and Guattari's formulation of a 'minor literature' makes sense, at least as it applies to such a literature's reception by the majority culture: minor literature is said by them to 'unmake' or 'deterritorialize' the language of the majority, to connect the individual 'minority' writer to a 'political immediacy' that gives rise to an implicit 'common action,' and to assemble the writers—and writings—thus connected into a 'collective assemblage of enunciation.'[23] In Zipes's terms, Jewish 'minor literature' in German presents a specific threat to German culture, but a threat that is also the promise of 'enrichment, transformation, and creation,' for the very questioning of hierarchies, power structures, and national history performed by this particular minor literature also means that the 'utopian component of culture in general' is preserved and thus, presumably, renewed.[24]

While it would be tempting to take over Zipes's formulation wholesale from the German into the Swiss context, there are some obvious historical and social differences between the two majority cultures that make it necessary to reformulate the concept for use within the Swiss context. For whereas Germany, despite its extremely fragmented and differentiated national history, presents itself to this very day as a cultural and linguistic unity, a Kulturnation, or ethnic nation-state,[25] Switzerland is by definition a sort of 'multicultural' society, a Willensnation, or state-by-treaty, made up of at least four distinct linguistic groups, within which there can be discerned further regional and dialectal divisions, not to mention sectarian differences. Switzerland is, therefore, in at least one of its political formulations, a nation of minorities in which a 'minor literature' would have trouble profiling itself against a virtually nonexistent major.[26]

Furthermore, while the Holocaust, 'that other historical demarcation [after the Middle Ages],'[27] reinforced the medieval social marginalization of the Jews in Germany in a drastic and virulent fashion, there has been no comparably radical 'caesura' in Swiss-Jewish history, for all that Switzerland's economic and even ideological complicity with the Third Reich has in recent times been stylized into a symbolic collaboration.[28] Such a break might have stimulated anew the special minor-literary situation Zipes glosses thus: 'Whereas major literature can assume social understanding and acceptance by the majority of people in a particular nation, the minor literature cannot connect automatically to the social milieu and takes flight, raising questions that call for links to commerce, economics, bureaucracy, and the law.'[29] But Switzerland's Jews, despite facing at the time certain undeniable legal hardships, such as restrictions on their freedom of expression or the imposed financial responsibility for those Jewish refugees who had been let into the country, were notably 'spared' the horror of the Holocaust, that ostensibly final project of rupturing the already tenuous connection of European Jewry to its wider social, and existential, milieu.

Finally, the very concept of 'culture,' on which Deleuze and Guattari's arguments rest, has begun to be reconsidered, a retooling due in part to the current discourse on multiculturalism. In a 1997 essay, K. Anthony Appiah, for instance, cast doubt on the use of the word 'culture' in discussions of the functioning of what he calls, citing Michael Walzer, 'regimes of toleration.'[30] Even in the United States, Appiah argues, where 'diversity' has become a rallying cry across the political spectrum and arguments are made on the basis of everything from African American to deaf 'culture,' what is really at stake might be better termed 'social identity,' since on the whole American society today is no longer divided and distinguished by anything holistically alien to it, such as the ways of Senegambian rice farmers or Italian peasants were during the country's founding centuries.[31] The same might be said of modern-day Switzerland, although it is, to employ Walzer's terms, a 'consociational' and not an 'immigrant' society. And yet Switzerland has, by means of prosperity and technical advancement, produced, at least in its native-born and longer-resident immigrants, a level of integration that makes possible a similar politics of identity against the security of a reasonably homogeneous consumer culture.[32]

Swiss-Jewish writers, then, are modern individualists within a de facto 'multicultural' society of minorities who resist organization into a cultural assemblage from within which collective statements of creed or purpose might issue and who are connected neither by place of origin (they come, after all, from such disparate places as the Argovian 'Jewish' villages, Alsace, and the classic East European *shtetl*) nor by common literary heritage. The Jewish writers of Switzerland collected here are united perhaps solely by their common will to make a cause or a topic of what, despite great recent exposure in the media, continues to be *kein Thema*—'not an issue'—in Switzerland: the fact of Jewish life, in all its venerability and all its banality. This is so even, or perhaps especially, among young and 'enlightened' non-Jewish Swiss, who may hope to demonstrate, by means of their blasé indifference to a formerly taboo topic, just how far they have progressed, but who instead often give the impression of merely avoiding a difficult encounter.[33]

In this insistence on facing the difficult and the taboo, Swiss-Jewish writers manifest their one correspondence to the model of the 'minor literature' as sketched above: their attachment to political and legal structures and to the force and presence of history within and throughout their narratives. This is not so much because, as Deleuze and Guattari suggest of Kafka and Zipes of Jews in Germany, Swiss Jews cannot rely upon the understanding and acceptance of the majority and so seek refuge in a positivist legalism. Rather, it is because they have determined, individually, that their Jewish heritage requires an actual, positive, modern performance, one set against the backdrop of their various present-day Swiss realities, if it is to be relegated neither to the exclusive mysteries of cult nor to the consensual precincts of the courtroom and the bargaining table. Thus the authors that I have collected here actually toe a fine line between the two models I have proposed: between a readiness for assimilation and integration, as enacted in a positive, synthesizing hybridity, or the creation of a recognizably Swiss Jewishness, and a will to differentiation and exclusion, as made possible by the crafting of a hermetically separate 'minor literature,' which is content—or perhaps condemned—to speak only to its immediate cultural community.

That there is in fact a tradition of just such a posture between the worlds and between the possible models for a Jewish role in Swiss society—the assimilationist and the separatist—will become clear with a look at the historical background of the present-day Swiss realities to which the literature of Jews living in Switzerland today reacts and with which it interacts. A survey of the literary productions of Swiss-Jewish writers of the post-emancipation period and until the later decades of the twentieth century will suggest the extent to which today's Jewish writers in Switzerland are heirs to the stance of earlier generations, as well as the way in which this posture reflects the Swiss cultural attitude on the international scene.

Jews in Switzerland: A Short History

The 'problem' posed to the nascent state of Germany during the eighteenth and nineteenth centuries by the existence of 'the Jews' within its variously shifting borders was one of existential definition. The discourse surrounding the definition of the Jewish folk, or culture, or nation, which preoccupied by turns such different thinkers as Moses Mendelssohn and Heinrich Heine (among many others), was one that could hardly be indifferent to non-Jewish Germans in the process of organizing their own version of a nation throughout the period of the Enlightenment, the Napoleonic Wars, and down to the founding of the second German Reich in the 1870s.[34] And the very disarray in which the German states and principalities found themselves on and off during this period had surely, if paradoxically, helped to foster such a discourse, both in keeping the question of national statehood alive and open and in allowing Jews settled in one region of the German world to observe the circumstances of their fellows in another and so to continue debating the existence of both Jewish and German nationhood in a forceful and prominent fashion.[35]

The 'Jewish Question' that arose from these inquiries was, of course, to be 'answered' during the twentieth century in the most radical fashion, with the Nazis' implementation of the 'Final Solution,' that system of camps of deportation, concentration, and extermination that has come to be known as the Holocaust and that was meant to silence once and for all the challenge to the integrity of the German nation represented by Jews, and other alleged outsiders, within the Third Reich's expanding frontiers. And yet today once again, more than half a century after the Holocaust, the question of Jewishness—and therefore of Germanness—is being considered in Germany in a host of publications, both literary and academic, as well as in cultural venues and events of the most varied sort.[36]

Switzerland, for its part, has not until very recent times had to pose itself much of a 'Jewish Question' at all; if not quite because, as Joyce's anti-Semitic Mr. Deasy says of Ireland, it never persecuted the Jews for the simple reason that it never admitted them in the first place,[37] then at least because Switzerland was, for a period of three centuries—a period that included both the crucial age of intel-

lectual and political development that was the European Enlightenment and the revival of Jewish intellectual life in Europe known as
the Haskalah—simply without Jews altogether and was therefore not
obliged to face the 'Question' that 'the Jews' were elsewhere alleged
to pose. For Switzerland had expelled its Jewish inhabitants from
its territories, except in the most circumscribed possible areas, the
Argovian villages of Oberendingen and Lengnau in the outlying
Protectorate of Baden, by the end of the sixteenth century. Jews were
burned in various places in Switzerland during the plague epidemic
of the mid-fourteenth century and were only gradually, and grudg-
ingly, to be accorded the right of residence, the free exercise of
trades, and the practice of religion in the late nineteenth century.[38]
This process was not to be completed until the 1860s and 1870s,
and then only under pressure from foreign powers, among them
France, which had begun the process in 1798 with its establishment
of a centralist Swiss Republic on the model of the French and its
forced extension of equal rights to French citizens of Jewish extraction resident in Swiss territory. There were, however, to be decades
of backlash and retrenchment, both political and popular, particularly in the traditionally reactionary cantons, before the Federal
Constitution was finally revised, in 1866 and 1874, to guarantee,
respectively, freedom of residence and profession and of religion.[39]
    The relatively stable political nature of Switzerland's cantonal
confederacy, compared to the German situation, made challenges
to its integrity less threatening during this period, despite the fact
that the composite linguistic and confessional character Switzerland was to take on during the middle decades of the nineteenth
century might just as easily have rendered it less secure. In fact, as
the influential German-born Swiss-Jewish philosopher and critic
Hermann Levin Goldschmidt was to formulate it in the 1950s in a
plea for a better and more coherent Jewish cultural presence in
Switzerland, it is precisely the heavily segmented regional and linguistic character of the Swiss polity that has prevented Swiss Jews
from achieving solidarity.[40]
    In any case, although the Switzerland created in 1848 and beyond
was a Willensnation and not a Kulturnation, like the putative Germany of the patriots and unificationists, the latter, figurative en-
tity was to remain quite without a political complement until the

last decades of the nineteenth century, while Switzerland had been reinforcing its boundaries and national characteristics for some time.[41] Finally, it must be noted that the Jewish population of Switzerland has never been large: from some twenty families living in the permitted Jewish zone of residence in the early seventeenth century, the number grew slowly, if steadily, to around eighteen thousand individuals, or 0.25 percent of the total Swiss population, in the last decade of the twentieth century, a percentage that had remained constant with only minor fluctuations since the period of the emancipation.[42]

Comparison with the Jewish population of the German states during the crucial centuries in which Jews were banned from Switzerland is instructive, if in some cases misleading. Whereas, for instance, there were 175,000 Jews in Germany at the end of the eighteenth century, making up some 1 percent of the total population, the actual numbers of Jews in the various states and duchies varied widely, with a kingdom like Prussia and cities like Hamburg, Berlin, and Frankfurt am Main possessing large and (financially or culturally) important Jewish populations.[43] In Switzerland, meanwhile, the zone of residence had been restricted to the remote villages of Oberendingen and Lengnau, in what was to become the Canton of Aargau, or Argovia. These towns relied for their livelihood on the nearby country trading centers of Baden and Zurzach, and thus the Jewish life that grew up there and, during the later period of emancipation, spread to the larger urban center of Zurich, was rural in character.[44] The first communities in other Swiss cities, such as Geneva and Basel, were composed of similarly rural Alsatian Jews, who had settled there as French citizens, their ranks later to be swelled by Jewish immigrants from various parts of Europe.[45]

Given the fragmented and unsettled history of Jewish life and culture in Switzerland until the late nineteenth century, it should come as no surprise that the few pieces of what might be termed Swiss-Jewish literature from before the period of emancipation are either not entirely Swiss or not entirely literary or, indeed, not even properly Jewish: a piece of medieval poetry by Süsskind von Trimberg, a German troubadour who has long been (mis)identified as Jewish, that was first collected in medieval Zurich; a commentary on a popular book of Jewish ritual and prayer, and thus not a work of literature at all in the strict sense, prepared by a fourteenth-century Swiss rabbi; and an eighteenth-century Protestant pastor's extended report on the history of Jews in Switzerland, including his hypothesis that a popular piece of Swiss folk literature may have its roots in allegorical verses sung during the Jewish holiday of Passover. A Jewish population kept small, rural, and unstable for several centuries, after all, could hardly be expected to produce much of anything requiring the ferment and interaction provided by the great urban centers of early modernity.

Pre-Emancipation: A Figure of Speech, a Book of Blessings, and a Song

Considering the crucial role that Zurich was later to play, especially during World War II, as a free transit center for literature in the German-speaking world, it is perhaps fitting that the Swiss metropolis's first involvement with literature by an allegedly Jewish author in German was as its promoter and distributor.⁴⁶ And that this 'Jewish' writer should turn out to have (no doubt unwittingly) created the sense that he was of Jewish origins by donning in his verse the 'guise' of a Jew in an evident effort to render his dejection palpable, has peculiar resonances in present-day Switzerland, where the case of Bruno Doessekker's literary masquerading as a Jew has in recent years rocked the Swiss cultural scene.

The *Manessische Liederhandschrift*, or Manesse codex, now in the possession of the University Library at Heidelberg, was a collection of courtly poetry compiled in the early fourteenth century in Zurich by the knight and councilor Rüdiger von Manesse and his son Johannes and contained, among its roughly six thousand verses, twelve poems by Süsskind von Trimberg, a medieval lyric poet who is thought to have lived in the German region of Upper Franconia in the second half of the thirteenth century and who, in one celebrated poem, appears to present himself as a Jew.⁴⁷ The mere possibility of there having been a Jew among the medieval German courtly poets has occasioned controversy at various junctures in the history of German studies, and the actual 'ethnic' origins of Süsskind have been investigated (and imaginatively reconstructed) by proponents of various academic, aesthetic, and political ideologies; he continues to be identified as Jewish in some of the scholarly literature,

despite strong evidence to the contrary.[48] Similarly, the central
question of just what it is about Süsskind's verses (or, more properly, their assumed moral stance, as the genre often involved taking
a position on social matters) that may be termed 'Jewish'—apart
from his one explicit use of the word Jew (iuden)—immediately
raises problems that go far beyond the aesthetic, presuming as they
do an essential and identifiable 'Jewish writing,' despite the spe-
ciousness of even the 'racial' premises for such a claim.

   None of this, however, should be allowed to obscure the fact that
a thirteenth-century poet, writing in German, had (posthumously)
'published' in medieval Switzerland at least one text in which
both Jewishness and the life of the creative artist are explicitly 'thematized'—that is, made a vivid and crucial vehicle in the conveyance
of the poem's central image. Indeed, Süsskind's is a text in which
figurative 'Jewishness' becomes the very sign of the hardships of
authorship and thus creates an intriguing nexus of tropes:

> I've been a-singing for my pay:
> A singing fool, I say.
> Now, if their lordships won't come through,
> I'll quit their court and flee.
> And let my beard grow all the day
> Of hairs full long and gray;
> I'll live the life of an old Jew
> And roam eternally.
> My mantle shall go flutt'ring long
> Deep underneath my cap.
> All humbly I shall limp along
> And seldom shall I henceforth sing a courtly song
> Now that their lordships have turned off the tap.[49]

The ostensibly causal connections among patronage, the figure of
the 'old Jew,' and social exclusion may be merely coincidental or
may indeed simply reflect the availability of the image of 'the Jew' to
express the status of the pariah; but it is certainly of interest to read
in this early representation of Jewishness in a Swiss literary context
an ironic consciousness of the commercialization of art, as well as
of the fickleness of the audience's favor, the whole packed within a
vision of the wandering Jew's exclusion from the craft of song.

The fourteenth century, for its part, saw the work of one Mosche of Zurich, a scholar who had studied with Rabbi Yitzhak ben Yosef, or with his student, Rabbi Perez, both of Corbeil, near Paris, before taking up a position as the rabbi of the Jewish community of Zurich. His work in France was to have as a result a commentary on Rabbi Yitzhak's so-called S'maq, an acronym formed from the Hebrew words *Sefer Mitzvot Qatan*, or small book of blessings, to be distinguished from the *Sefer Mitzvot Gadol* of Coucy and the most popular European guide to Jewish observance until the appearance of the *Shulchan Aruch* in the sixteenth century.[50] Rabbi Mosche's commentary on the S'maq was so extensive that it came to lend the name of its place of origin to the work as a whole, giving rise to the title Zürcher *Semak*, or Zurich *S'maq*.[51] A manuscript of the text, with Mosche's commentary inscribed in its margins, can be viewed at the Bodleian Library in Oxford. Rabbi Mosche himself, researches suggest, perished, along with the rest of the Jewish community of Zurich, in the burnings of 1349, the official Swiss reaction to rumors that Jews had poisoned public fountains or had helped to spread the Black Death.[52] This murderous outbreak of Judeophobia was eventually followed by the 1436 prohibition on Jewish settlement in Zurich; similar bans arose elsewhere in Switzerland. The prohibition would remain in effect until the 1860s.

Perhaps the most remarkable testimony to an early form of Swiss-Jewish literary hybridity comes, however, from an even more unlikely literary source than either a putatively Jewish minstrel or a decidedly nonsecular medieval rabbi. In 1768, Johann Caspar Ulrich, pastor of the Frauenmünster in Zurich, wrote a history of the Jews in Switzerland from earliest times to his own present day. He began with a summary of scriptural accounts and some surmises about the use by the Roman emperor Titus of the local populace from the Swiss town of Avenches for the siege of Jerusalem in C.E.70 and proceeded with an extensive history of Jewish settlement and fortunes in Zurich and elsewhere in the territory of contemporary Switzerland, basing his work upon legal and economic evidence and supplementing it with documentation in the form of letters and contracts.[53] (Florence Guggenheim-Grünberg, the late dean of Swiss-Jewish history, called Ulrich's work 'the most valuable source for the history of Jews in Switzerland.')[54] Ulrich's preface makes claims of sectarian impartiality, indeed of his own friendly intentions toward his subject, whom he says he pities for hardships past and present. Despite these claims, his text is in fact not free of terms of anti-Semitic abuse, nor of satisfied references to the harsh fate visited upon the Jews for their ingratitude to their Lord, their failure to accept his Son, and their crucifixion of this same. 'And so the Lord grew weary in the end of his ancient and now quite corrupted folk,' writes Ulrich, in his account of the causes of the Diaspora. 'His wrath was full upon this brood of snakes . . . and there was no more hope of clemency.'[55]

And yet such venomous and clichéd Judeophobia did not prevent Ulrich from making a remarkable—and, in hindsight, oddly generous—conjecture. In a section entitled 'Notes on Certain Old Jewish Easter Songs etc. Still to This Day Remembered,' Ulrich discusses, among other 'entirely Jewish documents,' the traditional Passover round 'Chad gadya,' 'An only kid.' Each strophe of that song introduces a new element (kid, cat, dog, all the way to 'the Lord God') in a chain of events involving violence and revenge: 'It was one kid, an only kid, that Father bought for just two bits: one kid, a lonely kid. Came a cat and ate the kid that Father bought for just two bits: the one and only kid. Then came a dog and bit the cat that ate the kid that Father bought for just two bits. . . .'[56] The song ends with 'the Lord God' triumphing over the Angel of Death, who has in turn destroyed the earlier elements in the chain. Ulrich considers various hypotheses, both Jewish and non-Jewish, concerning the song's origins and allegorical significance (the goat represents Israel, the cat the Assyrians, and so on, down to the Messiah triumphing over the Turks in the Promised Land, in a typological minihistory of Jewish travails). He then makes the following observation:

This song must once have been familiar to our own citizens' children, who must have had much commerce with the Jewish children. They brought it home with them, which gave occasion to vex the Jews, and as a pastime those Christian children composed this song, the which is still known to this day:

A peartree stands in the garden tall
The pears don't want to fall
The farmer sends Joggeli down

> To shake those pears off to the ground
> Joggeli won't shake the peartree tall
> The pears don't want to fall
>
> So the farmer sends his little dog out
> To give Joggeli one with his snout
> The little dog won't give Joggeli one —
>
> So the farmer sends his little stick out
> To give the little dog one over the snout
> The little stick won't give the little dog one —
>
> So the farmer sends a little fire out
> For to burn up that little stick stout
> The little fire won't burn the little stick stout —

And so this Zurich children's song follows the Jewish Easter song to the end, and thus proves to this day that the Jews not only lived here in Zurich, but also must have come to know the Christian citizens well.[57]

Ulrich then makes similar claims for a derivation of the Zurich children's chant 'Guter Gesell ich frage dich' from the Passover song 'Echad mi yodeah' as a proof of the Jewish presence in Zurich since before the Reformation, as well as of the commerce between Christian and Jewish children in the streets of Zurich.[58] What is striking about his derivation of the 'Joggeli' song from the Haggadah round is that it assigns such a controversially foreign origin to a text central to Swiss folklore (''s Joggeli will nüd d'Birre schüttle' is in fact recited to this day by Swiss children). And that Ulrich turns the Jewish song, which is a tale of violence and retribution, into a paradigm of Swiss neutrality and withdrawal—the Joggeli song is, after all, a pageant of restraint—may serve as an ironic adumbration of the variously uneasy Swiss-Jewish hybridities to come.

Post-Emancipation: The First Generations

This domestication of the foreign, its co-opting and transformation by a host culture, is, in Ulrich's formulation, an aggressive, even hostile business ('They brought it home with them, which gave occasion to vex the Jews'); and it is above all practiced by the host culture upon the foreign culture that it finds within its midst. But what of the reverse process: the creation, by increasingly more self-confident and better-off members of a minority culture, with their roots and often their birthplace in a sometimes very different national context, of a new and perhaps hybrid literature of their own, made up of the consciousness and traditions carried with them into their new homeland as it is brought into contact with the material afforded them by a fresh aesthetic landscape?

Although he resided in Switzerland only during distinct and discontinuous periods of his life, the Bulgarian-born thinker and writer Elias Canetti's own early encounter with Swiss culture may be emblematic of the experience of immigrants to Switzerland in general, if not of Jews in particular. Having begun life in a Ladino-speaking Jewish family with ancient Sephardic roots, in a small town in Bulgaria, then still a part of the Ottoman Empire, Canetti (1905–1994) went with his parents to England, where his father died, before going to Switzerland via Austria with his mother and settling in Zurich during World War I. The two stayed on there until 1921, when Canetti's mother decided to move herself and her sixteen-year-old son to Germany. Canetti was to return to Zurich only much later, as an adult, and to die and be buried there.

Canetti's feelings about Switzerland, or, rather, about Zurich, were evidently profound: he speaks of the move to Germany in 1921 as his expulsion from paradise and says that the years he had spent in Zurich were the only completely happy years of his life.[59] His first visit to a Swiss school, as he relates it, may account for some of the importance this milieu was to take on for him. While the classes were conducted in so-called *Schriftdeutsch*—that is, high German, or 'written German'—the instructor was accustomed to calling the role in the local dialect; and so Canetti came to hear the name of one of his schoolmates, Segenreich, or 'rich in blessings,' magically distorted by the local pronunciation (which rendered it 'Säge-rich') and thus for some time rendered cryptically fascinating to the thoughtful young man. Outside the classroom, meanwhile, the lingua franca was entirely dialect, or *Zürichdeutsch*, and Canetti himself began learning this strange new tongue, despite the strong objections of his mother, with her elevated literary passions and her taste for 'pure' German. She 'was given to considering as valid only those languages that had a literature'; and she had certainly not brought him to Switzerland so that he might forget all that she had taught him about the Burgtheater in Vienna.[60]

Nevertheless, Canetti continued to practice the dialect, albeit keeping his progress secret from his mother. Perhaps it was precisely the forbiddenness of this knowledge that made it so appealing, for its acquisition constituted his first act of independence from her—indeed, his transformation from her subject (*Untertan*) into a man.[61] His interpretation of the absolute appeal of the Zurich dialect, however, apart from its structural use in his relations with his mother, is significant. The language of his Viennese peers had been suffused with the odious talk of war (in which Canetti had himself participated, although mainly out of his zeal to win over comrades). In Zurich, meanwhile, 'the many words that had to do with war had not penetrated into the speech of my schoolmates.' The 'powerful and undecorated phrases of the Swiss boys' thus found a compensatory favor in the ears of the gifted Canetti, who had been moved ahead in Vienna and was consequently bored by his lessons in Zurich, where he had been denied recognition of his precocious achievements in Austria.[62]

Thus Canetti absorbed this allegedly literatureless dialect, this folk tongue, and learned to cherish it both for its savor of contraband and for its resistance to the bellicose and imperialist strains of the 'high' language as spoken in the capital of the Austro-Hungarian monarchy. This latter quality may serve to account for the appeal of Swiss dialect and culture to that entire generation of German-speaking Jewish writers to whom their linguistic 'homelands' of Germany and Austria were to become increasingly more hostile as the century wore on. Switzerland would come by contrast to seem a place where the German tongue might still be a plausible tool for the expression of ideas by writers whose 'ethnic' or 'religious' (not to say 'racial') heritage had rendered drastically problematic their relationship to it and, indeed, to the larger political entities in which that language was officially spoken.

Having demonstrated a brief flowering of 'tolerance' following the emancipation of the Jews in the late nineteenth century and the enthusiastic engagement of Swiss-Jewish citizens in the defense of their country during World War I,[63] Switzerland was subsequently

to become, during the interwar period and, infamously, throughout
the existence of the Third Reich and its perpetration of the Holocaust, markedly inhospitable to would-be Jewish immigrants.[64] The
campaign by the wjc during the 1990s to reclaim Jewish funds
deposited in Swiss banks, and the subsequent investigations by
the Independent Commission of Experts into Swiss relations with
Nazi Germany, have put an end to the long-nourished illusion that
Switzerland in the 1930s and 1940s was a paradise for Jewish refugees from, and opponents to, war (and eventually also racial persecution), as Canetti had experienced it in the early decades of
the century.[65] Furthermore, inquiries into the fate of would-be
immigrant writers to Switzerland between 1933 and 1945 have
made plain just how cooperative the country's intellectual attitude became during its delicate coexistence with the neighboring
Third Reich. A policy of collaboration between Swiss immigration
and employment authorities and the Swiss Writers' Union (ssv),
whereby the latter would prepare reports for the former on the
suitability of literary or journalistic candidates for immigration, led
to the rejection of about a third of those applications made between
1933 and 1945. Of the some one hundred candidates accepted,
nearly half were granted only 'conditional' work visas, which typi-
cally meant that the immigrant was permitted to write books but
forbidden to publish articles in periodicals, the latter being for
some their daily bread and certainly an arena for the expression of
ideas potentially hostile to the Nazi regime. In the case of Jewish
applicants, the representatives of the ssv making the recommendations were often led by guidelines handed down in the course
of international meetings with Goebbels's Reichsschrifttumskam-
mer, the Nazi organization for the promotion of literature, that
furthered the ssv's stated aim of preserving the 'Aryan' nature of
the Swiss literary body.[66]

Nevertheless, it was at least theoretically possible to subsist as a
Jewish writer in Switzerland during the period of the Holocaust,
something that had of course become practically unthinkable during the same time in Germany and its occupied and annexed territories. One German-Jewish intellectual refugee who did manage to
spend the Holocaust and war years practicing her trade in Switzerland, despite an 'evaluation' by the ssv that led to severe restrictions
on the public expression of her opinion, was Margarete Susman,

alias Reiner (1872–1966).[67] The literary critic, painter, and philosopher, born in Hamburg, had already spent part of her childhood
and youth in Zurich, where her father had established the family for
business reasons, before she returned there as a refugee from Hitler's Germany in 1933, having in the interim studied in Munich and
Paris.[68] In addition to groundbreaking essays on such contempo-
raries as Rosenzweig and Kafka (collected in *Gestalten und Kreise*
[1954]), studies of Romanticism (*Frauen der Romantik* [1929] and
Deutung einer grossen Liebe: Goethe und Charlotte von Stein [1951]), and a
book on the meaning of Jewish suffering (*Das Buch Hiob und das
Schicksal des jüdischen Volkes* [1946]),[69] Susman also published several
volumes of poetry, among them *Gedichte* (1892), *Mein Land* (1901),
Neue Gedichte (1907), *Die Liebenden* (1917), and *Aus sich wandelnder Zeit*
(1953). This last, late collection bears the traces of the philosophi-
cal engagement with Judaism that had taken a central place in
Susman's intellectual career. *Aus sich wandelnder Zeit* (From a time
in transformation) contains poems entitled 'Israel,' a prayer for
refuge, and 'Gesetzesfreude' (Joy in the law), in which allusions
to King David and the Ark of the Covenant introduce a meditation
on the redemption of the world through God's law, as well as an
elegantly rhymed series of four quatrains depicting Moses as 'Der
Knecht des Volkes' (The servant of the people). The poem demonstrates the complex intertwining of Jewish and Christian sym-
bolisms—a German-Jewish hybridity *avant la lettre*—to which Susman, a Jewish child of the German nineteenth century, was heir:[70]

> His hair and beard were both still wringing wet
> When he emerged from out the heavy vapor,
> The champion of his folk, a wrestler's labor —
> Wrestled so long that folk forgot its debt.

> Strode into light: and music met his ear,
> A lightly coiling, brightly festive medley;
> And smiling now he broke his silence deadly,
> So sweet that choir's acclaim and welcome here!

> He saw: he saw the glowing work erect,
> In naked desert sun the calf all golden
> Ringed round by his folk, lust- and bliss-emboldened,
> He saw his folk: this folk—he, God's subject.

Broke up the tablets, struck—till he was raw
And turned away from that accursed brood —
And groveled so that God his worship saw,
And in his folk's place offered up his blood.[71]

Here is a strikingly physical Moses to rival the ancient man of rage
who emerges from Freud's study of Michelangelo, yet who is also
provided with a readiness for sacrifice ('And in his folk's place
offered up his blood') that is drawn from Moses' Biblical offer to
expiate his people's sin (Exodus 32:32); an image that, however, as
evoked here without God's subsequent rejection of the offer (Exodus 32:33), surely also derives from the central role played by sacrifice in the Christian ideology. More striking still, in the post-
Holocaust years of the volume's publication, is Susman's poem
'Zorn Gottes' (God's anger), in which the Jewish people is compared to the innocently suffering Job—and found wanting: 'And
Lord, I know: Your folk is not like Job,/The blameless one. Your folk
has sinned immensely.'[72] This 'Jewish people,' tempted away from
God's path by the seductions of exile, by its love of the nations
among whom it was living, surrendered the light it was to have
brought to those nations: and so has had to suffer the attacks of
Leviathan and Behemoth disguised as humans, a common enough
contemporary figure for the Nazis.[73] Still, the poem goes on, God's
folk has now surely paid enough; and, with this likening of the
Holocaust to a holy pyre of reconciliation between God and His
Chosen People, Susman strikes an uneasy note in the chorus of
theological and historical interpretations of that event building
throughout the 1950s to reach a crescendo during our own age.

Such an elevated Jewish-German neoclassicism, however, was
bound ultimately to fail to give answers to the urgent questions
posed by the totalitarian era. And the Swiss-German dialects could
no longer provide a linguistic haven from the stigmatized German
tongue, having themselves, in the interwar period, been infiltrated
by the vocabulary of war and domination Canetti thought to have
escaped but which finally visited Switzerland during the existence
of the Third Reich, in the form of a perniciously tacit ideological
and economic implication with the Nazis. Yet the same symbolic
dynamics had never obtained with regard to the French spoken by
the Swiss of the Romandie, the six western cantons in which that

language is predominant. Both the greatly reduced differences between Swiss French and 'official' French, as well as the much less
glaring association of the language with the murderous project of
the Holocaust, mean that the relationship to their language of
French-speaking Jewish writers in Switzerland has been markedly
less thematized than that of the German speakers.

One notable French-speaking immigrant Jewish writer who
spent the period of World War I and part of the interwar years in
Geneva and who returned there from Paris and London after World
War II was Albert Cohen (1895–1981). Cohen was born on the
island of Corfu into a venerable community of Venetian Jews and
arrived in Switzerland by way of Marseilles, where his family had
sought refuge from the economic hardship and growing anti-
Semitism of their native land. In Marseilles he was introduced to
the French language by the nuns who ran his school; he was not to
be spared anti-Semitic insult in his adopted tongue, although the
celebrated and foundational incident of his first exposure to public
anti-Jewish opprobrium occurred in France and not in Switzerland.[74] Cohen took on Swiss nationality in 1919, and, apart from his
absence between 1932 and 1947, during which period he was active
in Zionist and pro-Jewish causes, he was to spend the better part of
his life in Switzerland, working for various international organizations and writing, among other theatrical and autobiographical
works, a cycle of comic novels centered loosely around his adopted
city of Geneva, with a recurring dramatis personae studded with
colorful Jewish characters.[75]

Cohen's four great novels, Solal (1930), Mangeclous (1938), Belle du
seigneur (1968), and Les Valeureux (1969), all include appearances by
members of the Solals, a widely dispersed Greek-Jewish family of
French extraction described in epic and occasionally grotesque
terms. There is, for example, Pinhas Solal,

known as Mangeclous [= nail eater]. . . . He was also given the epithet
Captain of the Winds, on account of a physiological characteristic dear to his
vanity. One of his other epithets was Word of Honor—an expression with
which he fairly varnished his speeches, wanting as they were in truth. He had
been tubercular for a quarter of a century but was hale and hearty, and was
endowed with a cough so resonant that it brought down the synagogue lamp
one evening. His appetite was renowned throughout the entire Orient, no less

than were his eloquence and his immoderate love of money. He almost always took with him on his strolls a little cart, in which he kept iced drinks and victuals for his own personal enjoyment. He was called Mangeclous because, he would claim, with his usual sardonic smile, he had as a child devoured a dozen screws to assuage his inexorable hunger.[76]

True to the method of their creation—three of the four novels started life as one single, enormous work, to be cleft later into their present forms[77]—the novels are episodic in their interweaving of picaresque adventures, comic set pieces, and opera buffa scenes of intrigue and deception against the backdrops of Cephalonia (a stand-in for Cohen's native Corfu), Marseilles, and Geneva. Cohen's great gift to Swiss-Jewish letters—indeed, to Swiss literature—is doubtless this heightened sense of the international potential of Switzerland, where the Greek-born Jew, who had grown up speaking Venetian dialect, lived as a respected diplomat among French-speaking Calvinists and managed simultaneously to build for himself a reputation in Paris, the Mecca of the French literary world.[78] His novelistic works clearly reflect this cosmopolitan experience, perhaps the special preserve of the diplomat, though certainly tinged with the irony of his having made a career in a neutral country. *Mangeclous*, the second of the novels, contains an exemplary, if characteristically burlesque, staging of Geneva as the coolly self-confident showplace of international encounters. In quest of a mysterious fortune, the Solals have made a detour to the Swiss city, where their old friend, the Catholic Scipion of Marseilles, has gone to make representations before the League of Nations concerning the independence of his hometown. By the manicured shores of Lake Geneva, Scipion, a vain and sensual enthusiast with the broad accent of the French Midi, an unstoppable loquacity, and the missionary's zeal in his friendship with the Jewish Solals, pauses to lick the wounds inflicted on him by the coldness of the Genevans: a boatman, a traffic policeman, and a tram conductor all have rebuffed his sociable advances; a gendarme has even forbidden him to sing on the street without a permit. 'He went to sit down on a bench and chew over his rancor. And his offended soul became Jewish.'[79] As if to underscore this symbolic conversion to the tribe of the excluded, Scipion is immediately reunited with Jérémie, a friend of his childhood and now the very picture of the Jewish refugee: 'With little scuffling steps, his back bent, a little old man with a meager red beard approached the bench where Scipion was snoring. . . . His thin face, yellow and ravaged, appeared scarcely Aryan to all who had eyes to see.'[80]

And, indeed, Jérémie, of absurdly mixed East European heritage, has recently been released from a 'German prison' (this in the last years before World War II!) and is making his way to Marseilles. There follows a scene of reunion between the two old friends in which the thick southern patois of Scipion is rivaled in exoticism by Jérémie's heavily accented French. ('Impossible to transcribe, continuously and completely, his strange pronunciation. The sentences would become incomprehensible,' admits the narrator in a philological aside, having attempted to render all of Jérémie's Yiddish vowel transpositions.) Presumably sensitized by his recent spiritual conversion to Judaism, Scipion springs for a new wardrobe to make the refugee more palatable to the hostile Genevans, although when Jérémie balks at having his temple locks cut off on the grounds that he will then no longer be recognizable as a Jew, Scipion assures him that he is in no danger of being thought an Englishman. In the ensuing exchange, Jérémie discourses on the Mosaic commandments and the folly of rationalizing religious prescriptions, and Scipion declares him a sanctimonious old thing. Then, having done his best to dress up the Jew in respectable garb and having found him to be as alienating as the Genevans themselves presumably do, Scipion at last feels at home in the city. Nevertheless, traces of Jérémie's Judeo-French remain, unglossed, in the language of the narrator.[81] This infiltration of the ostensibly neutral voice of the text by means of a free indirect discourse marked with otherness and particularity is, of course, a legitimate modernist legacy, pioneered as the technique was by such illustrious forebears as Flaubert and Joyce; but it is here surely also the sign of a burgeoning, if perhaps ultimately illusory, Swiss-Jewish literary hybridity.

The trope of the Jew in disguise recurs in Cohen's œuvre, notably in reverse, when, in the extended opening scene of Belle du seigneur, another member of the Solal family, himself a revered functionary at that same League of Nations for which Scipion is making in Mangeclous, dons the dress of 'an old Jew' (long coat, fur hat, dark complexion, white beard) and surprises his beloved Ariane, the wife of the pompous bureaucrat Deume, in the midst of a narcissistic reverie on her own gifts and position in Genevan society.[82] With an operatic flourish, Solal thus tests Ariane's regard—and finds it sadly wanting, when she (rather understandably) rebuffs with violence the unrecognized intruder, a gesture Solal implicitly interprets as anti-Semitic. The reader has by this time also been privy to Ariane's inner monologue, which displays a fairly insufferable Protestant bigotry and parochial snobbism. Nevertheless, one is made uncomfortable by Solal's wounded vow to 'seduce' Ariane 'basely, . . . as is your dessert and your desire,' and thus to wreak vengeance on her for all of the old and the ugly and the erotically inept.[83] And if the love affair that subsequently develops between the two has about it anything of a symbolic performance of that potential for a Swiss-Jewish hybrid suggested in the encounter of Scipion and Jérémie in Mangeclous, then the reader has further reason to be uncomfortable, for this romance will end in a suicide pact. The recurrence in Cohen's work of the motif of containment, of the secure but constraining enclosure, whether in the rhetorical form of the monologue or in the actual choice of setting, such as the room in which Solal and Ariane end their days, has also been noted.[84] Could it be that this was the internationalist Cohen's figure for the necessary evil of his adopted homeland's isolation and neutrality in a world of violence and ethnic hatred? Or was it perhaps the expression of his pessimism about the Swiss-Jewish cultural project?

Next to Canetti's sense of the self-fashioning promise of the folkloric Swiss-German dialect for his own development against an august 'high' tradition and Cohen's hybridizing assimilation of 'foreign elements' into a literature crafted in the adopted tongue of his new homeland, there was a third possible means for conducting a literary life as a Jewish immigrant in post-emancipation Switzerland: continuing to write in the language of one's distant culture. For while Canetti and Cohen had learned their respective literary tongues, German and French, before arriving in Switzerland, these were in turn both foreign to the language communities they had been born into—in Canetti's case, the Ladino or Spaniolish of the Sephardic Jews of the Eastern Mediterranean; in Cohen's, the Venetian dialect of Corfu—and the two dominant languages of their new country, Switzerland. The native tongue of Lajzer Ajchenrand (1912–1985), born in the Polish town of Demblin, southeast of Warsaw, was Yiddish, and it was in this language that he wrote and published poetry in his adopted country of Switzerland, beginning soon after his arrival in 1942 until his death there more than forty years later. (His time in Switzerland was interrupted only by a few years' sojourn with his Swiss wife in France and Israel, an interruption that was, however, to cost him the Swiss naturalization for which he later applied and which was conditional upon twenty years' unbroken residence.) His first poem had been published in a Yiddish magazine in Warsaw while he was still young; his burgeoning career was soon interrupted by emigration to France and voluntary service in the French army. Captured and bound for a concentration camp under the control of Vichy, he managed to escape to Switzerland, where he had first to endure internment in Swiss refugee camps before winning release and the regard of fellow inmates and writers alike.[85]

However, despite his championing by such local and international names as Max Frisch, Hermann Hesse, Isaac Bashevis Singer, and Paul Nizon and his receipt in 1967 of the Itzik-Manger Prize, one of Israel's top literary awards, Ajchenrand remained relatively unknown in Switzerland. This had surely to do with the specific foreignness of his chosen language, for as related as Yiddish is to German—and, indeed, to Swiss-German dialect, as some contend—it may be precisely this uncanny consanguinity (combined with the fact that it is traditionally set down in Hebrew, and not Roman, letters) that renders it alienating to the average German-speaking reader. One of Ajchenrand's first postwar publications, *Hörst du nicht: Jiddische Gedichte*,[86] was printed with facing-page German translations by Walter Lesch, and the book Ajchenrand published in the year before his death, *Zwischen Itzt un Keinmol*,[87] was reviewed in the mainstream Swiss press.[88] Nevertheless, as Ajchenrand himself maintained, there was a singular problem to be faced in the translation of Yiddish poetry into German. The Yiddish poem, according to Ajchenrand, is based 'in a profound, gentle, interior order. . . . It is simply not the vocabulary that makes the language that of the poet, nor that of the people; rather, it is the music that accomplishes this. In German everything becomes harder. To Germanify a Yiddish poem always also means to harden it.'[89]

Furthermore, despite references in the worldly Ajchenrand's verses to Dante, to the French Revolution, and to some of the best known figures of both the Jewish and the Christian scriptural traditions, the form and central preoccupations of his melancholy ballads, often devoted to a brutally clear-eyed reckoning with the Nazi murderers and with mourning for his lost family, were no doubt strange to his sheltered Swiss audience. And perhaps this is simply an index of the difficulty of the Swiss-Jewish hybrid cultural project, in which neither the will nor the material is always dependably to hand. Still, here is Ajchenrand, in 'Beim Rhein' (By the Rhine), a poem written during the final years of the war, confronting with a certain ambivalence the fearsome German cultural legacy, albeit from the perspective of a Jew in exile. And yet Ajchenrand's Swiss readers might well have found his divided tones of intimidated admiration and bitter resentment resonant with their own experience, having in recent and more distant times learned both to wonder at and to fear their imposing northern neighbor:

> Beat on your waves like wild steeds on the steppe,
> Drive them, like our lives, in the whirling flood.
> Unmoved, eternally you flow and ebb,
> In spite of old mad warrior cult and God.

> Up from your banks death marches grimly on,
> With fire and storms of steel to left and right;
> Igniting fear the way the sun the dawn
> Above the earth and oceans will ignite.

> Your streaming torrent bows the mountaintop
> As if by low'ring clouds, dead monuments—
> At which aspect within me welling up
> As from a body torn come raw laments.

> The poets sang you, 'Tranquil, quiet Rhine,'
> And God and Fatherland by you extolled.
> But your cold stream like poison flows in mine,
> And thus abused, such ravings leave me cold.

Beat on your waves like wild steeds on the steppe,
Drive them, like our lives, in the whirling flood.
Unmoved, eternally you flow and ebb,
In spite of old mad warrior cult and God.[90]

Or perhaps there had been just enough 'old mad warrior cult and God' ('Der umsinn fun uralte krieger un gott') in the Switzerland of the 1930s and 1940s to render such an unflinching condemnation of bellicose patriotism less than entirely palatable to Ajchenrand's potential non-Jewish audience.

Harder for such an audience to classify as foreign was the work of Jews born and raised in Switzerland, and thus shaped from their very earliest days by the same culture as their fellow citizens. Foremost among these, considering the sheer scope of his literary work, is Kurt Guggenheim (1896–1983), the Zurich-born son of a local businessman with Argovian-Jewish roots and the prolific author of an impressively varied corpus.[91] After his debut novel, the Bildungsroman Entfesselung (1935), came Sieben Tage (1936), Riedland (1938), a romance, and Wilder Urlaub (1941), a soldier's tale. Following World War II, in which he served on the Swiss border, Guggenheim published the autobiographical service novel Wir waren unser vier (1949); the four-novel historical epic Alles in allem (1952–1955); a series of studies of his youth around the turn of the century, Sandkorn für Sandkorn (1959), Die frühen Jahre (1962), and Salz des Meeres, Salz der Tränen (1964); a study of Gottfried Keller, Das Ende von Seldwyla (1965); Minute des Lebens (1969), a reconstruction of the relationship between Zola and Cézanne; a final novel, Das Zusammensetzspiel (1977), the story of a professor; and the three volumes of his diaries, Einmal nur. Tagebuchblätter (1925–1980).[92]

With Alles in allem (All in all),[93] Guggenheim's masterpiece, for which he received the Literature Prize of the City of Zurich in 1955, Guggenheim had set himself the imposing task of recreating the rise of his hometown in the twentieth century as a model of the modern experience. In this realist endeavor, in which the sometimes scientifically observed lives and fortunes of many of its citizens are used to depict Zurich's progress from modest provincial town to modern cosmopolitan city, Guggenheim faithfully recorded the attitudes of his countrypeople to their Jewish fellow citizens, alongside the efforts of immigrants and Swiss Jews alike to find their way in a rapidly changing world. Indeed, it has been argued that the Jewish characters in Guggenheim's monumental novel of Zurich in the first half of the twentieth century play an indispensable symbolic role. In his afterword to a reprinted edition of *Alles in allem*, the Swiss critic Charles Linsmayer notes the significance of the work's Jewish characters.[94] Suggestively entitled 'Foreignness in the Familiar, Becoming at Home in the Foreign: Kurt Guggenheim's *Alles in allem* and the Theme of Social Integration' and closing with an explicit citation of Georg Simmel's celebrated 'Excursus on the Foreigner,' with its attribution to the immigrant of a paradigmatic place in modernity, the essay assigns Guggenheim's Jews the role of a symbol both for foreignness, as non-Christian in their totality, and for potential integration, as representing a cultural group that is itself internally divided between the assimilationist western Jews of Argovia and Alsace and the separatist eastern Jews of Poland and Russia.[95] Furthermore, it is precisely the presence of Jews in Guggenheim's novel that, according to Linsmayer, allows the work to transcend the bounds of its immediate geographic frame and to become an emblematic and universal narrative of modernity: 'In the most beautiful, moving, and, indeed, model, fashion, Kurt Guggenheim has depicted the meeting of two cultures, or, rather, the organization of the foreign within the familiar, using the example of Jewish Zurich. For *Alles in allem* is always also the history of Zurich's Jews. And yet it is as little a Jewish book as it is, in the narrow sense, a Zurich book. Zurich stands within it as a model for a human urban society, and Judaism for the phenomenon of integration and socialization in all its nuances, facets, and extensions.'[96]

Jews in Zurich, then, for at least one contemporary critic, are at once a proof of the cosmopolitan diversity and modernity of the city; a guarantee of its tolerance, liberalism, and capacity for the assimilation of foreigners; and a symbol of the whole work's allegorical importance as a showplace of the modern experience.[97] Furthermore, as the title of Linsmayer's essay suggests, the presence of the other within the community of the familiar carries with it the hope of a corresponding process, the becoming-at-home in the foreign ('das Heimischwerden im Fremden'), a process of domestication that may just as easily be experienced by immigrants as by the members of the majority culture those immigrants have come to join. Thus the novels may be read as standing at once for diversity, that thoroughly (post)modern watchword of a 'globalized' culture, and for integration, the long-cherished ideal of the early modern, post-French Revolution society.

But the Jewish characters in Guggenheim's cycle of novels are more than simply Janus-headed figures for modern diversity and cohabitation within the family of humankind. The four novels are constructed chronologically, covering respectively the periods 1900–1913, 1914–1919, 1920–1932, and 1933–1945. The representation of these decades, despite the restriction of the novels' showplace to Zurich, inevitably includes scenes of some particular moment, considering the events transpiring both internationally and domestically and the historical actors passing through Zurich, and so through Guggenheim's pages (the German Kaiser, for instance, or Lenin and Tristan Tzara). Thus the cycle is positively drenched in the minutiae of contemporary political, cultural, and social affairs.

In his second volume Guggenheim gives us the following sharply observed encounter between the young Aaron Reiß and Josef Gidionovics. Reiß is the Zurich-born scion of a long-settled family of Argovian Jewish cattle and real estate salesmen, and a writer-to-be who will eventually be revealed as the author of the cycle, and thus Guggenheim's alter ego; Gidionovics is the son of immigrant East European Jews, a traveling salesman for the family's tailoring business and 'a lanky, curly headed young man of outspokenly Jewish type' who speaks with the local working-class accent despite his Polish name. The two meet at basic training in 1914, recognize each other as fellow Jews (however different their immediate social backgrounds), laugh together at the unfamiliar uniforms, and occupy adjoining beds in the barracks. But when Gidionovics asks Reiß about the possibility of release from service on Saturday, counters the secular Reiß's scornful reply with an incomprehensible Yiddish curse, and begins to discourse on the return to Palestine and on Switzerland as merely another station in the *galut*, or Jewish exile from the Holy Land, the real differences between the two become clear. Reiß, says Gidionovics, is a *Westjude*, an assimilationist, ready to feel patriotic about any land in which he can prosper, and thus practically a greater enemy of the *Ostjuden* than are the Christians themselves. In his comrade's rhetoric, meanwhile, Reiß detects the 'dialectic of the Zionist associations that had formed among the Galician immigrants in Aussersihl [the working-class district of Zurich]'; and he is impressed by Gidionovics's seeming indifference to his surroundings and his will to continue speechifying no matter his present context. When that context eventually does intervene, with a fellow recruit ordering the Zionist to shut up, the two drift off to sleep to the sound of nearby churchbells, 'a motherly, native sound' (mütterlich, heimatlich).[98]

Guggenheim here does something remarkable: in the midst of a heroic canvas of Swiss mobilization and valor, he paints a miniature in which an utterly minoritarian point of view—the Jewish—is allowed to split itself further, into its two great European streams, and stage a debate in which the pressing Jewish sociopolitical themes of the early decades of the twentieth century are taken up and thereby threaten to disturb the peace of the tranquil Swiss homeland. To be sure, there is irony in the scene of the two young Jewish men, who have just been discussing the relative merits of various homelands, being lulled to sleep by the 'motherly, native sound' of the Christian churchbells. Earlier in the same scene, when Gidionovics and Reiß laugh at each other's ill-fitting uniforms, there is an echo of a chapter from the first volume of the cycle, in which the young Reiß must march through the streets of Zurich in full festive Jewish regalia to celebrate Rosh Hashanah with his parents and is spotted in the foreign garb, to his shame, by his classmates.[99] But despite this implicit critique of the shaping power of institutions and costumes both civil and confessional, and of the aleatory nature of the identities thus produced, Guggenheim's faith in the ultimate rightness of the chemical reactions to which his city, as a representative of the modern urban experience in general, is host is everywhere detectable in the cycle, which will conclude years later with, among other things, marriage between descendants of the Gidionovics family and of the Mengs, a well-established clan of immigrant non-Jewish Germans.[100]

The reference to 'chemical reactions' is not incidental, for Guggenheim was deeply influenced in his realism by an unlikely source, the technical writings of the French natural scientist Jean-Henri Fabre (1823–1915), whose ten-volume Souvenirs entomologiques Gug-

genheim came to know well and which he eventually, according to
Linsmayer, made his realist model, in preference to the works of
Zola and Proust.[101] This tension—or perhaps marriage—between
literature and science was to provide Guggenheim with another
evocative scene of wartime encounter among Swiss soldiers, with,
however, rather different implications for the symbiosis of Jewish
and non-Jewish strains in Swiss culture. In his 1949 autobiographical novel of military service on the Swiss border during World War
II, *Wir waren unser vier* (There were four of us), Guggenheim splits
his own persona, as it were, among three of his title's four characters: the poet Martin Anwand, based on Guggenheim's friend Albin
Zollinger but bearing the symbolic weight of the literary life; the
Jewish biologist Michael Glanzmann; and the French-Swiss doctor
and first-person narrator Jean Loriol, whose humane interest in his
patients and fellows marks him as the author's kin.[102] It is Loriol,
who actually shares the fewest primary characteristics with Guggenheim, who will play a crucial role in a scene central to the
novel's tragedy, that of the doomed poet Anwand.

In one compressed chapter, Guggenheim presents us with a
scene of first news of the nascent Holocaust arriving in the early
1940s in Switzerland by way of the biologist Glanzmann, who has
relatives still in Poland and who has already experienced a hint of
exterminationist anti-Semitism from a German colleague at the
university. Glanzmann greets the news and deflects his own pain
with an extended disquisition on the biological development of
human consciousness, in an evident attempt to organize the behavior of the Nazis along comprehensible scientific lines. This is
followed by Loriol's and Glanzmann's visit to the bedside of the
ailing poet Anwand, who begins to read to them from the first draft
of a new work, a mordant satire of the current political situation
under the motto 'The Campaign against Stupidity,' only to sink
back in exhaustion, brought to the verge of a breakdown by the
stimulation of an audience. Concealing his negative diagnosis of
the evident frailty of his friend and placing the artist's task ahead of
his health, Loriol then counsels Anwand to complete his 'great
contribution to national fortification,' much to the poet's con-
tentment and Glanzmann's dismay. He himself, says Glanzmann,
'would have decided differently, as a biologist, and as a human
being, too.'[103]

The sickbed scene is a subtle rewriting of an earlier moment in German-Jewish letters, the climax of the first act of *Doktor Bernhardi* (1912), a play by the Austrian Jew Arthur Schnitzler (1862–1931) in which the Jewish physician of the title forbids a cleric to enter the room of a young Christian woman dying of the sequellae of an out-of-wedlock pregnancy. Bernhardi's rationale is that the presence of the cleric, come as he has to administer last rites, would immediately alert the delirious young woman to her moribund condition and thus rob her of 'the happiest hour of her life,' in which she believes herself to be well and healthy.[104] The ensuing scandal takes on, inevitably, anti-Semitic tones, as the Jewish Bernhardi, who had been moved by a desire to preserve the woman's happy illusions rather than by any explicitly confessional motives, is accused of obstructing the exercise of the Catholic religion and effectively damning the 'fornicating' woman's soul to a hell of missed absolution.

As reinterpreted by Guggenheim, the same motif, with the confessional motives now reversed, takes on a new meaning: it is the non-Jewish Loriol who 'lies' (passively) to a doomed patient in order to preserve his illusions—to wit, his production of literature—while the Jewish Glanzmann would have forbidden Anwand the exertion of writing in order to preserve for as long as possible his life on earth. Guggenheim makes the cultural-relativist point explicit with the chapter's last words, Loriol's thoughts upon hearing Glanzmann's judgment: 'They consider human life as sacred, in any form . . . beyond any morals or ethics. That's why they have preserved themselves so long. And that distinguishes the Jews from the rest of us.'[105] 'The Jews,' in other words, count human life superior even to literature, that beautiful illusion present in a primitive form in Schnitzler's patient and now matured to the sophisticatedly cynical *belles lettres* of Guggenheim's Anwand, who is a cross between Alexander Pope and Karl Kraus. But whereas it had been the Jewish Bernhardi who, in Schnitzler's rendering, had been willing to risk his patient's eternal soul for the sake of her last earthly illusions, here it is the Jewish Glanzmann who would be willing to sacrifice a last literary production for the sake of his friend's continued earthly life. The relative merits of literature and reality have thus switched positions, in other words, in their weightings by these two Jewish characters: Bernhardi prefers illusion to truth,

while Glanzmann champions truth over illusion. And so he un-
masks himself, in Loriol's assessment, as the agent of a Judaism
that is bound to reality, to the truth of earthly human life, and thus
unwilling to pay the ultimate price for literature.

By these terms, Guggenheim's dilemma was that of the born
member of such a (putative) community of devotees to human life—
even at the cost of the transcendence, indeed the sublimity, of
literature—who was himself also by trade a writer of fiction—that
is, someone whose primary commitment is to the creation of illusions rather than to the righteous preservation of life. He solved
this dilemma methodologically by modeling his craft on the natural
sciences and by cleaving in his themes closely to the concerns and
phenomena of quotidian life, thereby constantly exhibiting a hu-
manist's empathy with the lives of his fellows to counterbalance the
potential coldness of the techniques of observation he had learned
from the entomologist Fabre.

Radically different was the approach to literature and truth
adopted by André Kaminski (1923–1991), another native Swiss of
Jewish origins who made of his own life's experience and the observation of his milieu the subject of his eclectic written work.
Kaminski was born in Geneva as the child of Polish-Jewish immigrants, spent his childhood and the war years in Switzerland, and
followed his political sympathies to Poland in 1945, where he resided on and off (with trips to North Africa) until his expatriation as
a counterrevolutionary in 1968. Thereafter he returned, by way of
Israel, to Switzerland, where he lived in Zurich, working as a radio,
television, and theater producer, as well as an author, until his
death in 1991.

Kaminski's literary work, which he began to publish relatively
late in life, includes the collections of stories *Die Gärten des Mulay
Abdallah* (1983), *Der Sieg über die Schwerkraft und andere Erzählungen*
(1983), *Herzflattern: Neun wilde Geschichten* (1984), and *Flimmerge-
schichten* (1990); the novels *Nächstes Jahr in Jerusalem* (1986) and *Kiebitz*
(1988); and an account of his trip through Germany to promote the
1986 novel, *Schalom allerseits: Tagebuch einer Deutschlandreise* (1987).
Apart from *Schalom allerseits*, in contrast to Guggenheim's painstak-
ingly accurate fictional reconstruction of the past, Kaminski's work
is distinguished by a healthily ironic license in the treatment of

actual historical and autobiographical events. The note of narrative elasticity is struck in the very first lines of *Nächstes Jahr in Jerusalem* (Next year in Jerusalem), Kaminski's best-selling novel of his family's roots in Jewish Poland:

My Uncle Henner Rosenbach was, in the first place, a psychopath; second, he was the most splendid liar in the Austro-Hungarian double monarchy. In theory, he was my great-uncle, which I doubt, however, since he was incomparably more like me than his brother Leo, who was said to be my grandfather. At any rate, Uncle Henner was descended from the renowned Rabbi Shloimeh Rosenbach, who wrote his treatises in Bukovina three hundred years ago, and on whose gravestone the following saying is carved: 'Truth is the most valuable of all goods and should be handled with thrift and restraint.' It has been and remains my family's goal to live up to this maxim.[106]

Kaminski explains wryly that the family, whom the Iron Curtain now prevents from visiting its venerable ancestor's grave, is consoled by the fact that the maxim has now been taken up by 'the world Communist system, from the Elba to the coast of the Sea of Japan.'[107] The novel then goes on to trace fancifully the trajectories of the two branches of Kaminski's family, from Poland by way of Austria and America to Switzerland, and their embroilments with the various national and international regimes of the early part of the twentieth century. Along the way, Kaminski demonstrates a talent for burlesque humor as well as magical realism: for instance, Kaminski's (alleged) great-uncle Henner struggles (allegedly) for years to invent color photography, only to disappear in a Wizard of Oz–like confidence trick; Kaminski's father and ten uncles, notorious anticzarist agitators in their native Poland, flee to the United States and are soon organized into an unstoppable left-wing football team, the 'Kaminskiboys'; and when, at the end of the novel, 'Andrzej Kaminski' himself is born, the company assembled for the ritual of the *brith*, barely relieved that his parents have been dissuaded from naming him Vladimir Ilyich, is freshly chagrined to discover that the newborn is already circumcised.

Elsewhere, in similarly flamboyant style, Kaminski extends the autobiographical narrative that begins with his own birth at the very end of the novel. For example, in the short story 'Lea und der Gauleiter' (Lea and the Gauleiter, or Nazi district boss), the narrator, the Communist son of a Polish-Jewish immigrant in Switzerland, vies for the fiancée of the top local Nazi sympathizer during World War II and proposes an erotic duel to decide the contest.[108] But despite its often explicitly described connection to his homeland, as evidenced by plenty of local color and carefully depicted speech patterns, and Kaminski's obvious talent for both *yiddishkeit* and mordant observations on the state of German-Jewish relations, his œuvre has been treated with respect in neither Switzerland generally nor in intellectual circles in Germany, a fact that has been explained by Kaminski's frequent categorization as a writer of trivial entertainments, as well as by the relatively marginalized share of Swiss-Jewish writers in the postwar debates about Germany and 'the Jews' on the whole.[109]

Kaminski's breakthrough as a writer came with *Nächstes Jahr in Jerusalem*, which was a great success particularly in Germany, where it was published by Insel Verlag, an imprint of the estimable Suhrkamp house. When Kaminski followed this coup with a promotional tour of Germany that brought out large crowds to hear him read in the most out-of-the-way German towns, as well as in the metropolitan centers, the writer produced a further trump in the form of a best-selling account of the trip, *Schalom allerseits: Tagebuch einer Deutschlandreise* (Shalom everybody: Diary of a German voyage). In the reception of that book in the mainstream Swiss press, there is a hint of what may have made Kaminski unpalatable to the Swiss intellectual public: he is taken to task for his self-congratulatory tone (he consistently notes the good turnout to his readings), for his alleged posturing as a victim (he has cause, during the course of the trip, to go back on his initial resolve simply to let bygones be bygones by discussing the German-Jewish past avidly with the Holocaust and postwar generations), and for his evident pleasure at defying the Nazis' will that Jews be silenced forever.[110] The crankiness of the reception and the irritation voiced at Kaminski's ebullience no doubt reflect a traditional Swiss mistrust of success and foreign acclaim.

And yet the nonfictional work performs a subtle reversal of the precept guiding the novel it celebrates, that of the necessity of being sparing with the truth; and it is a reversal interesting for the meaning of Jewish writing in Switzerland. In a little frame narrative of two very short episodes at the beginning and end of the book, Kaminski recounts his visits, before and after the tour, to a Jewish fortune-teller in Zurich to seek advice on his trip. Kaminski has just declared his attachment to Heinrich Heine, 'that German Jew and Jewish German,' and illustrated it with a vignette from his own schooldays in 1930s Switzerland with a fanatical German literature teacher who had marked him down for his loyalty, however weakly expressed, to the poet the Nazis were in the process of eradicating from German memory. And, indeed, the personage Kaminski then goes on to describe in 1980s Zurich, Chajm Schlapkin, the Tarot card reader, owes a great deal to the grotesqueries of Heine's famous 1843 epyllion, 'Germany, a Winter's Tale,' to which Kaminski will refer explicitly in the next chapter. The fabulous figure of the Jewish clairvoyant, 'small, round, and bald-headed' and 'like a hedgehog,' with his fractured German and off-putting manners, but said to be infallible, recalls Heine's fantasied visit to Hammonia, the prophetic patron goddess of Hamburg who reveals Germany's future in Charlemagne's chamberpot. Schlapkin, meanwhile, is even more prosaic: to Kaminski's question as to whether or not he should accept his publisher's invitation and travel to Germany, he answers simply no. When Kaminski is unsatisfied and tells him that he intends to write a book about Germany, Schlapkin warns him against it because 'they'll hack you up like a fish.' 'They,' Schlapkin explains, are the Germans if Kaminski points the finger at them in his book, and they are 'our kind' if Kaminski praises the Germans. The solution? The book should be neither praise nor blame, but rather 'the truth.' Nevertheless, Kaminski is sure to be eaten alive (or celebrated to death, as Schlapkin wryly adds at the book's end) whatever he writes.[111]

Here is a little primer in the Swiss-Jewish literary imaginary: for all of its tangled past, Switzerland, as represented by Kaminski and Schlapkin (who is significantly likened to a hedgehog, Switzerland's unofficial totemic animal), is truly 'neutral'—that is, a zone outside of the great postwar debates over the role of 'the Jews' in modern Germany. It is the privileged site of the imagination and of literature (recall by comparison Guggenheim's French-Swiss narrator in *Wir waren unser vier*, with his assessment of the value of literature above that of life); and it is also—perhaps therefore—a place from which one ventures out at one's peril and where one is well advised to leave behind the luxuries of praise and blame, of confident moralism as well as of literary hyperbole, in favor of a cold-eyed objectivity, which effort, in any case, will not save one in the end from the savagery of the world beyond the border. In this, Kaminski's 'Jewish' view may not be so very different from the traditional, stereotyped Swiss 'hedgehog' outlook, to which the world beyond the borders appears tantalizingly busy, filled with event, history, meaning, and 'truth'—and yet also distressingly chaotic, violent, and amoral.[112]

The venerable, ambivalent posture of Jews in Switzerland, ready to meld their culture with that of the confederation in order to produce something new, something hybrid and vigorous, yet also filled with a will to preserve their singularity by separating and fencing off the Jewish culture from the non-Jewish and thereby create an insular 'minor' culture, begins to look rather like the attitude of Switzerland itself on the international stage. Switzerland's economic and cultural attention is—of necessity—focused on the world beyond its borders, and it has on occasion shown a strong desire to burst the constraints of its self-imposed neutrality by launching initiatives to join such international bodies as the United Nations or the European Union. But a deep strain of skepticism about the conditions obtaining outside, coupled with a firmly entrenched conservatism and a xenophobia often styled as patriotism, both with their roots particularly in the German-speaking regions of the country, has consistently defeated attempts to wean Switzerland of its attachment to a minor but singular status as a political loner. The vicissitudes of such Jewish authors in Switzerland as Albert Cohen, Margarete Susman, Lajzer Ajchenrand, André Kaminski, and especially Kurt Guggenheim are a parable of just such an ambivalence, a uniquely complicated balancing act between adherence to a tentative and minuscule minority identity in a country made up of minorities and whole-hearted commitment to a national project of just such a tentative and minuscule minority identity enacted on the international stage.

In remarks made in 1954, on the occasion of the fiftieth anniversary of the Swiss Federation of Israelite Communities (SIG), Hermann Levin Goldschmidt stressed the problematic affinity between the nature of the Jewish culture in Switzerland and the character of its host country. He drew from the comparison an unsettling conclusion but also a kind of hope:

Thus Swiss Jewry today shares with the rest of the population of this country the fateful question: does it have the strength and the courage to guard its own independence? And if Jewish Switzerland wants to survive these difficult decades, and to preserve the irreplaceable legacy of Europe and the Jewish Occident for coming generations and the future bearers of this heritage, then it must continue to exist thanks to its own sense of responsibility and accomplishment, to hope for as little as possible from the outside, and to provide as much as possible itself!

We find ourselves in a special relation to the rest of the world's Jewry, a relation defined by our Swiss situation; but we find ourselves also in a special relation to the other population groups of Switzerland: that of the Jewish segment of the Swiss population. It is only on the basis of this double peculiarity that questions of Jewish cultural activity in Switzerland can be correctly addressed—that is, we must determine our actual problems, and we must emphasize our particular accomplishments.

Three main difficulties attend this work: the extremely small numbers of Swiss Jewry, their uncommonly high order of fragmentation, and a quite disproportionate lack of means. Barely twenty thousand are the Jews of Switzerland as a group, and in comparison with the rest of the population, a minuscule number that finds itself in addition—as do the other inhabitants of the country—further splintered by very tangible cantonal frontiers and by two linguistic borders. Above all, the rift between the French and the German linguistic regions rends our cultural activity into two barely reconcilable halves.

That such a varied nature is entirely in keeping with a Swiss community is of little comfort when one cannot even count upon the whole of these small numbers for one's work with the group in question. In addition, it has to this day been only very seldom the case that hearers, readers, and patrons could be won from beyond Jewish circles. The severing of the Jewish accomplishment from the rest of Switzerland's cultural activities, a phenomenon that has a host of historical circumstances at its origins, causes the small number of Jews to seem even smaller and brings a further decrease in sympathy and participation from outside. And yet this rift, at least, is of no fundamental importance. It must, it will be repaired one day, in view of the evidence of our accomplishments![113]

Goldschmidt's account of the role of Jews in Switzerland is at the same time an account of the role of Switzerland itself: sure of its accomplishments and its importance, yet dismayed by its comparative weakness, by its internal divisions, by the small measure of sympathy and understanding accorded it by the outside world. Would it be best to produce itself on the international stage as a kind of hybrid, as the Swiss version of a postmodern, globalized culture? Or would it be better to retreat into its familiar status as a privileged but inscrutable minority, not bound by the same rules as its fellows because heeding the call of a higher power, a more venerable morality? With that 'varied nature' that 'is entirely in keeping with a Swiss community,' the Swiss-Jewish authors collected here, in their writing and in their public lives, worry over these same quandaries, perform these same attempts at hybridity, and are tempted in the same way by the appeal of their minority status. What they provide are a series of provisional answers to what Goldschmidt comes close to calling the 'Swiss Question'— answers, however, that are themselves always couched in the form of a question.

Notes

1. See, for instance, the use of the commonplace in an article by the respected Swiss journalist and editor of the German weekly *Die Zeit*, Roger de Weck: 'Weil der Freund so gerne Feind war,' *Der Tages-Anzeiger*, May 24, 1996, p. 2. For nuanced reflections on the vicissitudes of this relationship, see an essay by Jane Kramer, a longtime chronicler of European and Swiss affairs: 'Manna from Hell,' *The New Yorker: Special Europe Issue*, April 28 and May 5, 1997, pp. 74–89. In her 'Alpine Neurose,' *Die Weltwoche*, October 1, 1998, Kramer takes these reflections further by noting similarities in Swiss and American relations to their respective histories: for instance, a shared tendency both to personalize and to moralize the elements of their respective national mythologies.

2. Pierre Heumann, *Israel entstand in Basel: Die phantastische Geschichte einer Vision* (Zurich: Weltwoche-ABC, 1997).

3. John McPhee, *La Place de la Concorde Suisse* (New York: Farrar, Strauss, Giroux, 1984).

4. Serguei Hazanov, *Lettres russes* (Vevey: Editions de l'Aire, 1997), p. 38. For thoughts on the (imaginary) relations between Swiss-German and

Yiddish, see Rafaël Newman, '. . . eine Schau in die Welt . . . ihr nahe zu sein und ferne zugleich,' in *Zeitschrift für deutsche Philologie*, special issue on 'Deutsch-jüdische Literatur der neunziger Jahre,' ed. Sander L. Gilman and Hartmut Steinecke (Berlin: Erich Schmidt Verlag, 2001), pp. 174–88.

5. Binjamin Wilkomirski, *Bruchstücke: Aus einer Kindheit 1939–1948* (Frankfurt: Suhrkamp Verlag, 1995). Published in English as *Fragments: Memories of a Wartime Childhood*, trans. Carol Brown Janeway (New York: Schocken Books, 1996).

6. See in particular Birgit R. Erdle, 'Traumatisiertes Gedächtnis und zurückgewiesene Erinnerung: Zu Binjamin Wilkomirskis Buch *Bruchstücke. Aus einer Kindheit 1939–1948*,' in *Figuren des Fremden in der Schweizer Literatur*, ed. Corina Caduff (Zurich: Limmat Verlag, 1997), pp. 153–74.

7. The three cases dominating the news in the late 1990s were those of Eli Carmel, who was expelled by the Basel police in 1939; Joseph Spring, who was handed over to Nazi authorities in 1943; and Charles and Sabine Sonabend, who were deported with their parents from Switzerland to occupied France in 1942. The first claimant was awarded fifty thousand francs in damages by a local court; the cases of Spring and the Sonabends were tried in federal court and defeated on technicalities, although a loophole was invoked to award the claimants symbolic monetary damages. For a consideration of the discourse surrounding the two cases, see Daniel Wildmann, 'Die zweite Verfolgung. Rechtsdiskurs und Konstruktion von Geschichte in der Schweiz,' in *Gedächtnis, Geld und Gesetz. Vom Umgang mit der Vergangenheit des Zweiten Weltkrieges*, ed. Jakob Tanner and Sigrid Weigel (Zurich: vdf, 2000), Zürcher Hochschulforum, vol. 29.

8. See the series of articles by Ganzfried: 'Die geliehene Holocaust-Biographie,' *Die Weltwoche*, August 27, 1998; 'Fakten gegen Erinnerung,' *Die Weltwoche*, September 3, 1998; and 'Bruchstücke und Scherbenhaufen,' *Die Weltwoche*, September 24, 1998. See also Ganzfried's update: 'Binjamin Wilkomirski und die verwandelte Polin,' *Die Weltwoche*, November 4, 1999.

9. It was also rumored, perhaps most perfidiously, that Ganzfried was motivated in his revelations by envy of the success of Wilkomirski/ Doessekker's book, published in the same year as Ganzfried's own allegedly similar book, his fictionalized account of his father's survival of three Nazi camps: *Der Absender* (Zurich: Rotpunktverlag, 1995). On this issue and for a refutation of such a claim based on an analysis of Ganzfried's highly nuanced novel, see Rafaël Newman with Caroline Wiedmer, 'Odysseus' Tattoo: On Daniel Ganzfried's *The Sender* and Binjamin Wilkomirski's *Fragments*,' in *Literary Friendship, Literary Paternity: Essays in Honor of Stanley Corngold*, ed. G. Richter (Chapel Hill: University of North Carolina Press, 2002).

10. Stefan Mächler, *Der Fall Wilkomirski: Über die Wahrheit einer Biographie*

(Zurich: Pendo Verlag, 2000). Ganzfried was quick to criticize the report for emphasizing the role that an alleged 'trauma' had played in Doessekker's actions, and for not being hard enough on the 'accomplices' in what Ganzfried considered a deliberate act of fraud: see Ganzfried, 'Der Holocaust-Transvestit,' *Die Weltwoche*, June 22, 2000.

11. See, for a brief overview of this phenomenon, Sander Gilman, 'Ethnicity-Ethnicities-Literature-Literatures,' *PMLA* 113, 1 (1998): 19–27. In a fulminating article in the regional *Aargauer Zeitung*, Max Dohner came closest to framing the case of Wilkomirski thus by evoking the lackluster Swiss quotidian as a spur to creative autobiographizing and the 'dictatorship' of Zurich's 'unending cultural carnival' as the reason for the book's uncritical reception there. It is clear, however, that the discourse surrounding multiculturalism in any form would be suspect to this author, for whom the particular criteria of this identity performance were of little interest. See Max Dohner, 'Holocaust-Erinnerung: Wurscht, was wahr ist?' *Aargauer Zeitung*, September 4, 1998, p. 66.

12. Ganzfried, 'Binjamin Wilkomirski.'

13. See Homi K. Bhabha, *The Location of Culture* (London: Routledge, 1994). See also Newman, 'Binjamin der Lügner?' in . . . *alias Wilkomirski: Die Holocaust Travestie*, ed. Sebastian Hefti (Berlin: Jüdische Verlagsanstalt, 2002), pp. 175–96.

14. On the notion of 'subject position' and its use in the discourse surrounding the historiography of the Holocaust in particular, see Dominick La Capra, *Representing the Holocaust* (Ithaca: Cornell University Press, 1994), p. 46. For a discussion of the term's use in the light of other psychoanalytically derived models for Holocaust historiography, see Caroline Wiedmer, *The Claims of Memory* (Ithaca: Cornell University Press, 1999), pp. 1–10.

15. Article 25 bis, the prohibition on Jewish ritual slaughter, although by then for the most part a dead letter, was struck from the Federal Constitution in 1973 but remains as a law—nearly seventy years after the Schweizer Israelitischer Gemeindebund (SIG), or Swiss Federation of Israelite Communities, had been founded with the express purpose of defeating such legislation; see Ralph Weingarten, 'Gleichberechtigt in die neue Zeit: Die 'Gründerzeit' des Schweizer Judentums 1866–1920,' in *Juden in der Schweiz: Glaube-Geschichte-Gegenwart*, ed. Willy Guggenheim et al. (Küsnacht-Zurich: Edition Kurz, 1982), pp. 54–68.

16. One recent text that suggests the form a first literary reaction to Wilkomirski might take is Vincent Philippe's lyrical memoir of his mother, *Le Silence d'Ilona* (Orbe: Bernard Campiche Editeur, 1999). Part investigative journalism, part historical reconstruction, the ostensible 'novel' turns out

to be a report on the author's discovery of his own Jewish roots, which had been dissembled by his Hungarian-Jewish refugee mother.

17. In her earlier award-winning novel, *Le Salon Pompadour* (Yvonand: Bernard Campiche Editeur, 1990), which plays partly during the Dreyfus era, Roche achieves something of the same for Alsace as an ancestral homeland of European Jewish culture.

18. Daniel Zahno, *Doktor Turban: Erzählungen* (Basel: Bruckner and Thünker, 1996; reprinted by btb/Goldmann Verlag, 1998). (The volume also contains the story 'Yerushalayim,' a sensual Israeli travelogue.) See also Yvette Z'Graggen, *Les Années silencieuses* (Lausanne: Editions de l'Aire, 1982; reprinted by Editions Zoé, 1999).

19. Markus shares her connection to Celan with another immigrant Swiss-Jewish poet, Franz Wurm (b. 1926), who carried on a correspondence with Celan that has appeared as Barbara Wiedemann and Franz Wurm, eds., *Paul Celan–Franz Wurm 'Briefwechsel'* (Frankfurt am Main: Suhrkamp Verlag, 1995). Wurm, who was born in Prague and lives in Zurich, has published a distinguished body of work: difficult, occasionally neologistic German poetry that has been compared to Celan's, but in which the poet's experience as a Jew nowhere comes to the fore with the weight of Celan's 'Todesfuge.'

20. The (acknowledged) influence of Woody Allen is surprisingly common among Swiss-Jewish authors, as, for instance, in the case of the comic writers Amsel and Marianne Weissberg (private correspondence) and that of the drier social observer Yvonne Léger. See Ronald Schenkel, 'Woody Allens kleine Schwester,' *Neue Zuger Zeitung*, October 30, 1998, p. 51.

21. Benoziglio, Ganzfried, Hazanov, Werenfels: personal interviews. Markus: interview with Henrik Rhyn, broadcast on Swiss Radio DRS 1, November 27, 1999. Roche: cited in Isabelle Falconnier, 'Guerre et paix, poing à la ligne,' *L'Hebdo*, May 4, 2000, pp. 100–107. Hazanov also lists among his influences Mikhail Bulgakov. This, combined with the fact that Roche does not mention Kurt Guggenheim, who was concerned, like her, with the factual history of social democracy in the twentieth century, suggests the extent to which the famous *Röschti Graben*, or linguistic barrier between the French- and German-speaking regions of Switzerland, is upheld among Swiss-Jewish writers as well. See now, for a first attempt at bridging this divide between the Swiss-Jewish literary communities, Rafaël Newman, *Zweifache Eigenheit. Neuere jüdische Literatur in der Schweiz* (Zurich: Limmat Verlag, 2001).

22. 'The Contemporary German Fascination for Things Jewish: Toward a Minor Jewish Culture,' in *Reemerging Jewish Culture in Germany: Life and Literature since 1989*, ed. Sander L. Gilman and Karen Remmler (New York: New York University Press, 1994), pp. 15–45.

23. Zipes, 'Contemporary German Fascination,' pp. 21–23. See Gilles Deleuze and Félix Guattari, *Kafka: Toward a Minor Literature*, trans. Dana Pollan (Minneapolis: University of Minnesota Press, 1986). This does not, of course, mean that individual writers have no objection to being thus 'collectivized'; one need think only of Henryk M. Broder, who has vigorously defended his right to stand aloof from other Jewish writers and to criticize them.

24. Zipes, 'Contemporary German Fascination,' p. 23. See now too, for another view of this complex, Andreas Kilcher, 'Exterritorialitäten. Zur kulturellen Konstruktion der aktuellen deutsch-jüdischen Literatur,' in Gilman and Steinecke, eds., *Zeitschrift für deutsche Philologie*, special issue on 'Deutsch-jüdische Literatur der neunziger Jahre.'

25. Compare the German political rhetoric in debates over immigration, double citizenship, and training versus enlarged work-visa quotas throughout the 1990s and into 2000.

26. Compare the public remarks of the Social Democratic federal councillor Moritz Leuenberger at the synagogue in Endingen during the town's twelve-hundred-year jubilee: 'The whole of Switzerland consists almost entirely of minorities.' Cited in Peter Neumann, *Die Schweizer Judendörfer: Auf Spurensuche in Endingen und Lengnau*, documentary film (Switzerland, 1998).

27. Zipes, 'Contemporary German Fascination,' pp. 22–23.

28. See, for example, the reactions to then federal councillor Jean-Pascal Delamuraz's casually epigrammatic reference to Auschwitz in Madeleine Dreyfus and Jürg Fischer, eds., *Manifest vom 21. Januar 1997: Geschichtsbilder und Antisemitismus in der Schweiz* (Zurich: Thema WoZ, 1997), as well as Adolf Muschg's essay, *Wenn Auschwitz in der Schweiz liegt: Fünf Reden eines Schweizers an seine und keine Nation* (Frankfurt am Main: Suhrkamp, 1997).

29. Zipes, 'Contemporary German Fascination,' p. 22.

30. K. Anthony Appiah, 'The Multiculturalist Misunderstanding,' *New York Review of Books* 44, no. 15 (October 9, 1997), pp. 30–36. The article is a review of Michael Walzer, *On Toleration* (New Haven: Yale University Press, 1997), and Nathan Glazer, *We Are All Multiculturalists Now* (Cambridge: Harvard University Press, 1997).

31. Appiah, 'Multiculturalist Misunderstanding,' pp. 30–31.

32. Walzer, cited in Appiah, 'Multiculturalist Misunderstanding,' p. 34.

33. Compare, however, the experiences of the twenty-four young Swiss Jews interviewed in Philipp Dreyer, *Zwischen Davidstern und Schweizerpass: 24 Porträts jüdischer Jugendlicher* (Zurich: Orell Füssli Verlag, 1999), which include, among accounts of various sorts of indifference, the whole gamut of modern anti-Semitic remarks and behaviors on the part of their non-Jewish age mates.

34. See the argument of Willi Goetschel in his introduction to Hermann

Levin Goldschmidt, *Werkausgabe in neun Bänden*, vol. 4: '*Der Rest bleibt*': *Aufsätze zum Judentum* (Vienna: Passagen Verlag, 1997), pp. 11–18.

35. See, on the early years of this period, Raphael Mahler, *A History of Modern Jewry 1780–1815* (London: Vallentine, Mitchell, 1971), particularly pp. 134–35, where Raphael comments on the extraordinarily complex and malicious nature of the laws on Jewish life in place in various of the German states, foremost among them Prussia, as being in and of themselves a spur to 'the growing assimilationist movement amongst the German Jews which, through the absence of human and national pride, was unequalled anywhere else.'

36. See, among many others, Henryk M. Broder and Michel Lang, eds., *Fremd im eigenen Land* (Frankfurt am Main: Fischer, 1979); Dirk Blasius and Dan Diner, eds., *Zerbrochene Geschichte: Leben und Selbstverständnis der Juden in Deutschland* (Frankfurt am Main: Fischer, 1991); Gilman and Remmler, eds., *Reemerging Jewish Culture in Germany*; and Sander L. Gilman, *Jews in Today's German Culture* (Bloomington: Indiana University Press, 1995).

37. James Joyce, *Ulysses: A Critical and Synoptic Edition*, vol. 1, ed. Hans-Walter Gabler et al. (New York and London: Garland Publishing, 1986), pp. 72–73.

38. The various strains of the Enlightenment, both Jewish and otherwise, did make occasional incursions into Switzerland before the emancipation of the Jews there. Note, for instance, Mendelssohn's engagement, voiced in a letter to the Swiss inventor of physiognomy, J. C. Lavater, on April 14, 1775, in the cause of countering legislation aimed at further constraining the Jews of Oberendingen and Lengnau. See Moses Mendelssohn, *Gesammelte Schriften*, ed. G. B. Mendelssohn, 7 vols. (Leipzig, 1843–45), vol. 3, pp. 106–7. For their part, as the modern era dawned, German-speaking Swiss Jews had to manage a difficult balancing act between the compelling cultural and political movements emanating from Germany and Austria and a firm commitment to the smaller, less internationally prominent country of which they were gradually becoming equal citizens; see Sander Gilman and Jack Zipes, eds., *Yale Companion to Jewish Writing and Thought in German Culture, 1096–1996* (New Haven: Yale University Press, 1997), p. xviii.

39. For essays and tables on the history of Switzerland's Jewish population, see Augusta Weldler-Steinberg, *Geschichte der Juden in der Schweiz, vom 16. Jahrhundert bis nach der Emanzipation*, revised and annotated by Florence Guggenheim-Grünberg, 2 vols. (Zurich: Schweizerischer Israelitischer Gemeindebund, 1966 and 1970); Guggenheim et al., eds., *Juden in der Schweiz*, the companion to a national exhibit on Jews in Switzerland; and its French-language counterpart, Aaron Kamis-Müller et al., eds., *Vie juive en Suisse* (Lausanne: Editions du Grand-Pont, 1992), which contains material on the

Jewish settlements in western Switzerland not included in the earlier volume. For a congenial folk history of Swiss republicanism and the native movements supporting the 'Helvétique,' see Markus Kutter, *Die Schweizer und die Deutschen: Es hätte auch ganz anders kommen können* . . . (Zurich: Ammann, 1995). On the history of modern Swiss anti-Semitism, see Aram Mattioli, ed., *Antisemitismus in der Schweiz 1848–1960* (Zurich: Orell Füssli, 1998).

40. Hermann L. Goldschmidt, *Fragen jüdischer Kulturarbeit in der Schweiz*; Sonderdruck aus der Festschrift des Schweizerischen Israelitischen Gemeindebundes 1954 (Basel: Buchdruckerei Brin AG, 1954), p. 7.

41. It should be noted that the modern-day multilingual character of Switzerland was very much a product of the upheavals of the eighteenth and nineteenth centuries, with German the official language of the confederacy until 1798, the imposition by the Napoleonic occupiers of equal status for French and Italian, and the cementing of this status, along with similar rights for Rhaeto-Romanic, or Romansch, in the constitutional decisions of 1848; see Urs Dürmüller, *Mehrsprachigkeit im Wandel: Von der viersprachigen zur vielsprachigen Schweiz* (Zurich: Pro Helvetia, 1996), pp. 11–12.

42. For early numbers, see Florence Guggenheim-Grünberg, 'Vom Scheiterhaufen zur Emanzipation: Die Juden in der Schweiz vom 6. bis 19. Jahrhundert,' in *Juden in der Schweiz*, ed. Guggenheim et al., pp. 10–53; for later figures see Ralph Weingarten, *Schweizer Juden: Broschüre zur Wanderausstellung der Gesellschaft für Minderheiten in der Schweiz (GMS) und der Stiftung gegen Rassismus und Antisemitismus (GRA)* (Zurich: Weingarten and Partner, 1998), p. 7.

43. Mahler, ed., *History of Modern Jewry*, p. 130.

44. See Weingarten, 'Gleichberechtigt in die neue Zeit,' pp. 54–68, for notes on the gradual move of Swiss Jews from the country to the city during the last third of the nineteenth century. For a fascinating study of the later contributions of East European Jews to the cultural and intellectual life of Zurich, see Karin Huser Bugmann, *Schtetl an der Sihl: Einwanderung, Leben und Alltag der Ostjuden in Zürich, 1880–1939* (Zurich: Chronos Verlag, 1998). On the East European origins of Omanut, the Swiss organization for the promotion of Jewish culture, see Jacques Picard, 'Vom Zagreber zum Zürcher Omanut 1932 bis 1952: Wandel und Exil einer jüdischen Kulturbewegung,' *Exilforschung: Ein internationales Jahrbuch*, Band 10 (1992), pp. 168–86.

45. Guggenheim-Grünberg, 'Vom Scheiterhaufen zur Emanzipation,' p. 28. On the history of Jews in the Romandie (the six western cantons), see Aaron Kamis-Müller, 'Fribourg, Valais, région jurassienne,' and Alfred Berchtold, 'Ces voix de Genève,' both in *Vie juive en Suisse*, ed. Kamis-Müller et al., pp. 164–71 and 173–91 respectively. The Italian-speaking Canton of Ticino, as well as the Romansch-speaking areas of the Canton of

Graubünden, have historically and to this day extremely small numbers of Jewish residents, with Lugano the only city in the whole of the Swiss southeast to have an official Jewish community. There have been recent Jewish immigrants to these parts of Switzerland, such as the Hamburg-born novelist Wolfgang Hildesheimer (1916–1991), who settled in Poschiavo in 1957, or the Israeli historian Vittorio Dan Segre, who leads the Institute for Mediterannean Studies at the newly founded Università della Svizzera italiana in Lugano; but their intellectual community has been in large measure found beyond the cantonal borders. In Hildesheimer's work, furthermore, despite a tone that has been called 'Old Testament' (see Urs Widmer's obituary in Der Tages-Anzeiger, August 22, 1991), there is a marked avoidance of direct reference to the Jewish experience.

46. For notes on the interesting modern history of literary agencies in Zurich, see Franziska Schläpfer, 'Der Literaturagent, Freund und Helfer der Autoren,' Der Tages-Anzeiger, April 26, 2000, p. 65.

47. Also frequently adduced as evidence of Süsskind's Jewishness is an illumination in the manuscript that shows a man, identified as Süsskind and evidently wearing the distinctive garb of a medieval Jew, in conversation with a Christian official; see for discussion Ingo F. Walther, Codex Manesse: Die Miniaturen der Großen Heidelberger Liederhandschrift (Frankfurt am Main: Insel Verlag, 1988). For an exhaustive exegesis of the figure of Süsskind, as well as translations of his poems into modern German, see Dietrich Gerhardt, Süsskind von Trimberg: Berichtigungen zu einer Erinnerung (Bern: Peter Lang, 1997). See particularly pp. 272–82 for Gerhardt's negative verdict on Süsskind's Jewishness.

48. For a discussion of the twentieth-century controversy surrounding Süsskind's place in the codex, as well as that controversy's place in the shaping of German studies in Switzerland, see Bettina Spoerri, 'Ein jüdischer Spruchdichter im Zürcher Manesse-Codex?—Die germanistische Kontroverse um Süsskind von Trimberg,' in Germanistik in der Schweiz—Schweizer Germanistik: Eine wissenschaftliche Reflexion, ed. Corina Caduff and Michael Gamper (Zurich: Chronos Verlag, 2001). On continued references to Süsskind as Jewish, see Bettina Spoerri, 'Tausend Jahre unbestimmtes Deutschland,' Der Tages-Anzeiger, May 22, 2000, p. 50, her review of Rolf Schneider, Vor 1000 Jahren: Alltag im Mittelalter (Augsburg: Weltbild Buchverlag, 1999).

49. Unless otherwise noted, all translations of German, French, and Yiddish texts are my own.

50. This guide, prepared by Yoseif ben Ephraim Karo (1488–1575) in 1565, was in turn supplemented—or, indeed, supplanted—in European Jewish homes during the nineteenth century by the Kitzur Shulchan Aruch, an

abridged version of the guide prepared by the Hungarian rabbi Shelomo Ganzfried (1804–1866).

51. For brief histories of the scholars involved, see Erich A. Hausmann, 'Ein Denkmal für Rabbi Mosche von Zürich,' *Die Jüdische Zeitung*, no. 8, February 23, 1990. For a more extensive account of Rabbi Mosche, see Jizchak S. Lange, 'Zur rechtlichen Stellung des jüdischen Lehrens in Zürich vor 600 Jahren,' in *25 Jahre Jüdische Schule Zürich: Festschrift* (Jerusalem: Koren Publishers, 1980), pp. 108–22.

52. Hausmann, 'Ein Denkmal.'

53. Johann Caspar Ulrich, *Sammlung jüdischer Geschichten, welche sich mit diesem Volk in dem XIII. und folgenden Jahrhunderten bis auf MDCCLX in der Schweiz von Zeit zu Zeit zugetragen. Zur Beleuchtung der allgemeinen Historie dieser Nation herausgegeben* (Basel, 1768); republished in 1969 by Gregg International Publishers, Westmead, Farnborough, Hants., England.

54. Guggenheim-Grünberg, 'Vom Scheiterhaufen zur Emanzipation,' p. 25.

55. Ulrich, *Sammlung jüdischer Geschichten*, p. 3.

56. See *Seder Hagadah shel Pesah: The Haggadah of Passover Line by Line*, trans. Saadyah Maximon, notes Rabbi Charles B. Chavel, D.H.L., illust. Siegmund Forst (New York: Shulsinger Brothers, 1958).

57. Ulrich, *Sammlung jüdischer Geschichten*, pp. 136–37.

58. Ulrich, *Sammlung jüdischer Geschichten*, pp. 137–39.

59. Elias Canetti, *Die gerettete Zunge: Geschichte einer Jugend* (Munich: Carl Hanser Verlag, 1977), p. 375. To be sure, Canetti goes on to note, in the last line of the volume, that 'like the earliest human, I first came to be as a result of my being driven out of paradise.'

60. Canetti, *Die gerettete Zunge*, p. 193.

61. Canetti, *Die gerettete Zunge*, p. 194. For further reflections on the role of Swiss German in Canetti's relation to his 'mother tongue,' see Dagmar Barnouw, *Elias Canetti zur Einführung* (Hamburg: Junius Verlag, 1996), pp. 83–114.

62. Canetti, *Die gerettete Zunge*, p. 193.

63. See Weingarten, 'Gleichberechtigt in die neue Zeit,' pp. 65–66.

64. For a history of the wartime period in Switzerland, see among others Werner Rings, *Schweiz im Krieg: 1933–1945: Ein Bericht mit 400 Bilddokumenten*, 8th ed. (Zurich: Chronos Verlag, 1990). The standard history of the Jewish experience of the period is Jacques Picard, *Die Schweiz und die Juden: 1933–1945* (Zurich: Chronos Verlag, 1994).

65. See Unabhängige Experten Kommission Schweiz-Zweiter Weltkrieg, ed., *Die Schweiz und die Flüchtlinge zur Zeit des Nationalsozialismus* (Bern: BBL/EDMZ, 1999), part of the findings of the so-called 'Bergier-Kommission.' See also, on Swiss immigration policy during the period

leading up to the Nazi takeover in Germany, Uriel Gast, *Von der Kontrolle zur Abwehr: Die eidgenössische Fremdenpolizei im Spannungsfeld von Politik und Wirtschaft 1915–1933* (Zurich: Chronos Verlag, 1997).

66. For details and statistics, see Charles Linsmayer, 'Sie hatten den geistigen Verrat bereits vollzogen,' *Der kleine Bund*; cultural supplement to the *Bund* of July 5, 1997, no. 154, pp. 1–3, Linsmayer's publication of his findings in the archives of the ssv. Among those 'evaluated' by the ssv was Hermann Levin Goldschmidt, who was to go on to achieve a signal renown as the veritable dean of postwar Swiss-Jewish intellectuals; among those granted a conditional work visa following the recommendations of the ssv was Robert Musil in 1939. Golo Mann, in the same year, was denied entry altogether. In his book-length study of the ssv, Ulrich Niederer notes that the organization was guided, as early as May of 1933, by the simple will to protect the Swiss market from being flooded with 'economic' immigrants, which by no means, however, excludes the later application of ideological criteria in the ssv's fashioning of its reports on candidates. See *Geschichte des Schweizerischen Schriftsteller-Verbandes: Kulturpolitik und individuelle Förderung: Jakob Bührer als Beispiel* (Tübingen and Basel: Francke Verlag, 1994), esp. pp. 139ff.

67. Susman was classified by the Swiss authorities as 'left-extremist' and forbidden to speak publicly or to publish during the war years; she took on the pseudonym 'Reiner' so as to be able to continue writing. See Thomas Sparr's article on Susman in *Metzler Lexikon der deutsch-jüdischen Literatur: Jüdische Autorinnen und Autoren deutscher Sprache von der Aufklärung bis zur Gegenwart*, ed. Andreas B. Kilcher (Stuttgart and Weimar: Verlag J. B. Metzler, 2000), pp. 560–62. There were, of course, other Jewish intellectuals practicing their professions in Switzerland during this period, both immigrants, like Salcia Landmann (1911–2002), Hermann Levin Goldschmidt (1914–1998), and Paul Parin (b. 1916), and natives, like Jeanne Hersch (1910–2000) and Jean Starobinski (b. 1920); their estimable contributions are not discussed here because they are either primarily academic and not literary or, as in the case of Hersch's novel, *Temps alternés* (Fribourg, 1942), not concerned with Jewish topics. The same might be said of Swiss-Jewish artists, like Willy Leopold Guggenheim, alias Varlin (1900–1977), or Alis Guggenheim (1896–1958), both of whom also wrote material (diaries and/ or poems) that was either not obviously literary or had no obvious connection to Jewishness. Alis Guggenheim, a lifelong Communist and internationalist, was particularly eager not to be 'classified' as Jewish ('For the Swiss I am just a Jew,' she wrote bitterly in 1944), despite the traditional Jewish subjects of some of her paintings from her childhood in the Swiss-Jewish town of Lengnau. See Susanne Gisel-Pfankuch et al., *'Als ob ich selber nackt in Schnee und Regen stehe. . . .' Alis Guggenheim 1896–1958: Jüdin,*

Kommunistin, Künstlerin (Baden: Verlag Lars Müller, 1992), and Varlin, *Wenn ich dichten könnte: Briefe und Schriften*, ed. Patrizia Guggenheim and Tobias Eichenberg (Zurich: Scheidegger and Spiess, 1998).

68. Susman's sister was not so lucky: attempting to cross the Swiss border at Hohenems (Austria) in 1942, Paula Hammerschlag was arrested along with her companions and subsequently committed suicide. See Susman's account of her own life, written at the request of the Leo Baeck Institute and published as *Ich habe viele Leben gelebt: Erinnerungen* (Stuttgart: Deutsche Verlags-Anstalt, 1964). See also the proceedings of a conference held in 1997 at the Jewish Museum in Hohenems, taking as its explicit focus various attempts at crossing this particular border: Petra Zudrell, ed., *Der abgerissene Dialog: Die intellektuelle Beziehung Gertrud Kantorowicz - Margarete Susman, oder, Die Schweizer Grenze bei Hohenems als Endpunkt eines Fluchtversuchs* (Innsbruck and Vienna: Studien-Verlag, 1999).

69. See the 1996 reissue of this book by the Jüdischer Verlag at Suhrkamp; it contains a valuable foreword by Hermann Levin Goldschmidt.

70. See Susman's own melancholy reflections on this symbiosis, arising out of the years of German prosperity following upon the founding of Bismarck's Reich: Susman, *Ich habe viele Leben gelebt*, p. 14.

71. Susman, *Aus sich wandelnder Zeit: Gedichte* (Zurich and Stuttgart: Diana Verlag, 1953), p. 118.

72. Susman, *Aus sich wandelnder Zeit*, p. 126.

73. Compare, for example, the editor's formulation in his foreword to Jo Mihaly, Lajser [sic] Ajchenrand, and Stephan Hermlin, *Wir verstummen nicht: Gedichte in der Fremde* (Zurich: Carl Posen Verlag, undated, likely 1945).

74. For a compressed but useful account of the literary life of Cohen, including thoughts on the episode of insult in Marseilles, see Marta Caraion, 'Albert Cohen,' in *Histoire de la littérature en Suisse Romande*, vol. 3, ed. Roger Francillon et al., pp. 343–53 (Lausanne: Payot, 1998). For a more extensive biography, see Gérard Valbert, *Albert Cohen, le seigneur* (Paris: Bernard Grasset, 1990).

75. Apart from the four novels discussed here, Cohen's writings also include the early poetry collection *Paroles juives* (1921), the one-act play *Ezéchiel* (1930), the memoir *Le livre de ma mère* (1954), and the final two volumes of his autobiographical trilogy, *O vous, frères humains* (1972) and *Carnets 1978* (1979).

76. Albert Cohen, *Mangeclous* (Paris: Editions Gallimard, 1938, reprinted 1965), p. 16.

77. Caraion, 'Albert Cohen,' p. 348.

78. Cohen notably held, for one year, the directorship of the short-lived but illustrious *Revue juive*, an international journal of literature and critique based in Paris. Among the members of the editorial committee were such

figures as Einstein, Freud, and Chaim Weizmann, who would go on to become the first president of Israel.

79. Cohen, *Mangeclous*, p. 166.

80. Cohen, *Mangeclous*, p. 166.

81. Cohen, *Mangeclous*, pp. 170–72. For example: 'Mais lorsqu'il aperçut la tête de porc qui le regardait avec *impireté*, posée sur une assiette, Jérémie se sauva, suivi de Scipion' (p. 172, my emphasis).

82. Cohen, *Belle du seigneur* (Paris: Editions Gallimard, 1968), pp. 13–54.

83. Cohen, *Belle du seigneur*, p. 53.

84. Caraion, 'Albert Cohen,' p. 353.

85. See Maja Wicki's reflections on the poet and her interview with his widow, published as 'Lyrik ist etwas vom Anständigsten, was diese Welt noch zu bieten hat,' *Das Magazin*, no. 44 (1986), pp. 26–31. I have also consulted Jacques Picard, 'Landshaft fun Goirl,' *Zytglogge Zytig*, no. 82 (1983), p. 2.

86. Zurich: Carl Posen Verlag, 1947.

87. Tel Aviv: Verlag Tamid, 1984.

88. Sigmund Bendkower, 'Für wen schreibt der jiddische Dichter?' *Neue Zürcher Zeitung*, no. 152, July 3, 1984, p. 29.

89. Ajchenrand, 'Ein Blick in Geist und Werden der jiddischen Literatur,' probably unpublished; cited in Wicki, 'Lyrik,' p. 31.

90. In Mihaly et al., *Wir verstummen nicht*, p. 31.

91. Among Guggenheim's ancestors was the first state-licensed rabbi in Switzerland, a committed Swiss as well as Jew who had served the communities of Oberendingen and Lengnau at the end of the eighteenth century and petitioned the still foreign authorities in Baden for clemency toward the Swiss. Guggenheim's family moved to Zurich, as soon as residence in Switzerland proper was possible for Jews, in 1862. See Nicole Rosenberger's article on Guggenheim in *Metzler Lexikon*, ed. Kilcher, pp. 190–92.

92. This varied and well-received corpus was nevertheless not enough to win Guggenheim a place in the five volumes of *Harenbergs Lexikon der Weltliteratur* (Dortmund: Harenbergs Lexikon-Verlag, 1989), an encyclopedia of world literature of which Guggenheim's countryman François Bondy was one of the editors, a fact to be accounted for, perhaps, by Bondy's patriotic self-effacement.

93. Kurt Guggenheim, *Alles in allem* (Zurich: Artemis Verlag, 1952–1955, first as four separate volumes; reprinted 1957 in one volume).

94. Charles Linsmayer, 'Foreignness in the Familiar, Becoming at Home in the Foreign: Kurt Guggenheim's *Alles in allem* and the Theme of Social Integration,' in Kurt Guggenheim, *Werke III: 'Alles in Allem'*, pp. 1047–87 (Frauenfeld: Huber, 1996). The title in German is 'Das Fremdsein im Eigenen, das Heimischwerden im Fremden: Kurt Guggenheims Roman

'Alles in Allem' und das Thema der sozialen Integration.' In the discussion of Guggenheim and Linsmayer here I follow my essay 'Binjamin der Lügner?'

95. See, for the text alluded to in Linsmayer's essay, Georg Simmel, 'Exkurs über den Fremden,' in Soziologie: Untersuchungen über die Formen der Vergesellschaftung (Leipzig: 1908), pp. 684–91; translated in On Individuality and Social Forms, ed. D. Levine (Chicago: University of Chicago Press, 1971), pp. 143–49.

96. Linsmayer, 'Foreignness in the Familiar,' p. 1074.

97. There is a curious piece of negative evidence that Guggenheim himself intended this potential symbolism when he chose to structure his generational novel around Jewish as well as non-Jewish characters. While, as noted here, contemporary historical figures appear in Alles in allem on their way around or through Zurich in the course of accurately depicted visits or sojourns, the absence of one temporary resident of the city is conspicuous: James Joyce, who spent part of a year in Zurich while writing Ulysses (1922) and who returned later, to die there in 1941. Joyce's great novel is famous in part for its own use of a Jewish character to depict, and indeed to evoke in its historical entirety, another European city, and thereby to raise that city to the transcendent level of mythology. Does this elision, then, represent Guggenheim's 'anxious' suppression of a predecessor in the same project?

98. Guggenheim, Alles in allem, 1957 ed., pp. 292–97.

99. Guggenheim, Alles in allem, 1957 ed., pp. 257–60.

100. Indeed, Rosenberger sees in Guggenheim's staging of the encounter between the Zionist and the assimilationist in the barracks of the Swiss army merely another moment in the author's lifelong and ubiquitous meditation on the entanglement of confessional and national identities, a meditation that led him to preserve his faith in his multilingual, multireligious Swiss homeland despite its flirtation with fascism during the period of the Third Reich.

101. Linsmayer, 'Foreignness in the Familiar,' p. 1054.

102. Guggenheim had himself wanted to become a physician but was made instead to follow his father's business career; see Rosenberger, p. 190. The novel's fourth character, the clerk Vinzenz Umbrecht, is by social and educational background too different from Guggenheim himself to represent his experience, although he incorporates certain 'Swiss' virtues Guggenheim obviously admired. See Charles Linsmayer's useful 1981 notes on the novel's background, reprinted as an afterword to Kurt Guggenheim, Wir waren unser vier (Frankfurt am Main: Suhrkamp Verlag, 1990), pp. 217–52.

103. Guggenheim, Wir waren unser vier, pp. 135–49.

104. Arthur Schnitzler, *Das weite Land: Dramen 1909–1912* (Frankfurt am Main: S. Fischer Verlag, reprinted 1997), p. 157.

105. Guggenheim, *Wir waren unser vier*, p. 149.

106. André Kaminski, *Nächstes Jahr in Jerusalem* (Frankfurt am Main: suhrkamp taschenbuch, 1988), p. 7.

107. Kaminski, *Nächstes Jahr*, p. 7.

108. Kaminski, *Herzflattern: Neun wilde Geschichten* (Frankfurt am Main: Suhrkamp Verlag, 1984).

109. See Eva Lezzi's very astute, if rather harsh, article on Kaminski in *Metzler Lexikon*, ed. Kilcher, pp. 290–93, where further bibliographical references can be found.

110. See, for example, H. Schafroth in the *Basler Zeitung* of November 6, 1987, and G. Kübler in the *Neue Zürcher Zeitung* of December 5/6, 1987.

111. Kaminski, *Schalom allerseits: Tagebuch einer Deutschlandreise* (Frankfurt am Main: Insel Verlag, 1987), pp. 7–14 and 234.

112. It is interesting to note that Albert Cohen, too, the inventor of Mangeclous, the champion of liars, spelled out the ineffability of truth, or at least its inaptitude to being grasped in language: Salomon Valeureux, the innocent, asks his wise relative Saltiel, 'What is truth?' And Saltiel responds, 'It is what is between the words.' Cited in Valbert, *Albert Cohen*, p. 12.

113. Goldschmidt, *Fragen jüdischer Kulturarbeit*, p. 7.

Daniel Ganzfried

Daniel Ganzfried was born in Afulah, Israel, in 1958 and returned to
Switzerland with his Swiss-Jewish mother and Hungarian-Jewish
father in 1960. He grew up in Wabern, near Bern. During the 1970s
and 1980s he apprenticed as a bookseller in Bern and as a printer in
Basel, as well as traveling and residing in Israel, Spain, Portugal,
and Central and North America. Since 1983 he has lived in Zurich,
where he works as a journalist, writes for the theater, and helps to
run the Hannah Arendt Tage, an annual conference on democracy.
His novel *Der Absender* (The sender) appeared in 1995; since then he
has also published literary and journalistic pieces in the Swiss press,
most celebratedly a series of articles for the *Weltwoche* on the case of
the purported memoir of 'Binjamin Wilkomirski,' *Bruchstücke*, as
well as working on a science fiction novel, a collection of essays on
the 'Wilkomirski Affair,' and a play based on the ill-fated voyage of
the *St. Louis*, the ship bearing Jewish refugees from the Nazis that
was turned back from Havana in 1939. In the excerpts from his
novel that follow, he intertwines the history of pre-Holocaust Jewish
life in provincial Hungary with the account of a Swiss-Jewish man
searching for his survivor father's history while volunteering at a
Holocaust archive in 1990s New York. Thus Ganzfried sets the stage
for a sustained meditation on the meaning of the past, the problematic dominance in post-Holocaust Jewish life of the notion of vic-
timhood, and the propriety of representing the Holocaust—as well
as of the Holocaust's enlistment in the projects of national and
personal identity construction.

Daniel Ganzfried

EXCERPTS FROM The Sender

I

He had hurried. All the same, when he got to the Empire State
Building almost five minutes too early, his father was already standing in front of the elevator to the observation deck. The high forehead, gray hair, soft mouth: Georg recognized him from a distance.
With every step he took toward him time fell away, until only a brief
yesterday remained of the years they had not seen each other. Their
hellos were curt, two fleeting kisses. He had the tickets already, his
father said; you couldn't hold up the line. The uniformed employee
in the cabin let his gaze wander once over their heads, pressed the
top button, and sat down heavily in the stool next to the console
panel. A dry bell tone. The doors slid together. The passengers
could only guess at the gathering upward motion.

Georg felt a bothersome pressure in his back: a small man was
trying earnestly not to get in anyone's way with his obtrusive tele-
photo lens. Georg left his helpless 'Excusez-moi' unanswered and
surrendered to the fantasy of being stuck for hours. Furtively he
sized up the densely packed passengers, convinced that they were
all thinking about the same thing— how it would begin to smell
after a while and what they would do for so long without a toilet.
A couple was reading quietly from a guidebook. Only it was the
wrong section. To Georg's ear, they were citing from a passage on
the twin towers of the World Trade Center. Or they were in the
wrong tower, he thought. Now and then he looked over at his
father, who seemed to be focusing on a random point on the alumi-
num wall. Georg wondered whether anyone else would notice that
they belonged together. He was looking for clues himself—as if a
sense had yet to be wrung out of their meeting. Another bell tone.
Ready for the rush of weightlessness even as they were coming to
rest, Georg waited for the doors to open and the people to wander

out in the draft. Still, the heavy breath of the city hit him full in the face, and as always for the first few minutes up here, it was as if he had entered a great vault.

2

In the seventies I made my first trip to Hungary since 1949. My father had died. My visa had been granted, purely arbitrarily, too late for the funeral. So I made the best of it and visited Uncle Soli in Budapest. What else was I to do? We talked the way two people usually do when they haven't seen each other for a long time. He described his experiences in the Ukraine. They had had to clear away mines. Despite many casualties, everyone had had a decent chance of making it: at least they weren't under German control. As history had demonstrated, a walk through a minefield was in fact less dangerous than a ride in one of the Reichsbahn's cattle cars. And then somehow, Uncle Soli came to speak of Grandfather and Grandmother. I mentioned casually that, of the two of us, I was the one who had seen them last. From behind, together with the rest of the family. Their line had been moving gradually into the distance while father pushed me forward in ours. Soli stood up. He walked to the window and looked down at the street for a while, where my old Ford Taurus was parked. 'Nice car. If only for the foreign license plates. It would have been smarter if he had stayed in America back then, our father, your grandfather.'

My grandparents had always been seventy to me. Their death had seemed never to become factual. They were simply no longer there. Like all the others. With astonishment, I now realized that they had evidently already had a life beyond my recollection. So I let my uncle talk on.

In those days, the representatives of the Pennsylvania steelworks had spread out all the way to the remotest backwaters of Hungary, with promises of contracts and cheap travel. They were especially on the lookout for young people, for big, strong, healthy men. They must even have had an Orthodox Jewish community to offer, since Grandfather would hardly have signed on otherwise. Not long before, he had married Sali, my grandmother. She was just as observant as he was, and waited in their homeland while he worked in the foundry for a few years. One day he was standing at the door again, not exactly rich but with a small nest egg and, above all, a plan. The vast tracts in America must have reminded him of the land back home and made him imagine applying the newfangled grain-harvesting techniques to the fields here as well. So he had bought a thresher with his own capital, the first in the region. It took a while for the farmers to rid themselves of the belief that the monstrous thing would chew up their grain rather than thresh it. But after that, my grandparents traveled for a few years throughout the entire *komitat*, getting themselves hired on by the landowners; thus each of their seven children was born in a different village. Why the thing went up in flames one day remained unexplained. The fact is, many of the poorer farmers couldn't keep up any-more, and there was already enough unemployment among the groundworkers.

According to Uncle Soli, it had to have been impossible to bring in a machine that did as much work as five people without making plenty of enemies for yourself. At the same time, the Tisza-Eszlar trial for alleged ritual murder had taken place. A Jew was supposed to have made *matzohs* out of the blood of a Christian girl. 'The machine wasn't insured, in any case.' That's when they settled down in Nyír.

A pious shoemaker and a warm, good-hearted woman. That's how I recall my grandparents. Grandfather spent more time at his tiny workbench, bent over all manner of texts, than with other people's shoes. His lips moved as he read, or he would stand up in order to walk a few steps in a little circle, one hand on his beard, be-fore seating himself again and reading further. I fashioned ships out of wood nails and old soles, the workbench became the Dan-ube, Grandfather was a pirate, and I was the captain: or vice versa; he didn't notice the difference. The only window in the workshop was a hole in the wall, way up under the plain roof. In summer two pigeons cooed there and let their droppings fall on the dirt floor. The rest of the year a smudged pane covered the opening. Their apartment, a few houses down, darker still, smelled just as much of cold tobacco smoke and soot. The cooking stove right behind the entrance doubled as a heater. An oil lamp dangled from the low ceiling. Grandfather often bumped his head against it, and it would clatter loudly, but he would never have sworn. The floor was of well-trodden mud, but a perpetual cleanliness reigned nevertheless; in the second room too, with the big bed where I sometimes lay between them on a straw sack. If Grandfather's beard scratched me in the face, I would awake, push him a little away from me under the down coverlet, and inch closer to Grandmother's delicate body. Then they would both turn in their sleep. Waves of warm air would stream from their bedclothes.

Every Friday morning Grandmother cleaned with special attention. 'One gets the house ready as if a precious and respected person were coming, in honor of the Sabbath Queen,' she read me aloud. Before I made my way to a meal at their house, my mother would take me aside and put a knotted handkerchief into my pocket, which I was to give to Grandmother. Grandfather was usually already seated at the table; his temple locks brushed the pages before him. Fleetingly, he would hold out his cheek for me to kiss and pat me on the back of my head. I much preferred to embrace Grandmother, who always had a little rice pudding for me or sweet soup with cherry preserves. Even when I only came by in a great hurry, as on the day I had believed the kindergarten had burned down. We had been sent home earlier because the chimney sweep was overhauling the oil stove. 'Granny, Granny, give me my cherry soup, the kindergarten has burned down.' She turned. Her thin, pale face was framed by a head scarf, in the fashion of the market women. Without further questions, she pressed me to her. The wrinkled skin of her face was warm and soft and smelled of soap. In no time I had a plate before me. Hastily I spooned it up, said thank you, kissed her, and was off again.

3

The Ferris wheel on Coney Island was visible against a silver strip of the Atlantic. The horizon was a line between blue and blue.

'Do you hear all the sirens?' Georg shifted his gaze from the gentle curve of the Verrazano Bridge in the mist.

'Yes. Of course. I think if you pay attention, there's always one howling. It's normal here.'

'Do you think?' His father held his head emphatically to one side and asked Georg what had actually brought him here, why New York of all places, how long he'd been here and how long he was staying. 'Mrs. Fuchs gave me nothing more than a telephone number, from a young man I absolutely had to call. When I heard your voice on the answering machine for the first time, I was so confused I just hung up. I had no idea, you see, that you were in New York. And I think she didn't even know that I was your father.'

All Georg could think to offer as a motive for having come was his desire for a change.

'A change is always good. At your age I couldn't stay put in one place for long either. No better than with one woman. It keeps you young. Look at me and be honest; can you tell I'm seventy?'

Georg did his father the favor of saying no. In the past his father's awkward attempts at establishing common ground had always seemed to him misdirected. The basic reason for his departure was that, since the outbreak of the Gulf War, in the general deterioration of positions that had been deemed solid, it had emerged that affairs were going to take their course without his stir, and that he too would never stray so far from the average but that he could seek its protection at any time in the event of danger or lack of success. But he didn't care to explain that just now. Instead he described how his initial enthusiasm had yielded to the realization that New York in winter was nothing more than a damp, cold, temporary resting place.

'Well anyway, it's something for someone without a clear goal,' his father said conciliatorily. 'What do you live on actually while you're here? Were you able to put money aside? You are over thirty already, after all. Life is hardly cheaper here. Especially when you don't do your own cooking. Can you cook at all? Not so important. I haven't managed to get any further than scrambled eggs yet either. But scrambled eggs I can make. I swear it. Do you have a kitchen in your apartment?' Georg answered as well as he could while questions, answers, and more questions whirled through the air in a breathless, hasty round.

Sometimes they remained standing at the parapet, always a little longer on the side facing east, which was sheltered from the wind. A cold breeze blew from inland. A helicopter approached in its ascent over the Hudson. There was a quadratic order to what lay around and below them; it was only in the distance and in the flatlands that the city disintegrated. Then Georg looked at the surface before his shoes. Briefly he regretted having suggested the Empire State Building of all places as a meeting point, where the restricted area more than 1,200 feet in the air kept them unavoidably imprisoned next to each other.

Father's tenor babbled on familiarly, his suggestive smile flickered Georg's way, and every one of their trivially strung-together words seemed to underscore the fact that they didn't need to raise their respective masks in order to know who was underneath; it was in any case no more than traces of erosion that Georg had noticed. Tiredness overcame him, and his father's random, clumsy tenderness, the way he laid his arm around his shoulders for no reason, embarrassed him. He couldn't return it.

There came the obligatory discussion of his work. Caught up as he was, Georg managed to keep his remarks casual. He was a volunteer in an office planning a Holocaust memorial museum. His main duty was listening to cassette recordings of the Holocaust stories of people who had lived through the concentration camps; he arranged these stories by keywords and transcribed them onto the computer for the future Oral History Archive. 'A little boring. Always the same thing,' he concluded, curious as to what his father would respond. But he only wanted to know what the women on the staff were like. Georg even found an answer for him. They chatted on this way, sometimes interrupting each other, then each on his own again. Georg's inner resolve grew all the stronger to reveal to his father what had really been preoccupying him during the last month and was thinking of an answer in case his father should innocently ask why he hadn't simply called him up about the whole story.

First, however, he wanted to see if he could get a glimpse at his father's left forearm.

4

With time, Grandfather sank into ever deeper seclusion. It was Grandmother's task to make sure, quietly and efficiently, that they didn't go to rack and ruin, as much as it may have pained her that not one of the seven children she had raised was following the path of God to which she had been steering them. On occasion she would lament in the half-darkness at the kitchen table. My mother would be sitting on a stool, leaning against the wall. She wore her thick dark brown hair otherwise uncovered, but when she was visiting Grandmother she too tied on a kerchief. About Grandmother's hair color, on the other hand, I have to this day no idea. I only remember the nicely coiffed, near-blond wig she always wore outside the house.

At least once a year the whole family would gather at their home, for Passover. In the back room, where there ordinarily reigned a windowless twilight. The heavy bed had been pushed up against the wall. A white-covered table occupied the middle of the room. Platters, candlesticks, dishes, and glasses sparkled on the cloth. The odor of oil lamps and burnt wax lay in the air. A score of us waited around the table until Grandfather at the head had finished reading the portion about the Exodus from Egypt once again. Thereupon, as the youngest, I was permitted to steal the last piece of matzoh, the afikomen, and Grandfather, the man of the house, had to ransom it back for a few coins (which my mother had probably tucked into his pocket at the outset).

According to Uncle Soli, Grandfather must have been implacably strict in those days. On Fridays, he said, he would sometimes whip his children into their Sabbath clothes and on their way to synagogue with a leather strap. All seven of them, if need be, and Grandmother would make ready the kitchen all the while, as if she didn't hear the screaming. He must have really driven the fear of God out of them. Father, at any rate, forbade any religious temptation of my soul beyond the bar mitzvah preparation. Even on holidays. He especially hated them when they fell inconveniently during the Christian workweek. He didn't so much as want to know about Yom Kippur. Instead he poked fun at me when, spurred on by my overdimensional Uncle Kalman, who lived next to us with Aunt Borish, I wanted to fast like the observant people. Uncle Kalman worked as a bookkeeper at a shop selling fuel, coal, sod, and oil; he lived his religion as a bookkeeper too; he dedicated all his zeal to his faith without its ever for a moment becoming his passion. Around midday Father would come over quickly from the store. I would already have made it through the whole morning without a bite and would be sitting in the kitchen, where Mother would have prepared his lunch, although she herself would also be fasting. He would grant me a mocking glance and ask for scrambled eggs. My favorite dish. Make a lot of them, he would say; he was hungry. I would watch her—milk, eggs, flour, chopped peppers—and cast Uncle Kalman for a while out of my mind, with all his eager efforts to bring a life of godliness nearer to me. Finally Mother would have me bring the steaming dish to my father; she would have laid a slice of bread by it too. Uncle Kalman would be far away; I would be standing alone before God and my father, who would be chewing with pleasure. She would have made him so much that he could never have finished it all himself. I would wait until he had pushed the plate away, take up his fork, and quickly eat up the rest. He would laugh.

In the evening Father would allow me as an exception to go to the Orthodox congregation's synagogue with Grandfather. Grandfather himself would not say a word the whole way there. He wouldn't greet people from afar either, as was normally his custom. When someone would pass us, he would at most mumble a few words into his beard and hurry on. I would be uncertain whether it was joyful anticipation or nameless fear that drove him on. For the last part of the way I would have to give him my hand in order to keep up, and be careful not to stumble on the sidewalk cobblestones. In the courtyard of the synagogue he would silently make a path through the crowd of those waiting, with me hanging onto his hand behind him. His beard would tremble as he talked to himself, a private, absent smile on his face. Suddenly he would grip me tighter, stop in his place, bend down to me, and whisper insistently, 'Be full of awe, my boy, and regret, for this night HE shall decide.' I would have no idea what he meant. In my mind I would leaf through the past days as through a picture book, but I would hit upon no egregious misdeeds. Maybe at most the injured pigeon in the court, but Mathyi was as guilty as I, and no one had noticed it anyway, because it had flown to the edge of the woods and only there laid itself down to die. Grandfather would be silent. My hand would lie tightly held in his. Close to tears, I would tug on his arm, but he wouldn't let go. 'I know you can't do anything about it yet,' he would say finally. 'But HE decides about us all. Old and young. This evening!' He would gaze into the twilight sky and speak on, but no longer with me: 'Yes, today the Almighty will decide which of us may still live through another Yom Kippur.' It was only then that he would release my hand. I would suddenly become afraid of losing him and having to await judgment among all those pious Jews. Close behind him, I would enter the hall amid the throng of dark-clad figures. Some of them would already be wearing their prayer shawls over their heads and shoulders, but most would still be standing around in groups and gossiping loudly. Grandfather, too, would throw his tallit over his shoulders with a lazy motion when he had reached his place somewhere in the middle rows, and remain for the rest of the service in his own world. Around about me a dense forest of legs; in the gallery, the torsos of the women in the front row, their buttoned-up collars and wigs. I would be just tall enough to see the cantor at the Torah table despite the high wooden seatback in front of me. His song would already have begun to rise from him, and the next moment would be soaring with the other voices above me; soon individual sounds would be floating up out of the hundredfold whisperings and murmurings, all the way up to the vault. Most of the men would be wearing hats, some of them only a skullcap on the back of the head, and almost all of them had beards like my grandfather. Their lips would be flickering. Like him they would be rocking their upper bodies or turning halfway about their own axis, now left, now right, their eyes closed, the prayerbooks in their hands before their faces. Suddenly, in the middle of the prayer, they would all throw themselves to the floor, and a loud groan would arise from the congregation. I would hurry to kneel as well. Grandfather would be unavailable for questioning. Did some of us have to die now? Were the others praying to be allowed to live on? I would cower next to him and would already be envisioning the vault crashing down, as it did on Samson and the Philistines.

7

'Aunt Winnie, you must have known her too, actually.'

'But of course,' his father confirmed, 'how is she? Hey, you know, I think she must be eighty by now.'

The year before she had received her second artificial hip. Since then she had been dragging her bulk unsteadily through the house and had to be careful not to fall. That would be the end, her doctor had warned her. Georg reported further on the crooked house, whose windows needed resealing. She had three boarders: the youngest, in his thirties, she called 'Never-had-it'; the middle one, a fifty-year-old, 'Sure-would-like-some'; and the third, about her age, 'Can't-anymore.' The walls were hung densely with photographs of the long dead, most of them in grainy black and white, among them two husbands and her only son: testicular cancer. There was an eternal light in the socket, and Friday evenings, framed by two fat candles in silver holders, she would recite a short *kaddish* in a mixture of English, German, and scraps of Hebrew; after a few cups of sweet Carmel wine and a little chaser of sherry she would wipe away her tears with a lace hanky and finally begin to plead to be allowed to make up the old sofa for him. If he agreed to stay the night, she would coo like a dove and get out the linens with satisfaction. On one of those evenings she had given free rein to her conviction that it was not exactly proper for a healthy man of his age to be straying about the city for months on end. She could hardly introduce him to her girlfriends before he got himself at least a part-time occupation. An acquaintance of her neighbor, the daughter of the sister of the rabbi, had an extremely attractive daughter, but she wasn't about to go out with someone so young who slept in every morning. And then she had mentioned that there was a new Jewish museum being planned, and that the management was looking for help, or interns, all quite in passing, but Georg had heard the unmistakable challenge. Aunt Winnie loved to arrange things: in earlier days it had been houses and properties; now it was just marriages, jobs, and the like.

'Well that was kind of her,' his father said thoughtfully. 'You've got to occupy your time somehow, give the old *Yeckeh* credit for that.' He wanted to know whether he had a girlfriend somewhere out there, while the city heckled away at them from down below. Georg said no. 'All the same, a normal man of your age needs more than a bed and regular employment to keep him in one place. Especially in a city like this,' he insisted.

'So?' Georg answered, and wondered whether his father might be right. He recalled the first time he had listened to the cassette; he recalled the cardboard box in front of him on the desk, and as if it weren't of all people his father who was standing next to him, the story threatened to seep away from him before its conclusion. Georg lost himself in the thought that of all the myriad events, and precisely the more important ones, only their beginning truly endured in the memory. Anecdotes and trace elements made up the rest. Randomly tied together. Here too, in spite of everything he had thought he might discover. Maybe the sole result of his hectic search for the past would in fact remain simply that he had managed, along the way, to lend his present moment some justification.

Soon he really must get a look at that lower arm.

8

In the beginning it had been just a cardboard box.

Georg was taking a break at that moment. The coffee tasted like water-logged paper, and if you wanted to smoke, you had to go out onto the fire escape; as he had been out there already, there was nothing left for him but the newspaper on the desk. He sat down in Ben's soft leather desk chair and paged through headings, photos, and captions, until a cloud of sweet scent banished the war on the Gulf. Ben stood in the doorway. Smiling, in gray pants and a tie, his striped shirt buttoned all the way to the top. He let the cardboard box fall onto the desk and waved the back of his hand at the caked dust. 'Look what I've brought you. Showed up today.' At this he peered at him over the edge of his eyeglasses. In addition to his own field, the American part of the future collection, Ben managed the Oral History Project too, and was therefore actually Georg's superior. But Georg found his risqué humor much too amusing, especially when the uniformity of the office routine threatened to exhaust him. So now, caught up in one of Ben's off-color remarks, he inspected the uninscribed carton. 'What am I supposed to do with it?'

'Doesn't it look like a proper little present? Have a look inside,' Ben urged him.

Georg did him the favor and was amazed when, instead of a more or less successful practical joke, he saw nothing other than a new heap of cassette tapes.

9

Our house had high, thick walls of brick, whose reddish plaster was crumbling in places, and a tiled roof, while on most of the other houses low straw roofs shone dull yellow in the sun. Where their whitewashed plaster had fallen away, you could see the bare walls of straw-enforced mud.

A small supply room connected our store to the great kitchen, where there were also washbasin, bathtub, and heating barrel for the big monthly laundry. Our maidservant Anna came especially early on those days. Everything would have been pushed to the side, and the barrel would be standing alone in the middle. Heated up. The washing would be heaped on the table. The linens would be swirled in the bubbling water, driven by a piece of wood in Anna's hand. Among them, underwear, brassieres, and blouses were slung about. Anna would fish them out piece by piece with her wooden stick, slap them onto the wavy board, and scrub each one into submission with her reddened hands. Then it would be time to wring them out, and it wouldn't be long before the wash was hanging on long lines in the attic. The cellar was for storing firewood and coal. The great attic room we used to stock fabrics, sacking, or bales of cotton, and even the Christmas tree decorations we hadn't been able to sell the previous year. But there was still lots of unused space. Apart from Uncle Lajos, we were the only ones far and wide with electricity. In front of our house knotty birch trees stood irregularly at attention, along the street that came from the flatlands in the west and went on past the military airport on the outskirts of town. Some hundred yards past our house, at a hand-operated gas pump, the last tree dropped away. Now a dusty thoroughfare, the street bisected the Búza tér, reached the center, and led on, once again a proud avenue, eastward to town, and all the way to the distant border with the Soviet Union. It was usually thick with traffic. On Wednesdays and Saturdays, market day on the Búza tér, the farmers would stream into town on their horse-drawn carriages. Those were the most important days for our store. We had everything on offer you could need for your everyday life. 'From the cradle to the bier, Gal's store has it, never fear,' ran the sign over our shop window: work clothes, shoes, tools, rat poison, animal fodder, rope for calves, salves and unguents, even bread, or flashlights and batteries. My father may have been so beloved among the farmers because he shared something of their coarse, irascible temperament. At any rate, they were such a steady part of our business that as a little child, I would run screaming to Mother whenever a somberly dressed city dweller would come to the door.

On other days it would mostly be motorcars rattling by. After Hungary had entered the war, the traffic grew steadily, a flood heading east, but we just managed to see their hasty return three years later going in the other direction, or at least what was left of them. Best of all were the motorcycles with sidecars. But the most frequent were trucks. In my wildest daydreams I would mount my pitch black stallion and ride down the road toward town myself, a mob of vengeful pursuers hard on my heels (or perhaps only my strict father, when I had come home with a bad report card); the river at the border was already in sight on the horizon; I would hold the reins with one hand and with the other draw out my saber or shoot wildly, now forward, now backward, leap over the water with a last dig of the spurs, and dismount my horse in safety on the other side of the border while the mob remained behind, jeering, on the farther shore.

My relatives, especially Uncle Lajos and Aunt Rosie, my father's siblings, but most often my eldest cousin Emmi, all spoke of the border with the Soviet Union as if they were gazing down from Mount Nebo onto Canaan, the land that they, like Moses, would never tread.

I was going by foot once more. It was Friday. I had set off to my grandparents'. I heard a cry behind me. The front truck in an army convoy was stopped, motor running, in the middle of the street. The vehicles behind it rumbled impatiently. People hurried to the scene. I approached as well, filled with curiosity. The uniformed driver stood by the hood. He was poking the toe of his boot at a bundle on the ground. His superior came riding up. He brought his horse up short before the dense crowd of people. Brandishing his saber energetically, he shooed them back: 'Carry on, carry on!' Through a gap in the people I saw the contorted body lying on the cobblestones and recognized Uncle Potzkopf, a neighbor from across the way, with an expression as if he had just solved a difficult riddle. A thread of blood disappeared into his beard. Despite the flies on his face he was still.

The captain remained seated on his mount. He merely shoved the saber back into its sheath and cursed as he gave his horse the spurs.

10

Ben looked at him with something approaching pity. His trim mustache moved like a little brush between his full cheeks as he explained that the cassettes had not been included in the archive because of some sort of defect. When he had come in from outdoors on warmer days, like today, a slight redness would creep over his plump face, and his neck would spill out like a damp ruff over his collar. 'Maybe there's valuable testimony in there, survivors of the St. Louis or something like that. Just imagine if Mr. Hersh pops up and surprises us in the archive one day, spots the unprocessed stuff and starts nosing around. Just thinking about it makes me ill. With all our other problems.' Ben glanced at the ceiling.

The museum's collection was only very slowly taking shape. And there were people who were dubious about even that progress. For the last several weeks, a two-hundred-year-old tabernacle from Czechoslovakia had been at the forefront of all their efforts, their most important piece so far. But the donors were making conditions about its storage. And rightly so, people were saying under their breath around the office. Nevertheless, they had to figure out how to secure the object before someone from another museum snatched it away, as had recently happened with the diaries hidden in milk cans from a Polish ghetto: Washington had bid more for them. Mr. Hersh had a special role in all of these difficult negotiations. He was one of the 'Survivors,' as those who had lived through the concentration camps were familiarly known here. They made up their own species; one referred to them with pride and gave them special privileges. This was especially crucial in New York, where all the other communities, after all, could only avoid dissolving unnoticed into their surroundings by stressing their alleged uniqueness. Some of them shrilly, others with an elegant aloofness, each according to the share of authenticity reserved to that uniqueness. On the other hand, no one was exactly sure what was to be done with these 'Survivors'; their own silence about their history set them too distinctly apart from the rest of the family, which was concerned with nothing so zealously as the attempt to bear witness to the rest of the world. Not a few of them had made it to wealth and respect since the war. Now the moment seemed to have come, since time was threatening to ravage their legacy too, as it did all com-

moner things. Those who could afford it, therefore, started thinking about what would remain for posterity. For his part, Mr.
Hersh, whose fortune had been made in real estate deals, some of which
had made headlines for him, all too often and in all too close
company with other, more notorious names, had been moved to
start a foundation for an Oral History Archive on the concentration
camps; and as long as the costs were below the amount he donated
for it, the museum was anxious to lose neither his money nor his
good name. At any rate, this had been Georg's interpretation of
Ben's answer when, at the outset of his work there, still shy and full
of good will, he had asked him what the future purpose of the
Archive was.

Ben tapped his ballpoint pen playfully against his lower lip. His
gaze was fixed on the middle distance: 'I immediately thought of
your valuable contribution. And that this way I could keep you a
little longer.'

Georg was entirely the sort whose morale on the job could be
given a decisive boost with strategically placed positive evaluations,
even if he was only a volunteer in a museum whose funding might
well dry up before it was built. Yet you could never be sure with Ben
whether his praise was meant seriously or whether it sprang out of
that irony in which he enveloped everything around him as the
spirit moved him.

The more cassettes Georg had listened to since starting the job,
the more often he had heard repeated years, places, countries, and
the names of concentration camps entered on the forms; for some
time, in fact, he had had the impression, as he nearly dozed between the headphones, that he was listening over and over again to
one and the same story of survival of one and the same camp. When
details did nevertheless stand out, which was seldom the case, they
would stir about on the stew of voices like leaves torn from a tree
that float downstream while one watches for a while, until the next
branch comes and they are forgotten. The fifteen-minute breaks he
took between sessions at his listening post had recently been getting more frequent, without his noticing it, in proportion to the
extra effort it took him to get the headphones on again in his
windowless, soundproof studio. He had hoped this week to be
finished at last transcribing the mountain of cassettes he had been

handed, and to propose himself for some new, more diverting assignment. Georg was therefore now trying, in peace and quiet, to make some sense of this stew of voices, which had lately been threatening to ooze away from him.

'Gotta go now,' Ben said in conclusion, and picked up the receiver. 'My Molly is waiting for another call from me.' His high forehead shone, and the few strands of hair sticking to it glinted in rivalry. As he had told Georg not long ago, in her younger years Molly had been the lead in a Yiddish vaudeville revue whose cast further consisted of her husband and their two children. All that she had left today was her vanity and an apartment full of props. Posters, ticket stubs, photos: in short, everything you could desire.

'Well, there you are, you see. Nobody understands you the way I do. Your gift will be in the best of all hands. I'll take care of it personally. . . . The donations? Thank God, yes. Thanks for asking. There could be a few more of them, but considering the hard times, we can be glad. But I'm almost afraid people want to buy themselves out of the obligation to go on dealing with history, with these donations. And not only the Jews. . . . Yes, you put it very nicely. Can I repeat that?—*The thing is to show with great patience that the present is only a tiny snapshot in the eternal process of becoming, and that every day of the future is its precious result.*—Just a second, I'm going to write that down.' He scribbled away on his desk pad, but Georg could see that he was only doodling. After a judicious pause he continued: 'Maybe we'll use it to caption one of your photographs. . . . The contract for the gift? Of course, as soon as we've inspected the material.' His tone into the receiver was melodious, and he winked at Georg. 'And many thanks! On behalf of the director too.' When he had hung up, he rubbed his hands together: 'Soon she'll be ours. Just a couple more calls, a couple more visits, and her estate belongs to us.'

Ben stood up and left the office with the words, 'Have fun! And think about this: He who survives the Survivors has also survived the Holocaust!'

Georg was alone with his box of cassettes. He stared at it as if his look might have shooed it back into the corner it had surely crept out of. But it remained crouching on the table before him.

II

Uncle Potzkopf must have been on his way to the mikvah, to the Jewish baths, as was only proper for a pious Jew before the beginning of the Sabbath. Grandfather had taken me along once. 'Every human being is obliged to submerge his entire body, if possible, in the warm water of the mikvah. It is, however, forbidden for him to bathe together with his father, his father-in-law, his mother's husband, or his sister's husband; but where it is customary to cover one's nakedness, there it is allowed. A schoolboy is not to bathe together with his teacher, but if this last should require him for a servant, then it shall be allowed,' he read to me from a thick book.

The mikvah was a cement annex at the back of the Orthodox synagogue's community house. Rainwater was collected in a great cauldron on stilts. When we came in, the furnace stoker, in his dirty caftan, was just shoveling fresh coals into the hissing mouth of the furnace. Steam was whistling out of a vent. Grandfather drew me impatiently to the entrance and on through the door. Suddenly we were standing in a dimly lit room. My world had remained behind on the other side. This world here smelled of mold, sulphur, and sweat. I asked Grandfather to let me stay outside instead and watch the furnace stoker at work at his cauldron, perhaps I could even help him with work; anyway I had bathed at home just a couple of days ago. But he had already pushed me back into the farthest corner. Damply shining forms were whisking through the twilight; the paneling on the walls was damp, too; everything was damp. He forced me to hurry. I heard him right near me. His voice, otherwise firm, was trembling. Something must have happened to him, but I couldn't tell what. At this the entrance door opened again, the beam of light cut the darkness in two, and I saw him next to me on a bench fumbling with his belt, his upper body already bare down to his woolen, off-white prayer shirt. One of the tassels seemed to have gotten caught in his belt. He was trying to pull off his pants. Now he was sitting there, a specter, in mute desperation. The threads with their five knots each hung down along his hips like loose parcel string. When he had finally freed himself, he murmured these words, exhausted:

'Great is the commandment of the tzitzes, for scriptures have made it equal to all the others. You shall look upon them and

remember all the commandments of the Eternal One.' I saw that I
was the only one not wearing *tzitzes*, and I wondered whether HE
could punish me for it.

'Therefore let everyone make sure that he possesses a small *tallit*,
that he may clad himself in it the whole day long, and let it be of
sheep's wool, white and of the prescribed size. And great shall be
the punishment visited upon him who does not uphold the commandment of the *tzitzes*; but he who fulfills it conscientiously
shall have the good fortune to be permitted to appear before God's
bright emanation.' Grandfather answered me, now quoting from
memory from the same thick book. I was all the more relieved when
the door closed again and the clammy dimness hid my nakedness.
The walls were already thick with hung-up clothing. I crumpled
mine up into a ball and stowed it away. Grandfather took me by the
hand. There was a mildew-covered grating on the cement floor. We
were stepping on slippery stockings and stumbling over shoes.
Naked as we both were, we tapped our way into the next room. This
one was brighter. The light must have been coming from below,
from the steps toward which Grandfather was dragging me, and
from which clouds of steam were rolling up in our direction over
a whole series of steps. Naked figures were whisking about me,
bearded and hairy, their members bobbling before my eyes, and in
between children ran about every which way, squealing. Grandfather supported himself on the railing, and I held onto his hand.
Slowly, a vault peeled itself out of the steam, the outline of the
basin, with a sheet of frosted glass across its entire breadth to
almost halfway up the wall. On the lowest step Grandfather murmured a prayer, then we joined the other figures in the lukewarm
water. The sheet of glass was misted up, and the walls too; drops
collected on all the surfaces and left behind crooked traces of their
progress to the floor. Between the countless pale bodies there rose
up veils of silt with a coiling motion from the greenish floor—flags
in a foggy breeze. There was a general washing of beards and hair,
with conversation in that incomprehensible language that seemed
to flourish here in particular. My grandparents used it occasionally
when they were alone. Someone had once explained to me that it
was the language of the Jews, in distinction to the language of the
Torah, which was God's tongue and not for the use of us humans,

unless it were to praise the name of the Lord. Each man submerged himself completely at least three times, keeping one hand on his head the whole time so as not to lose his skullcap. When he came up again, his temple locks would be hanging down limply. Focusing my entire will on fighting down the disgust that rose within me, I splashed around alone a little while, and, when I noticed that Grandfather wasn't paying attention to me anymore, I got out again. I don't think I had been able to stand it for more than five minutes. From the edge of the basin I watched him washing his beard: he submerged himself once, lathered the dripping hairs, rinsed them with water, submerged himself again, lathered and rinsed anew, and submerged himself a third time. I noticed how thin he was, how sinewy and tall. I was getting cold. I wanted him to get out too; it was surely time. Instead of him, however, there emerged the *rebbe*. His member looked like a dripping corkscrew. I saw with amazement that his testicles hung down almost to between his knees. He dried himself with a towel, hardly an arm's length away from me. I was admiring his endowments with such an abundance of attention that for a moment I forgot Grandfather. A light slap on the back of the head interrupted my thoughts. From behind I watched the poor rabbi climbing up the steps. His parts resembled the dry udder of an old goat.

'Don't stare at the *rebbe*. It is a duty to honor your teacher more than your father. Your father brought you into the life of this world. Your teacher, however, will bring you into the life of the next.'

15

Hoarse tenor; eastern accent; probably a smoker, he noticed immediately, with his headphones on and waiting for the voice to give its name and present address at the very beginning. Many of the stories had this approach, even when the sender, except in this case, had already neatly listed all the information on the wrapper, in accordance with the museum's wishes. Georg turned the sound up a little—the eternal story, always the same: Auschwitz, Bergen-Belsen, etc. He stopped, fast-forwarded, and rewound lackadaisically, but no further information was offered. Back at the first passage, he stumbled over the place he thought he knew a hundred times over already: 'marked,' 'branded,' 'scratched,' 'etched,' they would say, when they came inevitably to talk about how a number had been tattooed on their left forearms shortly after their arrival. He wouldn't have given it any extra thought, even though the voice sounded familiar. It was only when this man's particular number was mentioned that Georg's ears pricked up. He rewound—and rewound again. Finally he noted down the number after the capital A. Then he started making various combinations of the individual digits. He compared them, crossed them out, and scribbled them down again underneath in a new order. But only the number from the report before him held up to his own memory. That was how he had seen it on that forearm. And from that moment on the voice continued with such naturalness, it was as if it was relating all the following to him, and to him alone.

He took the afternoon off to go roaming around the East Village. It made a difference when your purpose was suddenly clear.

There was a shy spring in the air. The trees on St. Mark's were blooming almost unbelievably. In Tompkins Square Park there were plastic tarpaulins lying over bundles of belongings. Oil drums and firewood were ready should the cold return. A black man was pushing his shopping cart, laden with garbage bags full of tin cans, through the entrance and on into Tompkins Square Park. The shrilly colored knitted cap on the back of his head was shaped like a taut octopus rump. A bearded old man stepped into Georg's path. Between the soles and the busted leather of his high-laced black boots, two crusty toes shot out right and left. With practiced naturalness he asked to be bought a drink, or at least to be given the money for a can of beer. Georg found a free bench. He stretched both his arms out along the back. For a moment the city was lost to him, when a woman in loose, colorful clothing drew near and in the next instant was sitting next to him. The cloths around her dark head had been wrapped up into a tower. 'Witchwoman, I am the Witchwoman,' she murmured. Over and over again: 'The Witchwoman.' All the while he felt her expectant gaze on him from the side. He was in a good mood, so he remained where he was.

'You can do magic, then?' he asked.

'Indeed. What do you need?' Her murmur had given way to a distinctly businesslike tone. It took him back to his normal life, with its reasons for everything. 'I'm looking for a certain man.'

'What's his name?'

'Sender,' he said teasingly. 'He's the Sender.'

She got up. 'Ask for Witchwoman if you ever need anything. Witchwoman, don't forget: Witchwoman.' Her clothes hung down as if they were on a rack, one that was getting ever thinner and more crooked the farther off she got, shaking her head as she went. After a while Georg left too. Next to the park entrance a couple of dozen people were standing in a line in front of two large, steaming tin pails. They were all holding paper plates and cups in their hands. Behind them two women moved up, and you could hear the muted sound as their ladles scratched against the tin. When the mush landed on a plate, the plate would bend perilously. Drippings of mashed potatoes glistened on the pavement between the tables. They ate standing up and without speaking, which gave the scene an unpleasantly worshipful air. Now an ocher Mercedes limousine rolled up. The chrome trim sparkled in the sun. Georg seemed to be the only one paying it any attention. A black man in a suit and stiff hat got out, got into line, and left the motor running. When he too had received his due, he went back to the car. There he covered the plate with a second, packed the whole thing away onto the rear window ledge, and got back in line. He spooned up his second portion leaning against a lamppost.

There was still some time left before the Friday evening rush into the subway.

Rose Choron

Rose Choron was born in the Ukraine of Lithuanian parents. She spent her school years in Berlin and Lausanne and learned art history at the Sorbonne. During the war she studied painting at the Institute of Fine Arts in Boston, where, in 1945, she earned her M.A. from Radcliffe. She went on to study psychology at Columbia and at the Institut für angewandte Psychologie in Zurich. Her poems have appeared in British and American literary magazines, and she has published three books: *Family Stories: Travels beyond the Shtetel*, *Between Tears and Laughter*, and *Scènes de la vie juive en Alsace*, the last her translation of a nineteenth-century work by Daniel Stauben. In the selection from *Family Stories* (1988) that follows, she mixes a naive narrative style (further honed in her writing for children) with a picturesque Yiddish vocabulary to paint a miniature of a privileged yet anxiety-ridden wartime in Switzerland.

Rose Choron

Swiss Transit

The world, at first, laughed off the warnings of *Mein Kampf*
As passing frenzies. My father did not laugh.
Instead, he moved our tents from Berlin to Lausanne.

Ice-capped in the beginning, like their mountains,
The Swiss warmed up to us
After we paid our bills and kept to ourselves.

Mother appreciated their unpretentiousness,
And the appeal was mutual.
We settled in a rambling groundfloor flat
With sunny terraces and garden and felt at home.

In Germany, most anxious to fit in,
We Lithuanian children had turned into Prussian brats,
Outdoing the authentic ones in arrogance and toughness.

This left our new Helvetian pals untouched.
They laughed and nicknamed us 'les Boches,' the Huns.

With Hitler on the scene,
We soon dropped 'Deutschland Über Alles.'
Embracing our new homeland with conviction,
We sang its national anthem, yodelled, ate fondue.
Spoke French and Schwizerdütsch,
And felt more Swiss than Wilhelm Tell.

My sister Feny, still a baby, was at home,
And Rachel started elementary school.
David and Sam joined the Ecole Nouvelle.

Among their classmates in this private school
Were Mohamed Reza Pahlavi, future shah of Persia,
And his brother, as well as the crown-prince of Siam.

Once, in a fit of temper and gratuitously,
Mohamed bade his brother to stand still,
And hit his face until it bled.

The class dragged the prospective monarch
To the cellar and paid him back in kind.
At heart, the dean approved his boys' reaction,
But to avoid a diplomatic scandal, they were punished.
Mohamed was transferred to Le Rosey,
A snobbish institute catering to names and money.

In contrast, Siam's prince
Composed and staged light musicals
And was the darling of his friends and teachers.

All children but myself had found their proper niche.
I was an adolescent, hard to handle.

A Jewish boarding school was recommended.
Although I was much younger than the other girls.
My mother sent me to it 'faute de mieux.'

The head of La Ramée, 'Madame' to all of us,
Held our reins with strong but gentle hands.
I liked her right away. Accepting her authority,
I felt secure.

For once I was the youngest, mothered and cajoled,
With someone always there to answer and explain.

We were twenty-five girls from all parts of the world.
Most had completed school, now wishing to learn French.
The Germans, though, were escapees from Hitler,
Their parents looking for new roots abroad.

I was the only one who went to the lycée in town,
Spending the week in La Ramée, weekends at home.

Sometimes on Sundays, mother asked the girls for tea.
She made them feel at ease
And they all called her 'Mutti,' as we did.

Madame had grown to be a good friend of the family.
Through her, our house became a refuge for lost parents
She sent to father for advice and help.

In due time, Mutti had acquired a Chevy,
Her driving teacher was Sérai, a wiry, hawk-nosed Greek,
Well-mannered and of many talents.

His love affair with the Greek consul's wife
Had stirred the tongues of gossipmongers.

Disowned by his shocked parents,
He stopped his legal studies and looked for work.
Mutti engaged him as our tutor.

A racy stallion, dark, young, whimsical,
He was more pal than teacher, and the boys adored him.
Excellent at all sports, he launched us
Into tennis, Ping-Pong, bob sledding and skiing.

On weekends and vacations we took to the mountains.
We hiked and picnicked, entered competitions,
Sometimes, alas, returning with limbs broken.

However little he had taught us otherwise,
Sérai blew a fresh, frisky wind into our sails.

Constantly in and out of feminine webs,
He finally got caught by a buxom Brunhild.
She brought a dowry of nine cats
And bore him two blond Goths.

Mutti, by now a fervent driver,
Took us for casual rides
Over high mountain peaks and valleys.

Sometimes we all went to Montreux to see her friends,
A family like us of Lithuanian origin.

With numerous relatives and neighbors,
They formed a *shtetel* within town, including
Shadchens, shnorrers, shtibel, and *yeshive,*
As well as open homes with *kreplach* soup and *latkes.*

Their only goal during those years
Was to keep constant contact
With the Jews in Germany and Poland,
Trying to get them out at any cost.

The secret links they had
With clergy and with governments abroad,
Enabled them to rescue many lives.

They even risked their own, forging passports and visas
And often smuggling escapees alone across the borders.
For bribing frontier-guards and the police,
Some, caught by Swiss authorities, were jailed.

On weekends, when our maid was off,
They used to send us fugitives to hide.
These people had arrived illegally,
And needed a safe roof and rest
Before continuing their journeys.

Some, though my age in years,
Had skipped whole generations overnight.
Their eyes mirrored the horrors they had seen,
And often in the morning, sheets were wet with tears.

Jean-Luc Benoziglio

Jean-Luc Benoziglio was born in Monthey, in the Swiss canton of Valais, in 1941. He studied law and political science at the University of Lausanne. He has lived in Paris for the last three decades, where he has worked for various publishing houses. Between 1970 and 1998 he published ten novels, among them *Cabinet Portrait* (1980), which won the Prix Médicis, and *Le Feu au lac* (1998), distinguished by the Fondation Schiller. His latest work, *La Pyramide ronde*, appeared in 2001. His works have been translated into German, Italian, Portuguese, Spanish, and Greek. In the chapter of *Le Feu au lac* (Fire on the lake) excerpted here, Benoziglio calls upon his own mixed heritage- his father was a Sephardic Jew from Turkey, his mother a Swiss Catholic- -and his experiences living in both France and Switzerland to evoke the ethical agonies of a Swiss Jew watching his French-Jewish relatives being rounded up by the French police during World War II. The chapter is staged as a sort of confession: the son, returned to the safety of Switzerland, recounts what he has witnessed to his impassive psychiatrist father.

Jean-Luc Benoziglio

EXCERPT FROM Fire on the Lake

' "Oh, show it to them, show it to them, for heaven's sake," Aunt Bouca shouted at me,' he says to the swivel chair. 'And I noticed, it's idiotic, given the circumstances, that she was at pains to pronounce and articulate every word properly. She and Uncle David, you know, I've already told you, they were always ribbing me gently about what they called my "ekzent." For my part, when they spoke French, I made a show of not understanding more than two words out of three, with the Turkish, the Spanish, and who knows what all. "A real Bower of Tabel," Nissim would say with a laugh, "not the marriage of the Centaurs and the Lapiths but the Switzers and the Carpaths; nor should we forget Anatolia and Lana Turner." He was killing us with his incessant puns and spoonerisms. You sometimes got the sense that, even if his own life was in danger, he would have gone on, at the risk of being counted out for good, punning on the password ('wasp erred') that could have made his escape possible. That said, compared with him and Zabo—that is, Elisabeth—both of whom spoke with a posh Parisian accent as if they had been living there at least since the time of Hugh Capet, it was I who most came across as the country cousin, the provincial, the foreigner, or the wog, as those bastards on the extreme right would have it. During the first months after my arrival, those two taught me everything, you understand, everything: street slang, police headquarters, film clubs, store opening hours, that you could toss your cigarette butts on the ground (yes: I smoked from time to time), and that you had to ask for a "noisette" if you wanted an espresso with just a spot of milk. I hadn't realized until that point just how much the usages of one language could change, if you know what I—. In quite another regard, I remember the first time I asked them how I was to get to the conservatory, and when, without even consulting a map, they answered, "It's a cinch; you get on at Château-d'Eau and go to Strasbourg–Saint-Denis in the direction of Porte-d'Orléans, and from there you carry on in the direction of Pont-de-Sèvres until Saint-Augustin," I thanked them so doubtfully that they burst out laughing; Zabo wound up accompanying me on my first trip, exactly as if I were a kid on his way to nursery school. "Our little cousin from another world," she would say. And it's true; I felt that I was a bit of a dolt because I had until then never done more than get on here at Saint-François (at least we had the string of all those Saint-Thises and Saint-Thats in common, it made a kind of a link) and take tram number 7 in the direction of the school. Of course, in the sense in which it is applied officially, in the sense in which an inscription in roundhand in I don't know what great book of state confirms or consecrates the matter, in the sense in which one can then, to the very ends of the empire, proclaim with pride, "Civis gallicus sum," and thus win the respect of the natives and the assistance of the authorities—in that sense, of course, neither I nor they were French. But if what counts is to know a country, its history, its customs, its literature, at least as well as the common run of those who make it up and who hold its passport, well then, you know, they were a hundred times more French than I. And nevertheless, it's they who got arrested. *Verhaftet.*'

Smoke ring.

Behind the swivel chair, through the window onto the chalet's balcony, he sees the flakes falling in more and more closely serried ranks. The storm came up not long ago, when he went down to get charcoal from the basement of the old fitted-up cowshed. Between the lingering traces of cows and the glacial cold outside, it makes for a medium temperature.

'Right at the beginning,' he says, still talking to the swivel chair, 'when I had had it up to here with their teasing about cuckoos, chocolate, and that eternal chestnut of Hugo's, that we milk our cows, you know, and live in liberty, I responded that, for people living in the rue des Petites Écuries, Little Equerry Street, after all, they weren't too well placed to be treating me quite like that. To which they retorted, equerry perhaps, but a *royal* one, good fellow. Republicans they certainly were, and fierce, but, like all their compatri— well, like all the French, not a little proud of the heredity, of the heraldry, of the hierarchy and the hemorrhoids, excuse me, when the noble fundament that grants them refuge is clad in ermine, for such is Our good pleasure.'

Smoke ring.

'During certain periods of History, or for certain fortunate peoples like our own, who do not, as it were, have one—that is, not always spelled with a capital—gonging off the months and years in the lives of the folk, sometimes over a pretty long period of time, does not represent to them anything major, docs not modify anything essential, unless, of course, that they grow old and that the deadline inevitably comes up beyond which the survivors will continue to gong, to garner, and to beget without all those who remain stretched out behind them. But It can also happen that events succeed each other at such a hectic pace in the course of one single and unique existence, that the reversals that mark it off are so profound, that one might legitimately ask oneself how it is that suicide, madness, alcoholism, and other deviant behaviors, as you would say, are still in spite of everything quite in the minority, are still in spite of everything the exception in the case of those who are hit full in the face by the events. What were they like, you know,' he says, still talking to the swivel chair, 'what were they like for young Mr. Marquis of V. during the first twenty years of his life, his perspective on the future and his vision of the world to which he could with justice aspire, and what became of him, born in Versailles with a silver spoon in his mouth and all the fairies bent over his cradle on July 14, 1769? I know: you'll think that I'm belaboring the point. But, if I tell you this, it's because they told me, up until the summer of '39, until before my arrival that is, that Uncle David was swearing that his naturalization was no longer anything but a matter of weeks away, of days even. From September '39 until May '40, I heard him say over and over that the procedure was going so well, he didn't doubt he would see it finished as soon as the war was over, soon. Between June and October '40, in a perhaps less confident tone of voice and without the "soon," still he continued in the same vein. And on October 13, I stayed home alone. You know why?'

Smoke ring.

'On October 13 I stayed home alone because on that day it was the turn of the Ns to get themselves on the list, and all four of them were lining up at the commisariat. "Can you imagine: the French Jews, too," said Uncle David as he came home, and you couldn't tell whether it was indignation or relief that had the upper hand inside him. I didn't dare tell them what had been gnawing at me since that morning. I didn't dare tell them that they had perhaps best never have obeyed the summons at all. French Republic or French State, I know well that, in spite of it all, no one was more respectful of the laws than Uncle David, and that, if they were to hide, he and his family would find themselves, this I know too, at the mercy of a denunciation or of an identity check, and God knows if one or the other was common currency at the time, with or without the wages of Judas. "With our name," said Uncle David, "how could we put them off our trail for even a second?" Ill at ease, I was thinking of my own name, with surprise (and at the same time comprehension) that he did not associate it with their patronymic and that, in the manner of the distraught or the egotistical, who lament their own experience of something painful that their interlocutor has already lived through, he did not quickly pause to slap himself on the forehead and exclaim, "But it's true, you're familiar with this as well!" But no. As Nissim said to me one day during the last days, and this time I truly believe I saw something resembling hatred in his look, there was the same difference between us two as between a born cripple and someone who comes back from a round of winter sports limping. Then he took off his jacket and flung it in the corner. Balled up the way it had landed, only three branches of the star were visible.'

Smoke ring.

'You will tell me that it is too easy to remake History in reverse and, now that we know, or rather, that we know nothing, to ask ourselves whether they should not have conducted themselves differently at the time. Perhaps, by refusing to register, they would have come through unscathed, or arrived more easily in the southern zone? They talked about it. And if they had done it, it would have been another black day on Uncle David's head, because since November there is no longer a free zone. Perhaps, I don't know, boats, visas, money, they would have been able to flee to South America; they talked about it: it seems that we have distant cousins—you know this better than I do—in Buenos Aires. They also talked about seeking refuge here. Just five hundred kilometers, after all, six hours by train separated them from here, that and the red-and-white wood barrier, a barrier that a customs guard just doing his duty would have raised, or not, and that he would more probably have left closed, to judge from what the newspapers are saying under their breath, to judge too by what I saw at the border on my return. They talked about it, in any case, and also, in the end, about the possibility of a clandestine departure, of a more or less honest, more or less interested smuggler. They said, with a glance at me, that once they were here, you could perhaps do something for them.'

Smoke ring.

'Whatever the case, what right had I, you understand, I who was risking nothing, I who was supposed to understand not the first thing about their situation, what right had I to give them advice? And when, shortly thereafter, they were each summoned to have applied to their residence permits a pretty little JEW stamp in fat letters, what on earth could I do: lock them in and forbid them to obey this new summons?

'That evening, Aunt Bouca and Uncle David told me that it would no doubt be preferable for me not to live there with them any longer, but to look for a room in the neighborhood of the rue de Madrid, near the conservatory,' he says to the swivel chair. 'I wasn't in much of a mood to be funny, but I asked them all the same whether they were that sick of my scales and my practicing. Their place wasn't very big, as you well know, and at night my bed was made up in Uncle David's office. I can still smell the odor of resin, of dental glue and cloves. Later on, as a result of the restricted enrollment, Uncle David had to take down his shingle and do replacement stints for a colleague who was, uh, Aryan, and who paid him more or less whenever and however he pleased. "Tells his patients that his colleague's name is 'Newman,'" said Uncle, "doubtless because if they heard my real name they wouldn't open their mouths, except in shock, and then not long enough for me to take care of their cavities." At any rate, that evening they didn't so much as smile, and told me that I knew very well that that wasn't it at all. Without wanting to be dramatic, they simply wondered whether I was still properly secure at their place, in view of the

circumstances. So I told them that they had always insisted that I
wasn't risking anything, didn't have to register myself, and wasn't
Jewish as far as the law was concerned. "Quite so," said Nissim,
"quite so: according to the statuesque statute of our senescent
Seneschal, he shall not be considered Jewish who is recognized as
having a religion other than the Jewish—d'you see, little Papist?—
and who has no more than two Jewish grandparents. So let's see if
we can recap your case: Grandfather Nathan, one! Grandmother
Sophia, two! Two, two, two, who will offer more? Two once; two
twice; two three times: sold! And go in peace, my good fellow: you
are not of the accursed race, so in his infinite wisdom has decreed
Partial Crétin, Automat-in-Chief, and so says his government. Unless, of course—." And here,' he says to the swivel chair, 'here he
paused briefly, for effect. And I think that for an instant I was afraid
of what he was going to say. And I am quite sure he noticed.'
    Smoke ring.
    ' "Unless, of course," he continued, "our seductive cousin here,
he of the Greek profile, the red knife with the white cross, and the
superb gold watch, has been bedazzled—who knows?—at the conservatory by the charms of some ravishing cellist, singer, or pianist
from the music class next door, has secretly joined with her in legal
matrimony, and the lucky woman, without perhaps his even knowing it, without perhaps his taking account of the gulf that opened
up beneath his feet the day he pronounced his timid 'I do,' unless
that lucky woman, therefore—*fatalitas!*—turns out to belong herself
to the deicidal folk. For in that case, my dear New Testament with
only two forebears from the Old, my dear Mr. Bet-On-Two-Horses,
Mr. Foot-In-Both-Camps, because of that simple, stupid little ring
on your finger, and if I've correctly understood what-passes-for-
the-thinking of the Maaarrrshall at Vichy, in that case—whoops!—
like a boxer who's lost too much weight, you would have changed
categories, like, and would be well and truly returned to the swarm-
ing camp of rats and octopuses all rich as Croesus, and *shalom* to
you too! So tell us, cousin: married?" And perhaps his voice carried
a little more vehemence than the subject of the conversation mer-
ited? As a matter of fact, I had noticed an alto player with long black
hair in the violin class who, well. I had never exchanged a single
word with her, and if I had, it wouldn't have been to ask her where

she came from, I didn't give a hang about that, but rather to try and find out where she was going after school, so—. In response to the question, then, I shook my head and gave him a little smile. But he wasn't smiling so much anymore himself. He could be rather quick to anger, you know. "And do you know why," he exclaimed, "do you know why those whom one would imagine, in the present circumstances, to have better things to do, do you know why they have deemed it necessary to make this supplementary precision in the definition of what they call our statute, and what, for them, is never anything other than the common and maniacal labeling of a heap of anonymous meat for the cold rooms: do you know why? I'm going to tell why, I am!" There was in truth no doubt that he was going to tell us, you see,' he says to the swivel chair. 'And he told us. "It's because the two grandparents you already have profaning the Papa's holy wafers would be increased by the Mama's two or three or four cosmopolite grandparents—ugh!—and, if we don't sterilize her, or if we don't castrate him, think about it now, just imagine now the frightful gnome that such an unnatural union would engender, imagine his oily locks, his crooked fingers, his hooked nose, and the horror of it when he drops his pants and—."

'Aunt Bouca cried, "Nissim!" '

Smoke ring.

The larch wood from which the walls of the chalet are made is warm in color, like honey. The dark brown knotholes dotting it recall, in their symmetry, the spots of ink produced on a sheet of paper one has folded, smoothed out carefully, and then unfolded. Contemplating them leads to a kind of revery, which can on occasion approach hypnotism.

Smoke ring.

Smoke ring.

Ring.

'Yes,' he says. 'What was I—? Oh yes: this business of religion, you see. Mama and you wanted, or she wanted and you let her have her way, that I be a Catholic, a baptized Catholic, flung wriggling into a font of cold water, raised Catholic, catechism, First Communion, religious schools, the whole program, the whole hoop-de-lah. My "entrance ticket to Christian society," as I believe Heine said. The result is that today, it's like this: I'm neither proud nor

ashamed; the result is, for all that I'm Catholic, I might as well be
Protestant, or Jewish, or Anglican, or Muslim, or Sun Worshiper, or
Whoknowswhatian, or nothing at all. Except for, of course—but it,
it bothers me to acknowledge it—that sort of indelible impregnation that was imposed on me in spite of me and which, whether I
like it or not, has throughout my whole life a—. Gregorian chants,
things like that. The odor of incense. But anyway. It is nevertheless
the case that, at Uncle David's, until the war, I thought I understood
that they weren't either, very, and certainly not Zabo, who, to the
great irritation of her father, claimed to be a Communist. Synagogue from time to time, at Pesach, for example, because, *after all*,
Yom Kippur, about whose existence I learned because it fell on
precisely that day on which they were summoned to register for the
first time, Rosh Ha Whatever, mmm? Yes: Shanah, a Sabbath more
or less adapted to their French customs—that is, that they basically
had their Saturday on Sunday—and there you are; as far as I know,
that's it, except that, of course, they didn't exactly fight over the
prosciutto. So, just between us, you see, it wasn't like those medieval discussions where, resting on their dogmas and their certi-
tudes, the most celebrated experts of the two camps would vie with
each other in argument to prove the supremacy of one particular
religion over the other. For a long time, at least until the promulgation of Statute No. 1, I would even say that the topic was simply
never broached in our conversations. My religion was as foreign to
them, or of as little moment, as my nationality, with this minor
difference: that, whereas we never talked about the former, they
would sometimes, without malice, tease me about the latter. Thinking back on it today, at this distance, I should perhaps nonetheless
have taken a certain number of little things into account, nothing
really, less than nothing, trivial matters. But for example, in conversation, while they would always use your first name to refer to you,
they never did for Mama. They never even said, I think, "Our sister-
in-law." No, it was always, "Your mother." "Your mother might
be quite right," they said at the beginning of the phony war, when
she wanted me to return and you left it up to me until I was mobi-
lized here. "Your mother" this, "your mother" that. They actually
pushed her to the very edge of the frame on the family photo—
unconsciously, you might say. In their imagination, in fact, I sup-

pose that she was sort of cut in two, and that they weren't particularly sorry about it. Anyway, as I said, they might try as they liked, out of a sense of delicacy in my regard, to appear as warm as possible, yet they could not prevent a sort of distant and muffled hostility from making itself evident as soon as they mentioned Mama, which they did as rarely as possible. At first, I thought such a reaction was due to the fact that "your mother"—they weren't ignorant of the fact—was a practicing Catholic, as one says when one single word isn't enough anymore to mean what it means. Now, in whatever way they understood it (and how, tell me, are we to understand it?), I think quite simply that they reproached her — and this is not the same thing—for not being Jewish.'

Smoke ring.

'And then, in the street, in the neighborhood, in the district, in Paris, in the occupied zone, in the French zone, these little posters started appearing all over the place, on walls, on windows, full of crap, sorry, idiotic things, you know, like, "The Jews are in line for a trip to Palestine," or, "Hey, Jewboy, don't you understand French?" or, "Pack up, Jews, or you're dust!" '

Smoke ring.

'Now, in the rue des Petites-Écuries, where we lived,' he says to the swivel chair, 'I had for the first time noticed people who were recognizable as Jews. Here you never see that. Earlocks, you know, black clothes, beard, kippa. If there is such a thing as the call of the blood, or, as far as I'm concerned, of the bl, of the ood, of the hld, of the oo, I mean, of the half-blood: but you see what I mean; it worked so that, to say the least, I was only half attracted to them. Some element of nature should perhaps have compelled me to feel some respect for them, if not sympathy. In spite of everything, when I beheld something so savage, so disturbing and so Biblical (for the Bible eructates, you know, it vaticinates, it assassinates), some element of nurture made me prefer our chubby, apple-cheeked priests, with their sensible shoes and the six hundred buttons on their cassocks, gently going about their business, sprinkling incense in the direction of the pews. I should have thought of Torquemada, I know, or of Isabel the Catholic; instead, I thought of Rabelais and the Little Sisters among the Paupers. And if that's the way I reacted, I could only imagine with a wince what sort of a welcome they would get in the southern zone, and not only there, from people perhaps no more malicious than average, but steeped in that filthy anti-Semitic propaganda, when, on the rue Saint-Louis, at the place de l'Eglise, or in the auberge du Bon Secours, they see for the first time, fallen from the sky or mounted up out of Hell, these Christ-killers dressed up like the Bogey Man. "Jews in Germany," they said, you know, "and Krauts in France." That said, and right up until the promulgation of the statute that, from one day to the next, placed under the same familiar sign the Pole who arrived last night and the Frenchman whose father fell in 1917 and whose great-grandfather fell in 1870, you couldn't really say, you see, that Nissim—and still less Zabo—had paid any more attention to such practitioners, or to their practices, than I had. Next to those kinds of fellow worshipers, their religious mind seemed to have been made up: they were oblivious to them. And why would I have wanted to come off as more royalist than the king, even then? All the more so because, you understand—and it would be funny in other circumstances—they would have granted me, those ultra-orthodox defenders of the faith and guardians of the temple, without hesitation and with much greater ease than the Marshal's bully boys, my "certificate of nonappurtenance to the Jewish race"; since I did not have a Jewish mother, I was in their eyes nothing, nonexistent, zero, a *goy*.'

Smoke ring.

'To get back to the street,' he says to the swivel chair, 'I don't know, and with good reason, what the street was like where you yourself were born; you've never spoken to me about it, and something tells me that, even if I were to pause briefly in my monologue, today would certainly not be the day you would begin. Fine. In Paris, in the neighborhood where a lot of Jews lived, recognizable or not—and I'm not talking about the "specifically Judaic features" yet; I'm talking about those few Hassidim who seem to be in perpetual quest of a wall to lament against—in those streets where people often spoke Yiddish or Ladino just as well as French, I, for my part, did not find it remarkable that vendors of Sulpician images, for example, were rather underrepresented and that tailors, hosiers, and clothesmakers were somewhat overrepresented, or that the majority of the foodstores, the lunch counters, and the restaurants were kosher. After all, if the whims of History were to move French chefs to settle in a region of Papua already frequented by many of their compatriots, wouldn't they be more likely to put steak, quiche, and hotpot on their menus than, say, serpent, grasshopper, or black ants? As a consumer of fondue, holy wafers, pig meat, Bernese bear cookies, Röschti, and all manner of Oriental specialties, my gastronomic neutrality, you see, turned out to be just as passably confused. At any rate, I must admit that I have never succeeded in understanding what "kosher" actually signifies. When I was very young, you probably don't remember, but I asked you about it one day. We were on our way out of Mr. Sarkissof's tiny shop, here at Petit-Chêne, tucked in between a very Protestant bank and a brasserie trying more or less to be Bavarian. I suppose you had purchased your usual exotic wares –rose preserves, smoked sprats, those sesame things, those eggplant things, those eggs, black all over, that sometimes intrigued or amused Mama's family. In any case, your response to my request for information, on this subject as on many others, was a shrug of the shoulders. So I tried my luck with Uncle David. "Look at our little cousin," said Nissim, "he wants a crash course in kashrut!" And Uncle told him that he was wearing us out. Then he tried his hand at—. When he had gotten to the bit about clawed feet, cloven shoes, and the kid that mustn't simmer in the milk of its mother, I told him thank you very much, but either he wasn't any better pedagogically than his brother-in-law, or it was me who had a decided block, as you would say. Nature or nurture, I couldn't help thinking that the Catholics (actually I have to confess that I thought "we Catholics") had it rather easier: fish on Friday, no human flesh unless in extreme emergencies, a special effort at Lent, and that's all.'

Smoke ring.

'I'm probably telling it badly. Out of order. Too quickly. But we've had so little time to talk since my return that the events are getting a bit jumbled in my head. And then, in a week's time, and God knows for how long, I'm called up to go to the border and play the fife under Adolf's nose, and just imagine his terror when he hears the news. "Ach," he'll say between bites of carpet, "zat iz too mach vor me; I vill ztop ze var!" '

Smoke ring.

'As the recruitment officer said the other day, after much deprecating commentary on my state of health, "Iv you blay ze vlute as a zivilian, you can alzo blay ze five vis ze drommers in a vanvare." You would have thought it was Balzac, you know, when he launched into his exasperating attempts to imitate Yiddish. He would have done better to avoid spelling Rothschild twelve different ways. At any rate, the other repeated my name several times in a peculiar way, and I could tell he was holding himself back from asking whether I would indeed agree in advance to fight on the Sabbath. But anyway. While we're on languages, one morning when I was on my way to the conservatory, I noticed for the first time the signs in two languages—can you guess the other?—announcing that, henceforth, the shops I was talking about, the restaurants, the watchmaker, the haberdasher, the furniture store, were declared "Jewish businesses." "*Geschäft*," I knew the word; I'd learned it at school. Useful, you see, those secondary studies in a trilingual country. I was ready for Mussolini as well. Helpful in making out the barking of the pack of dogs surrounding us. Well. Little by little, over the course of weeks and months, these same posters, in an ugly yellow, a Jewish yellow, were replaced by others in the display windows, in red this time, the color of life and of triumph. They made known that, most often for no more than a song, and not in an eastern mode either, *above all not* eastern, the shop in question had passed into good hands, not crooked hands, Aryan hands. If, until then, boycotting the store had been strongly recommended, and there had been no particular interdiction against stones thrown through the windows by our valiant commandos on the extreme right, now things were returning to *Ordnung* once again. *Business as usual*, you might have said, if English hadn't had such a bad press at the time, with not a single publication in that language at the kiosks. At the conservatory, whether it was true or not, the story was making the rounds that trumpeters were being forbidden to use the mute, on the pretext that it produced Negro music. Business did, then, pick up again as before, with the slight difference that, from now on, supply had blue eyes and demand had blond hair, or vice versa. Imagine an ax brandished in the air—you know just the sort of picture—loosening the stranglehold of the octopus tentacle by tentacle.'

Smoke ring.

'So then Uncle David and Aunt Bouca advised me once again to move to a less vulnerable area. They said that they didn't always pay attention to details during the roundups and that days or weeks or even months could go by before I would even be in a position to prove that I had been wrongly arrested. "Because arresting us, that would be right, I suppose," exclaimed Nissim, to whom his parents replied that that wasn't the point. With time, and especially since he had been excluded from the law school, he had become more and more aggressive toward me, never missing an occasion to put me in a corner on my nationality or my Catholicism. For example, I remember the peculiar way he looked at me the day he remarked that, in I don't know what edition of the New Testament, a misprint had produced the sentence, "At evening time Jesus pissed on to the other shore," instead of "passed on to." He spared me—but only just—the old story of Jesus son of a who—, of a woman ot easy virtue and an alcoholic Roman legionary. In any case, I found his laugh hardly forced, and he never wanted to believe that, if I could only manage a grimace in place of a smile, it was merely because I thought his story didn't merit anything more and not because I condemned it as sacrilegious. On the contrary: I told much worse ones, though not in their presence, it's true. And if I abstained from telling them in their presence, it is without a doubt, you see, the "impregnation," as agnostic as I claim to be, the residue of my education at the knees of the Fathers that made me judge it somewhat indecent, or perhaps too cheap, to deride Christ in front of Jews, an audience I imagined to be won over in advance to such a project. On the other hand, though, I remember my discomfort when Mama, who I know was in agonies here, absolutely insisted on sending me my baptismal certificate through that engineer of Grandfather Louis's, the one who was always going from one country to the other on factory business. It was the same Mr. Fortisse, you know, who brought Uncle David the money you sent him for my upkeep in the rue des Petites-Écuries. "Keep it in absolute security," Mama wrote concerning the certificate; "it could come in handy one day." In the bizarre and somber period we were going through just then in France, where you were sized up, judged, and classified according to the alleged races to which you had not, until then, known you belonged, or so-called religious confessions you had long since abandoned or forgotten, I was of course aware that some people were moving heaven and earth to get their hands on this sort of document and that notaries and priests had never before been so much in demand. And that rotten bastard, excuse me, our compatriot to boot, even if he has been naturalized as a Frenchman, "the eminent Professor" Montandon, whom one had to go and see when, in a dubious case, there was, as they said, "suspicion of Jewishness," so that he could measure the length of your nose, for shit's sake, excuse me, the protuberance of your ocular globes, or your brand of circumcision, and, out of the goodness of his heart and for plenty of money, you can be sure, deliver—or not—a certificate of "nonappurtenance," *limpieza de sangre*, purity of the blood; you know all about it. And while we're about it, do those sod— those idiots still exist, who actually believe that all Jews have one eye smaller than the other? Along with that other lunatic from Geneva, Dieudonné, who splutters away on the German radio in Paris, we're quite something, aren't we, we really export our best, don't you think?'

Smoke ring.

'But that a religion, you see, with all that that term suggests in the way of the subjective and the private, that a religion or, rather, this piece of paper attesting to my belonging, or to my having been inscribed in due and proper form, like in a golf club, could, from one day to the next, because somewhere at the bottom of an undrinkable bottle of Vichy water some octogen— some senile old man has decreed it thus, could, therefore, mark such a radical break between an uncle and me, an aunt and me, a cousin and me, the rest of the family and me, the Jews and me, a category of human beings and me, and make all the difference between protection and persecution, freedom and prison, the right to practice the profession of my choice and forced labor in who knows what penal colonies in Poland, well you see, I had as much trouble understanding that as I did accepting it. And furthermore, I haven't had any recourse to this Catholicism for years now; I don't observe any of the practices anymore, which didn't make things any easier, and I had, in addition to my incomprehension, a vague sense of crookedness, that I was becoming a little like one of those people who, at the end of a

Voltairean life of hardy spirits, demand in loud quavering tones that a priest be summoned to their deathbed. And I thought I saw the proof that all of this was quite definitely nothing but hypocritical bloody garbage, simply designed to get as many Jews as possible to fall into the trap, in the fact that, at the heart of this Marshal's France, with the Sacré-Coeur constantly on everyone's lips, as they claimed to be restoring and honoring religion, it was enough to have four Aryan grandparents, which was after all the case for the immense majority of the population, to pass the most peaceful days imaginable, if you were discreet about your atheism, but that, if you were militant about it, like a freemason, to be the victim of harassments or persecutions (which I did believe, however, were without connection to those being undergone by the Jews). Because, you understand,' he says to the swivel chair, 'you, here, the way you are, you, here, if you hadn't had the chance to be naturalized here twenty years ago, being simply who you are, son and grandson of who you are, whatever your current beliefs are, your language, your confession, or your ideas, if you lived in Paris, now, just as I see you before me, or even barely a hundred kilometers from here, on the other side of the white-and-red barrier, you wouldn't have any right to that radio there, you see; you would have had to give it up to the authorities, and your bicycle, too, if you had had one, even though you, on a bike, I, well . . . and they would have forbidden you to practice, and you wouldn't have a telephone, nor the right to use a phone booth, and no cinema, of course, no theater, no cafés, no restaurants, no public parks, no swimming pools or things like that, no shopping in stores outside of certain hours, when there isn't anything left, no libraries, no exhibits, and only a few scarce places at the back of the bus, and only the last car on the metro, what they called the "synagogue," and, since this summer, when you went out, that obligatory filthy yellow spot on your clothes; or indeed, in the streets, roundups, where any cop at all, or not even a cop, who finds your nose too much this, your skin coloring too much that, too Levantine I suppose, would have the right to stop you or to arrest you, and our mysterious neighbor, you remember the one, who smeared a swastika on our letterbox before the war, well, his equivalent could write a nice little letter all about you to the Commissariat for Jewish Questions, and they wouldn't send it back to him and make him eat it, glue, stamp, ink, and all, oh no: they would read it with the greatest of interest; they would thank him kindly for having proved himself such a good citizen—and they would be happy to discuss our apartment with him later on—: I, you, the way you are, you understand, this is what would happen one hour by car from here, *one hour*. I'm not making any reproaches, you know; I am probably not the stuff that martyrs or heroes are made of, and, to tell the truth, it's actually a relief, "a bashful relief," perhaps, to quote you-know-who, that the luck of the draw, or of History, or of who-knows-what, has placed you, has placed us on the right side of the border like this. But after all, as long as this privileged situation lasts, from which a measly four million of us benefit as citizens of this country, and in which, in comparison with what is going on today in the rest of Europe, a handful of Jewish citizens—one of whom you are, and me only half, as it seems—in which they should be able to live as freely as possible, well, tell me, have you reflected on this situation at all; in the end, have you posed yourself any questions; can you help me to understand something?'

Smoke ring.

'In the end, you see, Nissim was claiming that, even if I had had fifty Jewish grandparents—a genetic aberration, he would say with an awful grimace, that he himself well understood would terrify Goering, Goebbels, Himmler, and that whole clique of Wagnereal diseases—the Germans would still not have touched a Jewish hair on my Jewish head. According to him, there existed between our two countries—ours, of course, and Germany—lots of common interests, if not far too many mutual sympathies, for Hitler not to think twice before attacking some local Jud Süss, even a hundred times Jewish in his eyes. There aren't many of them here, after all, and in the present circumstances he could afford the luxury of appearing magnanimous, to avoid a diplomatic incident and to cast himself in a good light and save us for dessert. "Because," Nissim would say, "the last Jew in the world could live in an inaccessible frozen grotto on the obscure peak of an obscure peak in the Himalayas if he liked; he would still get him, Hitler would, he would GET HIM." While we waited, such generosity had its price, whether it was durable or not, and that was our forever stroking the beast the right way and avoiding, to the best of our abilities, any word or deed that could provoke its wrath in the least. "And here," Nissim would say, "among other reasons, is why, to prevent who knows what kind of ghettos from springing up again on the edges of Germania, here is why, in order not to unleash the Furor's *führer*, your government turns us back at the border, under the pretext that we are not at risk in France. Not-at-risk. But hell, is he blind, your ambassador: hobnobbing in Vichy, buddies with Mussolini, buddies with Roosevelt, buddies with Hitler, buddies with the Pope, buddies with the Grand Mufti of Jerusalem? Does he use a white cane?" After "your" mother, you see,' he says to the swivel chair, 'from now on it was "your" country, interminably: "your" government, "your" ambassador, and I thought there was in each of those possessive adjectives all the bitterness and provocation, and perhaps the jealousy, of someone who believes himself to have been unjustly dispossessed. In the same sense, I had noticed since the outset, in regard to those little things I was talking about before, that Uncle David just couldn't help himself: as soon as the talk turned at all to Catholicism, he would never just say, for example, "A priest," or, I don't know, "Holy Communion," but rather, "A—how do your people call it?—priest," or, "Holy—how do your people call it?— Communion." How-do-your-people-call-it? As if he didn't know. Little trivial things entirely, you see, but they rankled. That said, Nissim was starting to bother me, and, that evening, I became a little unhinged and answered him that, instead of always looking at things so narrowly and constantly sniffing out the most humiliating ideological compromises, he would do better to understand, or to attempt for one second to understand, that our government, surrounded on all sides by warring parties as we were, dependent on their good will for our survival, political as well as economic, was indeed obliged to think first about its own nationals, just as any other would have done in the same circumstances, and to pursue its interests by tacking with the wind and living from day to day. And then, to load up the boat with thousands upon thousands of extra mouths to feed and keep, Jewish or not, Jewish above all, Jewish on top of everything, didn't that mean risking the whole thing springing a leak and thus scuttling the whole country, Jews and all, driving it into famine, disorder, and a sort of anarchy that the SS, with all its divisions, would not hesitate a second to come and put right? It was then,' he says to the swivel chair, 'it was then, you understand, in the heat of the moment and in anger, that I, that I said that after all, you Jews, you're not alone in the world. "You," Papa, that's what I said.'

Smoke ring.

'Neither inside nor outside; it's always the same, you see,' he says to the swivel chair. 'Because in fact, I didn't really think that way, that the boat was full, or at least I did only in part. In spite of everything, in fact, I dreamed that a great burst of generosity would submerge this country. That, as privileged as we had been so far in this Europe of blood and fire, we would open our arms a little wider to the wretched and the persecuted. That we would all squeeze together to make place for the people we were cramming in, tighten our belts to offer a piece of bread to the people they were starving out. Is that Jewish, or Papist, or utopianist? And if such an attitude was bound to provoke the rage of that carpet eater up there in Berlin, I dreamed that we would all team up to laugh in his face, and that we would go down, maybe, under his blows, but that we would at least do it with our heads held high. Because after all, doesn't everyone here, the Protestant baker from Appenzell, the Catholic shepherd from the Valais, the watchmaker from the Jura tempted by the Church of Jesus Christ of Latter-Day Saints, doesn't everyone here, after all, believer or not, today, in this country, couldn't they, shouldn't they, even without believing in it particularly, at least fleetingly, share my wish? Or the Red Cross, now, tell me, is it going to develop color blindness when it comes to the yellow star? Or those who are not put off by the white cross painted on the door of the leper, but go in to bring him aid, those whose high calling on the field of battle is supposed to be to operate on the wounded, without distinction and with identical devotion, whether they wear the swastika or the Croix de Lorraine, even if one of the two sounds a little more, shall we say, harmonious to their ears; those people, and with them a great number of our compatriots, would they be content in that case to cross themselves furtively and to walk on with averted eyes if the victim were Jewish? If Hitler had got it into his head to persecute German families—why not?—Polish, Czech, Soviet, Yugoslav, Romanian, Dutch, Danish, Greek, French, and so on, to persecute all the families with names beginning with K, would I have to be called Towhomitmay Koncern to be appalled by this insane decision, and only the Ks of this country along with me, and, in this Klan, would we be the only ones to want to be able to reach out a hand to all the Ks of the world, as long as we remained spared? And how much time, by the way, in parentheses now, how much time should be required, in the face of this criminal insanity à la Caligula, how much time, one month, two months, three months, before some putsch sent the Reich's Lone Deranger into an asylum or a prison, never to be seen again? It's ten years now, however, *ten years* that Adolf has been raging. Tell me, must one be like me, in other words, half Jewish, a small k, if you like, or, who knows, a kwadroon, an oktaroon, must one be such, to hope that our government would show a little less pusillanimity and, raison d'état or not, feel some shame and anger at the discovery that, today, they have no other thought than to close the borders as hermetically as possible? I was dreaming then. And I don't dream that much anymore.'

Smoke ring.

'Yes, sir. The grand principles, you see, idealism, words. And then, when it comes time to put them into practice, whoosh, nobody left, everybody into the ark, let the flood begin. Because, at the moment that Aunt Bouca yelled at me to show it to the police, I barely hesitated before doing it, when in fact I could have, I don't know, made *the grand gesture*, hurled myself upon them knife in hand, or something like that. Sure. And when the door had closed behind them, did I fling myself down the stairs after them to try and convince the cops that they were making a mistake, or to suggest to them, like in the movies, that they arrest me in exchange for one of the two women? Did I at least run to the window to alert the neighborhood, itself, by the way, no doubt being rounded up too, or unhearing? Even though I knew it was useless, vain, desperate, did I make the least attempt to come to their aid? No, and no again. While everything separates our compatriots from the Jews, or nothing connects them, and I deplore the indifference here and the cowardice of the majority, still, what did I undertake, me, there, at the scene, for my own family, Jewish or not? Nothing, nothing, nothing. Or rather something: stupid and dazed, I squatted down on my heels and caressed Alleycat, wondering what would become of her after my departure and thinking, right up until that moment, that I was going to have to get hold of some scraps for her. Some *scraps.*'

Brutally, a gust of wind mixed with snow makes a shutter bang shut and plunges the room into half-darkness. The swivel chair pulls the plaid cover a little higher up over his midriff.

'There you are. Rest assured, it's over, or almost. The last months, as you might suspect, were the most difficult. Rumors, alerts, arrests, roundups came one after another and, again and again, Uncle David would advise me not only to change neighborhoods, but now also to leave the country, to come back here to seek shelter. He would say that it was certainly my nationality and my religion that had permitted me to escape from the roundups and the internment camps until then. But what would happen to me if our country, for example, were to abandon its neutrality, willingly or by force, were to side with Germany and declare war on France? "What would happen is," laughed Nissim derisively, "they would roll out the red carpet for our little cousin, the occupier's ally." And Uncle David said that, yes, that was true, and it was the opposite of what he had wanted to say. "Them," Nissim went on to exclaim, "them, declare war on Germany; you're joking, right, Papa?" Whatever the case, I admit that I mulled over this return more and more often from then on. I felt a sort of discomfort, indeed, at the thought of abandoning them to their fate, but you know, when a week doesn't go by without the people you live with being deprived of another freedom, without their ability to come and go being reduced, without some new chicanery being devised to humiliate them, you can't help but ask yourself whether the very presence at their side of an individual whom none of these measures touches—even if, at first, in good faith, they are happy for him, even if he does his best to let them benefit directly or indirectly from his privileged situation—whether his very presence, then, a constant reminder to the victims of a state they have known and lost, doesn't finally mean for them too painful an evocation, which, quickly becoming an intolerable challenge, forces them to confound in one single ejection and one single hatred both those their executioner spares and that executioner himself. In any case, I think this is a little what Nissim felt about me during that last period. And, as if that weren't enough, I think it's perhaps also this that the whole rest of the warring world feels about our country and its inhabitants. As for us here, you know, I have the impression that, for the moment, Hitler is behaving like that profoundly anti-Semitic mayor of Vienna who had, after all, his own couple of good Jews. When this was cast in his face he would reply, haughtily, "Wer Jude ist, das bestimme ich"—that is to say, because, you and German, "I shall decide who is a Jew." '

Smoke ring.

'Contrary to what had been foreseen at first,' he says to the swivel chair, 'I decided, therefore, not to wait until the end of the conservatory year to leave. Anyway, during that time, things were moving fast, and a lot of the teachers, including my favorite, Mr. Bloch, you know, interpretation, had been asked, for reasons you can guess, to go and teach, or hang themselves, somewhere else. Most survived for better or for worse by giving private lessons to pupils who were not too horrified by their status as pariahs. And it wasn't only teachers who were disappearing overnight. Pupils too. Like the alto player with the long black hair that I—. One fine morning, whoosh. But well. I—. She—.'

Smoke ring.

Smoke ring.

'Good. At that same time, and that was Uncle David's last black day before the arrest, one of our neighbors told us with dismay that he had just been denaturalized and that he had had to give up his passport and identity card at the prefecture. He was one of those whom the Gringoire and the guys from the extreme right called "paper Frenchmen." Their own titles, of course, going back to the Trojans by way of Aeneas, what they felt for the "paper" of the recently naturalized was that hateful contempt for what you crumple, tear, or burn before tossing into the garbage. Uncle David murmured that, if one could thus withdraw your nationality, with the stroke of an indifferent bureaucrat's pen, well then, all things considered, he still preferred that his request had not gone through. "Think about it," he said; "just think about it: you would have had a party, opened champagne; you would have stopped looking at your shoes in front of the foreigners' office at the prefecture and would instead be looking straight into the eyes of the employee at the voting office; and then one fine day, the mail arrives, an official letter, and you don't tremble any longer when you get an official letter, except perhaps from the Ministry of Finance, but it's a trembling you share from now on with forty million countrymen, and, thinking of something else, you slip open the envelope's flap with a careless motion of your finger, and you read that—. And the sky falls on your head." You can say what you like about our current government and the real or supposed Germanophilia of certain of its members,' he says to the swivel chair, 'but have you ever, you, the way you are, it's got me again, you see, have you ever thought that if, here among us as in France, some old sod of an anti-Semitic general—they're all over the place—if he had taken power, you could also, here, the way that I see you before me, receive a similar letter and, overnight, become Turkish again yourself—that is to say, expulsable or deportable or I-don't-know-what, under the pretext that your naturalization is posterior to this or that date?'

Smoke ring.

'Hey, haven't you had enough of those things? You know as well as I do what Freud died of in London three or four years ago.'

Smoke ring.

'And couldn't you try to do a triangle for a change, or a star?'

Smoke ring.

'Well, if I were an Indian, I would say the guy on the hill over the way was off his rocker, sending me the same message O O O all the time.'

Smoke ring.

'Fine, fine, fine. Fine. It's over, by the way. You know the end. They banged at the door early one morning. French cops. "Agents capteurs," they were called. Nice name; made you think of those guys, you know, whose job it is to remove certain animals from a territory where they are too populous and reinstall them somewhere else. They had a list of four people to arrest, and there we were, five of us. Ouch. Administrative problem. Look for the mistake. Papers'fyouplease, m'sieurs-dames. Nice and polite and everything. Still better than hearing it barked in German. Through the open door I saw a neighbor lady on the landing, on her way out with a child in her arms and another hanging onto her leg. So then, five foreigners' identity cards, everything in Ordnung, everything valid. For four of them, however, marked with the JEW stamp, this

validity is no longer on the agenda; they might just as well be ten
years out of date, for all that would matter. Right then, off they
go then, and pronto 'fyouplease, off they go all four of them and
pack two medium-sized suitcases each, *medium*, mind; no steamer
trunks, one for underwear, shirts, woollens, things like that, and
the other, or a bag for that matter, with a minimum, a *minimum*, of
two days' provisions until the end. What? What did I say? "Until the
end of the journey," don't you understand Fre—. There was a cry in
the inner court, and it sounded as if the window down below had
shattered into a thousand pieces. Tssst. Right: back to you. You,
that was me,' he says to the swivel chair. 'That would be you, then,
the non-Jew? That would be. "In point of fact he is not Jewish,
officer," said Aunt Bouca, reappearing on the threshold with a
suitcase in her hand; "he's a distant relative by marriage, neutral,
Catholic; we were putting him up here with us temporarily." His
back to the wall, his arms crossed, a suitcase at his feet, Nissim was
staring at me with a peculiar smile. What would I respond when the
cock had crowed, once, twice, three times? With another look at my
card, the cop said, yeah, yeah, not really Jewish, with a honker like
that. . . . Was he talking about my name or my nose? At any rate he
said it without particular aggression. As if I didn't look precisely
like my photo on the card. Just doing his job; one day it's traffic,
one day it's checking for perverts in the urinals, one day it's the
parade for the King of England, one day it's kids playing Django too
loud, one day it's the Jews. So then he asked whether it couldn't
in fact be the case that I, a Jew, had perhaps neglected to tell?
"William," said Nissim, and everyone looked at him quizzically. In
the stairwell of the apartment house there was a general descent,
with tears and the noise of children hurrying into the playground.
One of the cop's two colleagues said, Hey now, they weren't supposed to be having discussions with the people they were arresting,
and that there was nothing for it but to take all five of us in; they
would sort us out later. Nissim asked who "they" were, and they
shrugged their shoulders in response. In the bedroom Uncle David
asked Aunt Bouca to come and help him fold a blanket, and Zabo
was feverishly opening drawers, looking for ration and textile coupons. Alleycat had curled herself up on the sofa, which was normally forbidden. "Wait, wait a sec," said the first agent; "have you

by any chance seen where he comes from?" They bent over my papers anew. Aunt Bouca and Uncle David reentered the room. She had a shawl over her shoulders and he was carrying the blanket. In the middle of July, it was enough to give you cold shivers down your spine already. "Okay," said the first cop, "it is established that, Jew or not, you are not on the list of countries whose nationals we have been ordered to apprehend." But for extra security, would I please show them my passport? And for an instant, one of those instants, some people claim,' he says to the swivel chair, 'that can make all the difference between cowardice and heroism, for an instant I hesitated. Should I claim that I had mislaid it, lost it? Last chance not to abandon them, to link my fate to theirs. There were certainly stories of non-Jews who, braving the risk of being arrested, had sewn on pretend yellow stars with the words "Breton" or "Swing" or "Goy" instead of "Jew" emblazoned on them. Nissim was still fixing me with his strange smile. "Passport," I repeated, questioning, stalling for time. It was then that Aunt Bouca seemed to sense the stupid tempest that was raging in my brain and cried out to me to show it to them, for heaven's sake, show it to them! "And chop-chop," said one of the cops; "you're not the only ones we have to take care of." So rather than following them, my suitcase in my hand, I went to search for my *passeport suisse–Schweizer Pass– passaporto svizzero.'*

Smoke ring.

'What could I do,' he asks in a muffled voice, still with his back turned to the swivel chair. 'What would you have done in my place? What *did* you do in my place? And then something else; listen, it's made me sick, this other thing that I have to tell you before I go off to join the military band, a *musical band*, to participate in the struggle against their persecutors. Listen, they were already all four on the landing, their bags and suitcases in their hands; I had kissed them, eyes full of— and then, just like that, carelessly, one of the cops said to me that, when he was young, he had been at camp near Villars, did I know it? He obviously had to pronounce it "Villarsssss," but there, you know, we'll never change them. I nodded my head, unable to speak. Then he imitated, very badly, the accent of the Vaud, all the while staring at me, frowning, waiting. Waiting. Waiting. Password. Pass-accent. Shibboleth. I won't forget, I will never forget Nissim's smile when I repeated the cop's sentence with an intonation worthy of a local rustic: "Where's the fire on the lake?" '

When he turns around brusquely, only the back of the swivel chair is facing him. In the ashtray poised on the low table, a cigar butt is just burning itself out. Holy Havana: it needed no fewer than twenty-eight smoke rings to get to the end.

Yvonne Léger

Yvonne Léger was born in 1941 in Lucerne and has dual Swiss and French citizenship. She is a regular contributor to the Rote Fabrik in Zurich, an alternative cultural center. She illustrates her works herself, in fabric and paint, with a process she calls 'setting to silent music.' Her publications include poetry (*Ich schenk Dir mein Lächeln*, 1986), ballads (*Malva Rosetta nimmt ein Bad*, 1993), and novels, for one of which, *Eljascha* (1990), she was awarded prizes by Pro Helvetia and the canton of Lucerne. In the excerpts that follow, from the beginning and end of that novel, Léger recounts in fictionalized form her mother's wartime marriage to a French Jew and her ordeal crossing the border into Switzerland with a group of Jewish refugees. Through it all, the Swiss passport glows with the magical power of safety.

Yvonne Léger

EXCERPTS FROM Eljascha

Without changing his expression, the registrar of the ninth arron-dissement in Paris paged through Eljascha Rosenthal's Swiss pass-port. From front to back, and from back to front. As though he couldn't locate something he was intent on finding. He glanced at Joschi Levy's *carte de séjour provisoire*, his temporary residence permit, and continued to flip through the passport, occasionally eyeing the pale woman sitting in front of him. He checked. He turned pages. 'Excuse me, Madame,' he said suddenly, 'but for the Swiss authori-ties your name is no longer Rosenthal; it is Levy.' And, with that, he reached for the pen that lay beside the documents, dipped it into the ink, struck through the name Rosenthal, and wrote Levy above it. Eljascha wanted to open her mouth, implore him to stop imme-diately, insist that it wasn't up to him at all, and certainly not in her passport, which had been thereby rendered invalid. *Invalid, Monsieur.*

The situation was exceedingly difficult. Joschi was a refugee Theoretically still a German citizen, and as such, given the current political situation, without rights. An unwanted Jew, a deserter, for he was serving as a conscripted 'volunteer' in the French army. And, although he couldn't have returned to Germany even had he wanted to, he had thus made himself punishable under German law.

According to Swiss law, Eljascha Rosenthal had surrendered her Swiss citizenship by marrying him. She knew this quite well, but, camouflaged as the fetching young Mademoiselle Rosenthal, she had planned to retain her legal status with the help of her old passport, at least on paper. But now the registrar had botched it all up.

The small man in the proper suit and dark necktie was entirely guileless. Proudly he considered his work of art and began looking around for something else to change, this time in Joschi's *carte de séjour.*

Célibataire: single. With a bold stroke of his pen, the word was replaced by *marié:* married. This habit was unique to the French. Instead of issuing new documents, they scribbled into the old ones, so that many residence permits and passports looked like corrected school essays. Of course, this work wasn't ordinarily done by a registrar, and certainly a foreign passport was never to be tampered with. But people seemed to have accustomed themselves to the times, and thus the official appeared to enjoy an absolutely clear conscience. The only thing that still evidently worried him was that he didn't know how to write *marié* in German. He wrinkled his forehead and gave Eljascha a look more probing than beseeching. She shrank from his glance and turned her head toward Joschi, who was sitting beside her in a chair. He had to do something to prevent the official from rendering her passport still more invalid than it already was! After all, Joschi was a lawyer and would find the appropriate words.

The room in which they were to be married had been very high and white. At the front, under one of the three widows, stood a longish wooden table and a green upholstered chair, where the official had taken his place. Eljascha, Joschi, and their witnesses, Madeleine and Armand, had sat in front of the official on somewhat smaller chairs, also upholstered in green, and when they had looked out of the large windows, they had seen another part of the city hall. Behind the bride and groom and witnesses were row upon row of benches for the wedding guests, who in normal times might have kept Eljascha company as she walked down the aisle.

Drops of sweat had collected on Joschi's forehead and were running into his eyes. Probably the drops had blurred his vision, and he hadn't even noticed what the official had done, for Joschi just mutely held her hand and smiled at her.

From the rue Fontaine it wasn't far to the registry office. Together with their witnesses they had walked to the Place de Saint-Georges, passing the church of Notre Dame de Lorette to arrive at the rue du Faubourg Montmartre. After ten minutes they had reached the street named Drouot, the one that leads to the registry. Through a portal they had entered the cobbled courtyard of the official building. While Joschi asked where the registry was, Eljascha had glanced at the clock under the eaves, which was approaching nine thirty, the time appointed for the wedding ceremony. Mademoiselle Eljascha Rosenthal, soon to be Madame Levy, had pressed her black pearl bag to her body and asked her witness: 'Were you excited, too, when you got married?' The concierge had laughed: 'Not me, but Armand was.' 'That's what you think,' her husband had retorted. Madeleine had turned up her nose. 'Armand used to be charming and nice, but since we got married, he's become like all husbands.' She had waved her hand dismissively. Joschi, the husband-to-be, had stepped through the door marked *Information* and walked over to Eljascha. 'Madame, may I offer you my arm?' He had gestured toward the door in the middle building: 'That's where we go in.'

They had ascended a broad marble staircase with wooden banisters, under a ceiling set with stone roses. Eljascha should not have looked up because she had stumbled, and her black pearl pocketbook had opened. A handkerchief had fluttered to the ground, along with an open pack of cigarettes. And if her Swiss passport hadn't fallen out, all their troubles could have been avoided. For Eljascha hadn't put the passport back into the bag, but had instead kept it in her hand and laid it on the table along with her other documents. That wouldn't have been necessary at all. The marriage license, Joschi's residence permit, and his military papers would have sufficed.

Whyever had she done it?

In order to show the official that she came from Switzerland. That she was Swiss. Born in Lucerne. Raised in Lucerne. On the third floor, Kauffmannweg 27. He should have seen the balcony, an architectural jewel, with the beautiful ocean mural. But she couldn't say any of this to the official.

Why had she committed the unforgivable stupidity of parting with her passport? Of course she hadn't thought that the official would go beyond his competence. She had thought he would be impressed. Because she came from a country that was like an island protected by mountains. A singular place in the world. Because the island was unconquerable. The mountains scared off enemies, rendered them incapable of fighting. Papa, too, had thought that Swit-

zerland could not be taken. He should have known; after all, he had
lived through World War I as a sergeant. 'But,' Papa had always
added, 'Switzerland is a false diamond.' What could he have meant
by that?

The official pulled his *dictionnaire* out of his desk, paged through
it, and finally pointed out a word. '*Marié* in German is *verheiratet*.'
Ponderously he took up his pen, dipped it into the inkwell, scratched
through the word *ledig* with a fine, clean stroke, replaced it with
verheiratet, and nodded with satisfaction. 'Now everything is as it
should be.' Then he replaced the dictionary in its customary spot.

Eljascha's palms turned moist. She was having trouble breathing. It isn't so bad, she reassured herself. She had to think of Papa,
when he had told the family: 'I am bankrupt.' Mama had covered
her face and begun to weep. The children had stared at Papa, who
was standing in front of them with his hands stretched out in a
gesture of hopelessness. What did it mean? Suddenly Papa had
screamed, 'Stop crying, Aliska; stop staring at me. It could be much
worse; I could be terminally ill. Terminally ill, do you hear me?
Then you'd have something to complain about!'

It really isn't so bad, Eljascha thought, no longer to possess a
valid passport, and she even managed a smile.

The official had stood up and was looking at the bride and
groom. 'Joschi Levy and Eljascha Rosenthal, there's no garden of
roses waiting for you. You, a young woman, barely married, will be
alone much of the time. For our general will soon be calling up all
the officers and soldiers who are now on leave.'

He had fixed his gaze on Joschi. 'You, too, Monsieur Levy. You
have found a new home here with us, and I am convinced that you
will show your gratitude and fight honorably for France. In the
event that it should come to that.'

What was this man going on about? What homeland should
Joschi fight for? He had left his. He hadn't a home any longer.

The official had not yet finished his patriotic speech. 'We are
between war and peace. The pace of events is accelerating, and
every hour the situation changes. Everyone must keep calm, for it is
the destiny of Europe, and of civilization, that is at stake.' He had
paused for a breath, taken out a handkerchief, and wiped the sweat
from his brow.

Eljascha had squirmed back and forth on her chair, longing for a cigarette. If he would only get on with marrying them! Furtively, she had looked about her. How plain the room was. No canopy above their heads; only a crystal chandelier suspended from the ceiling, into which roses had been carved, as in the stairwell. She had suddenly noticed how joyless the room was. Almost offputting. A picture of the Place de l'Etoile had hung on the wall.

Behind her she had heard Madeleine sigh. Perhaps she, too, would have liked to smoke a cigarette. Eljascha had wondered whether the official was married. Poor woman. Instead of kissing her, he would have lamented over the destiny of Europe, and his wife would have smiled at him, all the while thinking of a soft hotel bed and her lover.

'I do,' she had heard Joschi saying. 'I do,' she had said and couldn't remember whether the official had asked her a question. He had slid the marriage license across the table and asked them to sign it. Joschi had taken the pen and passed it to Eljascha, who had written her new name on the paper. Armand and Madeleine had approached the table and confirmed with their signatures that Eljascha Rosenthal had now become Eljascha Levy.

'*Félicitations*, Madame.' The official had stood up and offered Eljascha his hand. Then it had been Joschi's turn. '*Félicitations*, Monsieur.' The concierge, too, full of emotion, had come to Eljascha and kissed her on the cheek, turned to Joschi, and, standing on tiptoe, had kissed her new husband. The concierge's husband, a skinny Frenchman with a pencil mustache, had shaken hands with the newlyweds.

'Monsieur Levy must kiss Madame,' Madeleine had said. Joschi had held out his hands to Eljascha. 'Come, my dear, let me embrace you.' He had taken her in his arms. She had looked into his gray-green eyes. 'Joschi, my poor Swiss passport.'

'What about your passport?' He seemed not to understand. For a moment, she, too, was confused. She had told him nothing of her plans to remain Eljascha Rosenthal with the help of her passport. Surely Joschi, a lawyer by training, would have objected. He would have tried to talk her out of it. 'Darling, you're breaking the law.' Now everything was legal, but she had lost her Swiss citizenship.

Joschi repeated his question. She attempted a smile. 'It's nothing, Joschi. I'm just afraid that the Swiss won't much like the changes made by a French official.'

'What sort of changes, dear?'

He really hadn't noticed. His military service at the Camp d'Auvours, the wedding, the whole thing must have confused him. She stroked his hair. 'This scrawl in my passport. I just hope I don't get into trouble because of it.'

Joschi looked at her, shaking his head. 'Darling, what do you want with your passport? You've exchanged your Swiss citizenship for me,' he said, and kissed her on the mouth. 'Bravo,' cried the concierge, and flung her arms around Armand's neck.

December 1940

The train arrived in Annecy, ten minutes late, at five o'clock. The women had followed their own thoughts and had not spoken to one another throughout the entire voyage. Only a few people in civilian clothing were waiting on the train platform. Two German officers stepped out of the stationmaster's office. They walked along the side of the train, seemingly expecting someone. Eljascha and the other women sank down into their seats.

I have my Swiss passport. My valid Swiss passport. Nothing can happen to me. Even though my name is Levy. But what if they arrest me anyway?

Outside the train the officers stood at attention. A man in a leather coat nodded at them. One of the officers took his suitcase, and the three left the platform. The women breathed a sigh of relief. The train began to move. Katia reached into her bag and took out a revolver. Oddly enough, Eljascha wasn't shocked. Perhaps because the revolver looked like Papa's revolver, only without the mother-of-pearl handle. Ute and Marianne looked at their companion with disapproval.

'I would sooner kill us than let us be arrested by the Germans.' Katia weighed the weapon in her hand, extended her arm, and pointed it at the door.

Shall I change compartments? Maybe Katia will suddenly lose her mind, even if no Germans appear. Or maybe she wants to get at my passport. Katia must have guessed her thoughts, for she winked at Eljascha. 'I won't kill you,' she said, and calmly put the revolver back into her bag.

For a moment, Eljascha saw herself in Dr. Heim's office. *I need cyanide, Doctor. Just in case we fall into German hands.* The vial lay carefully enclosed in a crystal pendant around her neck. Eljascha fingered it and thought regretfully of the beautiful, secretive Clem. She would have known what to do, Eljascha thought, but do I? She waited for inspiration, some kind of sign from Papa, a signal from Uncle Louis or from her patron saint. Nothing happened. The train clattered along the tracks.

Outside it had grown dark. A weak lamp submerged the compartment in ghostly light. Katia dozed. Eljascha thought she felt the eyes of the other two resting on her.

You're seeing ghosts. These women won't harm you. They are neither demons nor witches. They are escaping Jews, just like you. Try to concentrate on something else. Think of Joschi. . . .

*

The door opened. The conductor asked to see their tickets. Katia started out of her sleep and fixed the man with a gaze, unmoving. His uniform had probably frightened her. After the official had gone the rounds, punching their tickets, he stood with his hand outstretched in front of Katia. 'S'il vous plaît, Madame,' he asked. Katia opened her handbag slowly, and for a fraction of a second Eljascha held her breath. But Katia only fished out her ticket. 'Bon voyage,' the conductor said in parting. 'The French are always so polite,' Ute observed. She began unexpectedly to tell them about New York, 'in order to distract our thoughts and calm our desires.' . . .

*

'Whatever happens, the most important thing is to stay together,' Katia said. Everyone nodded. Why am I nodding, Eljascha asked herself; I have nothing to fear; but her heart beat so ferociously it seemed to want to leave her body. *Just don't panic. Nothing will happen. You'll show your passport to the official, and he will return it to you. Do you hear? But what will happen to the women?*

She suppressed the thought.

The train slowed down. When it came to a halt, they remained seated. They would be informed if they had to get out for the French passport control. Were they really in Annemasse? It wasn't even a train station. Eljascha pressed her face against the window. As far as she could tell, they were standing in the middle of a field. Surely the train would continue its voyage soon.

*

A few people had assembled in the corridor. The train had been standing still for fifteen minutes already. Ute opened the door and overheard snatches of conversation.

'Where are we anyway?'

'Why isn't the train continuing?'

'Has there been an air raid warning, perhaps?'

Katia was quick to make up her mind. 'I'll see what's up.' Marianne and Ute followed her.

On no account will I leave the train. So close to my destination. . . .

The people in the corridor began to cluster together. Eljascha stood up and turned to the elegantly dressed man who stood in front of her compartment, holding a briefcase. 'Can you tell me what is going on?'

'I don't know any more than you do, Madame. It seems to me that the train can't enter the station. This often happens. Don't worry. I ride this route regularly.'

Although the anxious passengers were crowding the platform and speculations about the unexpected halt were growing more outlandish as time wore on, Eljascha sat back down and waited. What could be taking the women so long? And what if the train suddenly continued on its way?

Eljascha became agitated. She pulled down the window. Raindrops fell on her face. Some of the passengers from the rear wagons were stumbling along the embankment toward the front of the train. Fragments of cloud blew through the night sky. In the far distance, lights could be made out. Eljascha strained her eyes and longed for the warmth of a living room. What time was it? Her watch had stopped.

Finally she saw the women. They were running along the wagons, searching for the right door. Then they spotted Eljascha. A few seconds later, soaked to the bone and out of breath, they sank back into the upholstery.

'Have you learned anything?'

'Nothing, except that it's still raining,' Katia answered, and began to chew on her fingernails.

'Stop it,' said Ute; 'it makes me nervous.'

Marianne closed the window.

'It's a trap,' Katia said.

Marianne hissed, 'Spare us your wisdom.'

A trap. It would snap together like Anna's mousetrap, the one she had put out at night in her kitchen. In the morning, Eljascha and her siblings had run into the kitchen, and the sight of the dead mouse had given them goose bumps.

The locomotive made a shrill sound, and cautiously, as though it didn't quite trust the situation, the train began to move again. . . .

Outside, the elegantly dressed gentleman was still standing. He opened the door and turned to Eljascha. 'We are coming into Annemasse.'

'Thank you very much. We are going on to Geneva,' Eljascha answered with a smile.

He made an incredulous face and seemed for a moment to debate with himself. Then he stepped into their compartment and closed the door behind himself. 'Haven't you been told? The tracks between Annemasse and Geneva have been barricaded with barbed wire.'

No, I don't want to believe it. Not so close to our goal. Anna's angels will give the train wings. Clem will pray at the Wailing Wall and work a miracle. Papa and Uncle Louis will send out the Heavenly Host to do away with the barbed wire.

'Don't look like that, ladies. You won't be the first to travel to Switzerland on foot.'

The train stopped. The stranger seemed to be in a hurry and told the women under his breath about the situation at the border. There were about six roads over the border, but, with one exception, they were all closed, blocked off with barbed wire. The simplest way led from Annemasse along the tracks until the vicinity of a small river, the Foron, which they could ford as the water level was now low. He wished them *bon courage*, opened the compartment, and took his place in line to leave the train.

He has it good. He can just get out, perhaps he'll be met by his wife, and then he can go home.

People were pushing to get out. French border patrols were on duty. They must know their Swiss colleagues, who were checking the documents of travelers on the other side, Eljascha thought. But if the train connections were interrupted and the streets were closed, then the Swiss border patrol must be out of work. Surely they had been given the task of catching refugees. If the borders were closed—and she didn't doubt this any longer—there could be only one reason for it: they wanted no refugees. 'All passengers must exit the train,' a loudspeaker commanded; 'the train will not continue. Annemasse. Terminus.'

★

Fear begets fear. Fear exudes a special perfume. It seeped from coats, suitcases, hats, from two women and three men who, like Eljascha, Katia, and Marianne, were standing on the platform uncertain what to do. Fear draws invisible circles. No agreement is needed to enter this circle. No mutual introduction. Everything is clear. Refugees hope for one thing alone: freedom.

A precious stone, carefully tucked away in their heads and in their hearts. The circle had closed. The French customs officials scrutinized the small group of people, who were whispering among themselves.

'Let's leave the platform, for starters,' one of the men suggested.

'Eljascha, stop dreaming.' Katia nudged her. 'We're going to enter your country on foot.'

'But you don't even know how to get there,' she dared to object.

'My dear child, of course we don't know the way; we must rely on the directions of the friendly man on the train. No one is forcing you to come with us. You can go to one of the French patrols and ask it to accompany you over the border. After all, you have a passport.'

Eljascha tried to get her thoughts in order. *I am pregnant. I really could ask an official to help me. But what if he refused? Stumbling around in the dark, rainy night with Katia and her friends and a few other helpless people is madness.*

Nevertheless, her decision to go along came spontaneously. It had to do with Papa, who was suddenly standing in front of her. In his hand was the little glass of transparent liqueur with the gold leaf floating in it. He handed it to her, like the time he had when she was still a child. She dipped her forefinger into the liqueur glass, and marveled at the sparkling dots of gold. Papa encouraged her: 'Have a little bit, Eljascha; it will give you magic powers.' She took a small drink and was surprised at how sweet gold tasted.

'Yes,' Eljascha said. 'I'm coming with you.'

★

One of the men led the group. They took the path that wound along beside the tracks. The earth was damp with rain and Eljascha tried hard not to slip, but suddenly her plimsolls, which she could no longer tie because her feet were so swollen, slipped out from under her and she fell flat on her face. The man walking behind her immediately helped her up. 'Have you hurt yourself?' Eljascha shook her head. She felt no pain and concentrated on the path again. *I hope Walter keeps his nerve and doesn't send a telegram to Joschi: Eljascha not arrived. Dear Saint Anthony, I haven't asked you for anything for a long while. Help me. Help me. Let us all arrive safely in Switzerland.*

★

Eljascha almost collided with Ute, who was walking in front of her, when the line of people unexpectedly stopped.

'We've arrived, we're at the Foron,' Ute whispered. 'We're at the Foron.' Eljascha passed the word on down to the ones walking behind her.

In front of them was the little bridge. Like a peculiar briar hedge, the barbed wire circled it. The river was narrow, and its water was in fact shallow. On the other side the silhouettes of houses and trees were discernible.

They joined hands. The human chain began to move. Carefully they descended the riverbank down into the river. *We all belong together. If one is lost, we are all lost. Our blood is a source from which we take our strength. From our breath we draw life.*

Charles Lewinsky

Charles Lewinsky was born in 1946 in Zurich. He studied German literature and theater and apprenticed as a director with Fritz Kortner. He has worked as director and writer in various venues, including Swiss, German, and Austrian television, for which he has written over a thousand shows. He created the successful Swiss TV series 'Fascht e Familie'; he has written plays and has provided the lyrics to numerous songs for various composers. He has been the recipient of many prizes, including the Chaplin Prize of the city of Montreux and the Prix Walo for best television series. His books include *Hitler auf dem Rütli* (1984), *Mattscheibe* (1991), *Der Teufel in der Weihnachtsnacht* (1997), and *Johannistag* (2000). He has most recently written a play based on the experiences of Fritz Löhner-Beda, the Austrian-Jewish librettist murdered in Auschwitz, as well as the text of a musical, *Deep*, produced in Zurich. In *Hitler auf dem Rütli* (Hitler on the Rütli, the legendary birthplace of the Swiss confederation), with coauthor Doris Morf, Lewinsky creates an imaginary oral history of Switzerland under fictitious Nazi occupation; the 'interviews' that follow present us with sharply observed elements of Swiss life, both Jewish and non-Jewish, through the prism of an extraordinary counterfactual situation.

Charles Lewinsky

EXCERPTS FROM Hitler on the Rütli

Schabziger-Schottisch

Do you know the Schabziger-Schottisch?

Of course you do. Maybe not the title, but you've certainly heard the melody a thousand times on the radio. Stand up for a second; let me get my accordion.

That's it, that's the Schabziger-Schottisch. It was composed here, in this room.

When they play it on the radio, the announcer says, 'Composed by Sepp Roetheli.' . . . Only a very few people know that he wasn't called Roetheli at all.

I think I have to begin the story differently. We've always made folk music in our family. My father and both his brothers all played the schwyzerörgeli. Another uncle, a clarinetist, was one of the big names in Ländler music.

Mostly they played just like that, for fun and by ear. Reading music is for schoolmasters, we always said. In that respect, however, my father was cast from a different mold. He was so thorough in everything he did, he always wanted to know everything exactly.

He taught himself to read music. He could play anything from sheet music if there were notes. But mostly there weren't any, of course.

Every Sunday afternoon he went into town and took lessons. Harmony and things like that. He was thorough, as I said. He wanted me to learn these things too, but as a kid you don't have any interest in stuff like that. I just liked to make music.

I still remember one mnemonic: Father Charles Goes Down And

Ends Battle. Each time another sharp. Do you understand music at all?

Doesn't matter. I just wanted to explain to you what kind of a man my father was. So that you can understand the rest of the story.

When all that Hitler business started, my father saw right away where it was heading. He read lots of newspapers; he always wanted to know everything down to the last detail.

Not long after the German invasion he returned one night very late from his music lessons. After it had become completely dark. He came into the house alone at first and looked around to make sure there were no strangers there. Then he went outside again and led the other man in.

'This is Sepp Roetheli,' he said. 'He'll be staying with us for the next while.' That the man's name wasn't Sepp Roetheli, that he wasn't a real Swiss at all, you could only tell that from his way of talking. If you were a musician, I could explain it better. His Swiss German was actually quite correct, the words and the pronunciation too. But the melody, the melody just wasn't right. At the end of every sentence his voice went up a little bit. Just the wrong melody. He didn't have much luggage with him. Actually just the case with his violin. He could play the violin, let me tell you; the rest of us might just as well pack it in. Even my uncle, the *Ländler* king on his clarinet.

You always hear about Jews being hidden in the cities, in the attic or behind a secret door. On a farm it's all so much simpler. First of all, there was only our family living there anyway. We didn't need a farm hand; we were six children after all, and four of us boys, at that. And later on, when my elder brothers had to go into the army, and to war, you didn't get any personnel anyway.

And when a stranger comes, then it's only into the parlor or the stable. Women sometimes would come into the kitchen, too. I think no stranger has been up on the upper floor where the bedrooms are for a hundred years, except the midwife and the pastor, when someone has died.

It's easy to hide someone on a farm. Countryfolk may be as curious as cityfolk, but they do it more with gossip.

That's why my father insisted that we only speak about Sepp

Roetheli. So it would still sound harmless, even if one of us muffed it.

So that was the music teacher he was always going to see. What he didn't know about music you could write on a tiny piece of paper. And could he tell stories! He helped out in the symphony orchestra. And when that wasn't enough, then in some little ensemble in a restaurant. In those days there were still ensembles everywhere, not like today, just a jukebox.

He always had stories for us children about the great composers. Funny ones, too. How Mozart was always writing his cousin indecent letters. Or the story about the farewell symphony. He was a real Swiss, except that, as a Jew, he couldn't be a Swiss anymore, of course, when the Swiss were all German citizens. A real Swiss, for many generations, like he was always saying. Still, I have to admit that, for me, he always had something foreign about him.

He lived with us for almost two years. He almost always sat here in the parlor, mostly alone. We couldn't take him out to the field with us. He helped out in the stable, and with time he wasn't bad at it at all, even if that wasn't exactly his calling.

But mostly he sat alone in the parlor. He played the violin a lot and composed. Mostly sort of sad eastern things. Just once, for my father's birthday, he wrote the *Schabziger-Schottisch*. It must have been an enormous job. We didn't have any manuscript paper, naturally, so he drew all the lines with a ruler. And an old-fashioned pen.

That evening he presented my father with the sheet music, with a great deal of ceremony. And then they played it together. You have surely never heard the *Schabziger-Schottisch* on the radio in its original scoring. Just for *schwyzerörgeli* and violin.

But that was all Sepp Roetheli ever composed in the way of folk music. He died soon afterward, probably of a lung infection. I don't know exactly, because of course we couldn't call a doctor. No one was to find out, you know, that Sepp Roetheli was staying with us. We buried him ourselves, too.

I don't know if you can use the story for your book. It might be a good thing if people came to know that folks got help in the country, too, and not just in the city.

What was his name? Joseph Rothschild. But not one of the rich Rothschilds. They're not the only ones.

Hitler on the Rütli

Actually you were supposed to be eighteen, and I was only sixteen. But I was tall for my age. Tall and blond and very athletic. That was the best thing you could be in those days.

I dug out a picture for you. My parents had it made specially, as a keepsake. That's me, there in the front on the left. The one behind me there in the uniform, that's Bucher. He was our Hitler Jugend leader, and later on he became a teacher. One of my sons had him at school.

Bucher is wearing a uniform, instead of a singlet like the rest, because he had a bad back. No, really, it's not a joke. Bucher had a bad back and was forbidden to strain himself because of it. That's why he wasn't there on the Rütli. The thing that drove him the craziest about the whole business was that he didn't get a medal. Everyone who was on the Rütli got this medal with the Swiss cross and the swastika and the inscription, 'A New Covenant for a New Era!'

No, I don't have mine anymore. Things like that, you just threw them all away after the war, naturally. Today you could get a lot of money for them. I saw one of the medals in an antiques store for two hundred and fifty francs. I wonder who would buy something like that. Exactly the same medal.

We were running for Schaffhausen in the torch relay. There were six from each canton on the Rütli. Six times twenty-two.

No, twenty-two. I'm not making a mistake. You think because the Ticino and Vaud and Geneva didn't belong to the Reichsgau of Switzerland, right? But they thought up an elegant swindle so that it would remain twenty-two all the same. Because we were accustomed to that number. Each half-canton was permitted to send a full delegation, as simple as that.

Of course it was a coincidence that it worked out just that way. If, for instance, Neuenburg, which belongs to French Switzerland, too, after all, hadn't come over to the Reichsgau. But Neuenburg used to belong to Prussia.

Should I tell you about the federal ceremony too? I mean, surely you know all about it from books. That was a big deal, a big deal, the 650th anniversary of the Confederation. But it's not every day that you meet someone who was actually there.

All right. The mustering point was in Brunnen. Bucher traveled there with our group. With our pack, as they said back then. Accommodations were in an athletics building. Lights out at nine, so that we would all be fresh the next day and make a good impression. But we didn't sleep much. First of all we were all so excited, and then there's always chaos anyway when a lot of young fellows get together. It was like all your school field trips at once.

The next day, that is, on the first of August itself, Bucher brought us to the ship. But he wasn't allowed to go along himself. He congratulated us and told us one more time that we should represent the canton of Schatthausen with dignity. But you could tell that he was upset about it all.

Our ship was one of the first to dock at the Rütli. We young vaulters were more or less the least important part of the whole thing and therefore had to stand around waiting a long time in the sun. The Föhn wind was blowing that day, so it was hot. But that didn't bother us. You have to picture it: sixteen years old, and the farthest I had been outside of Schaffhausen was on a field trip to the National Museum in Zurich. I could hardly take it all in.

We had a sort of place of honor on the field itself. The usual spectators had already secured themselves places that morning on the slope of the Seelisberg. There was a line of soldiers preventing access to the edge. They must have been nice and sweaty in their heavy uniforms and their steel helmets.

Next, one after another, in the order in which they had entered the Confederation, there came the representatives of the cantons, marching up from the lake. The cantonal sergeant-at-arms was always out in front with his colorful coat, and behind him were the officers. Someone behind me—a Bernese, judging from his dialect—said under his breath that the ones in the dark outfits were the Swiss and those in the uniforms were the Germans. But that wasn't true, of course. God knows there were enough Swiss walking around in the brown uniform in those days.

When all the cantonal delegations were complete, there came another pause. We passed the time trying to figure out who the various flags belonged to. We recognized the official ones with

the swastika, of course. But there were lots of others. The finest
of all, we agreed unanimously, were the ones from the student
fraternities.

Then fanfares were blown and we all thought that Hitler was on
his way. But it wasn't him yet. First came the oath scene from Tell. It
was performed by the actors from the Tell pageant in Altdorf. They
came up from below and they came down from above, through the
forest. Only it should have been nighttime. The sunshine was somehow wrong.

At the end they played a trick. A real theatrical effect. The scene
didn't end like in Schiller. They were all in the pose of swearing, the
way you know it, and someone called out, 'When will the savior
come into this land?'

Right at this cue there were fanfares to be heard again from down
below. There were fanfare blowers and drummers along the whole
route from the lake to the Rütli, and they played in such a way that
you had the impression the sound was coming nearer and nearer.
And right when the music was at its loudest, Hitler appeared and
went to the podium.

I'm not very good with words and probably haven't described it
very well. You can cheer just on the spur of the moment, without
really being enthusiastic. Like a sort of reflex that carries you along.
We all cheered like crazy.

Mahnke, the Gauleiter, came a few steps behind him. That was
natural, because he was such a big man, and if he had walked
next to Hitler, you would have noticed how small the Führer actually was.

You can look up Hitler's speech in a book. But if it says there that
the people cheered, you have to see this the right way. The speech
itself wouldn't have mattered much. For a Swiss it always sounds
even funnier when someone speaks high German all too well. It
was more all the brouhaha. I want you to understand that the whole
event just bowled you right over. I can explain it to you with a
personal example.

The day before, at breakfast, before we had left for Brunnen, my
father said that the Germans had bitten off more than they could
chew with their attack on Russia. Nobody had ever beaten Russia,
he said. The country was just too big.

And now here stood Hitler in the flesh in front of my eyes and told us that the Wehrmacht had enclosed the Russians at Smolensk and destroyed them.

The rest, that Switzerland had returned home after 650 years to the bosom of the German nation, that it was a new beginning, a new covenant that was being forged, as important as the oath on the Rütli, only bigger—all of that you just let roll off you. For us children it was another patriotic speech, like we knew them already and especially since the Nazis.

Something else made a much bigger impression on us. There was Hitler, waging a world war, and he still found the time to take part in Switzerland's 650th birthday party. Things had to be going well for him.

Our turn came right at the end. The thing went on, of course, but we didn't catch any more of it. We were already on our way by that time.

One group of torch relay runners after another had to step forward. The torch was lit on a flame burning in a metal bowl. Just like at the Olympic Games. Then someone from the cantonal government handed over a copy of the Articles of Confederation. In a leather casing, like a fat relay baton.

I still know by heart the speech that was made, as usual, on that occasion. First of all, we had been practicing for weeks, and then Schaffhausen comes pretty far down in the ranks of the cantons.

'This casing holds the Articles of Confederation, the soul of our fatherland; preserve the noble document faithfully, with which this community entrusts you as an embassy unto our friends.' And then someone from our group had to say, 'We thank you. The fire from the Rütli in our hearts and in our hands, we shall preserve the Articles faithfully, and may the Führer preserve our country!'

It was someone from Schleitheim who had to give the answer for us Schaffhausers. I've forgotten his name. He was so nervous that he spoke very quietly. You could understand almost nothing. But it didn't matter in the general celebration.

Yes, that's how it was on the Rütli on the first of August, 1941. And there was something else strange about it. We returned to Brunnen by ship, and that's where the real relay race began. We ran ten kilometers, and then we handed over the torch and the Articles of Confederation.

We were of course already long since at home by the time the baton arrived. And can you guess who the runner was who carried the torch ceremoniously up to the Munot at the end?

It was Bucher! He may have had a weak back, but he knew how to get the hero's role: by pulling the right strings.

The Best Cardplayer at Wauwilermoos

The best cardplayer I've ever known was named Elias Marmelstein. And as long as I played with him, he only won one single time. And we weren't even playing cards at the time.

Marmelstein was actually a chess player. A master or a grand master or however they're called. He was a wee little thing, with a face the color of skimmed milk. If you had blown on him, he would have fallen right over. Or if you had put him to work.

It was his good fortune that he had come to the office. We needed someone for all the paperwork. So we were lucky to have Marmelstein ourselves.

He had a memory like you can't even imagine. A proper computer he was. Tell him a number once and he would never ever forget it again.

And he could juggle with it; it was enough to drive you crazy. There was always reckoning to be done, real bean counting, real exact, and you had to draw up lists. Once I said that if it went on like that, I was going to start cooking nothing but alphabet soup, for all the counting.

I was in the camp as a cook, just as a cook. You had to take work where you found it. And there's been a lot of exaggeration in the stories that get told these days about Wauwilermoos.

So anyway, Marmelstein. He worked for the head of bookkeeping, and that wasn't easy. Every sack of potatoes had to be on the books, every kilo of meat. But the SS men stole like magpies. The top brass more than anyone else. Actually magpies isn't right; I once had a tame magpie, and he never ate anything that I hadn't set out for him at his very own little place.

So there was always something missing, and yet the books had to add up just the same. If you could have won the world war with forms, there would be Nazis running the show all over the place today. The numbers had to add up; that was all that mattered.

Marmelstein made sure that the numbers always added up. You could check up on him all you liked, everything was in good shape in the books. Of course, Marmelstein had to know exactly what was missing; otherwise he would never have been able to doctor the accounts properly. He knew so many secrets that everyone thought they would come for him sooner or later.

But it wasn't on account of that, in the end.

I should explain that in the entire camp there were only three Swiss—apart from the inmates, of course. Two from the SS, and me. The higher-ups had all come from Germany. Service in Switzerland was very popular, and they didn't really trust us, either. If there had been four of us, then it might have gone differently for Marmelstein.

The German SS men only ever played skat, and you can't play Schieber with three. Bieter gets boring after a while, if no one goes more than fifty points over the minimum without being sure to take all the tricks, and four-of-a-kind in hand, too.

I don't remember how I got the idea of asking Marmelstein whether he could play cards. Probably it was just because I had so much to do with him because of the accounts.

He said no, he didn't know how to play cards, but he was sure he could learn very quickly; it couldn't be harder than chess. You won't believe it, but he learned Schieber before he had ever so much as seen a pack of cards. Just in his head, without writing anything down. While we did the accounts for the groceries, I explained the cards and the rules. That you can only renege with the jack of trump, and that you don't have to declare the king and queen of trump until you play them, and all that stuff. He got it all in his head, you can hardly imagine.

So we had our first card game one evening after roll call. Actually it was forbidden with an inmate, but there's a lot you can get away with in a camp like that, if you know how. As long as none of the top brass caught on.

Marmelstein really played well, first time off. Not the way he would later, but not like a beginner, either. We played together, and apart from the fact that at first he didn't play the suits I had indicated, I had no complaints. We lost, but only by this much, and once we were even able to take all the tricks; I remember it to this day because I was so amazed by it.

It didn't last long, and Marmelstein played like the little lord Jesus. Cards are above all a question of memory, and he had that. He knew every card—not only what was the highest card in the hand or how many trumps had already been taken, but everything. He wasn't the one to make only a hundred and fifty-seven points instead of a hundred more, just because the other team has managed to scratch together one stupid little trick.

He never won. I mean, a hand or two or even a couple in a row, but never a whole evening. Sometimes when you were way ahead with him, you thought, maybe this time. But then the others would always just scrape through. There were always a few points missing in the final tally.

He did it on purpose. I got along well with him; he explained it to me once. He didn't want to win because an inmate who wins against SS men, well, that couldn't be good for him. But losing by just that much, without anyone noticing that he had thrown the hand, that made him popular.

If you ask me, that's an even bigger accomplishment than just playing to win. You really have to be able to keep everything in your head for that.

We went on from Schieber to Differenzler, and then it got even crazier. Differenzler is the hardest card game there is. That's why they still play it today on the Saturday card shows on TV, because you can really see whether someone's got it or not.

It was the same again with Marmelstein: he lost by just that much. Every time. The two SS men were very proud. They thought they were much better cardplayers than they actually were.

And that's how things started going bad. One of the two—Kari was his name; the other one I'd rather not say—he got all fatheaded. He got all puffed up like the Kaiser himself and started making speeches about how the Jews were inferior after all, and the Germanic peoples were superior, and card playing proved it. He needed it bad; it was no secret to anyone how he had gotten into the SS, a pretty ugly business, but that's another story.

Marmelstein didn't say a word; he just shuffled the cards and lost the next hand. And Kari just got louder and louder.

To tell the truth, it was my fault. Kari was getting on my nerves so badly with his boasting that I finally told him that Marmelstein was a chess master and that chess was the hardest game of all; you could read about it anywhere.

The next day Kari brought a chessboard along and demanded that Marmelstein play a game with him; he wanted to show him who was the superior race. Marmelstein didn't say a word; he just put away the cards and sat down at the board.

It lasted a very long time. I could never play chess; it would get to me to spend so long on one game. Like I said, I don't understand anything about it, but as the pieces kept disappearing, you could tell that Kari was winning.

At the beginning of the match he had been very quiet and concentrated. Then he became louder and louder and started talking about the superiority of his race again. Marmelstein didn't show the slightest reaction, as usual. He couldn't very well, could he, being an inmate.

Until Kari screamed that Lasker was an asshole and that he had become world champion only by rigging the match. At that time I didn't recognize the name, but I've learned since that Lasker was a very famous chess player; Emanuel Lasker was his name.

You didn't notice it then as he did it, but Marmelstein went to work on the board, and tack, tack, tack, Kari's pieces started disappearing. And then Marmelstein said, very quietly and very acidly, 'Mate!' I can hear it to this day.

And Kari went through the roof.

After that we had nothing but trouble. At the next check they noticed that half a pig was missing, and it was supposed to have been me, because as the cook, I was responsible for the provisions. That was a bad time. I'm lucky that I got through it.

We never found anyone else to doctor the books as well. And card playing was over too.

Yes indeed, the best cardplayer I ever knew was Elias Marmelstein. Although he was never permitted to win.

Roman Buxbaum

Roman Buxbaum was born in Prague in 1956 and emigrated to Baden, Switzerland, in 1968. He studied medicine at the University of Zurich and went on to receive training in psychiatry and psychotherapy, as well as pursuing studies at the Academy of the Visual Arts in Munich. Buxbaum is active in Zurich as a visual and performance artist and as a psychiatrist. His publications include (as editor) catalogues of shows of his own paintings, as well as companion volumes to mixed media shows and performances, often with direct or indirect reference to the Holocaust, in Switzerland, Spain, and the Czech Republic, among other places. In the summer of 1999 he presented at the Zurich International Theater Festival 'Mein Kunst. Hitler/Redlich. Buxbaum,' a performance piece based on dreams he had had while traveling in Southeast Asia and elsewhere and that he had previously published in a volume of essays by himself and others, Blei (1999), a companion to a show at the Rudolfinum in Prague. In the translations of those dreams printed here, we hear both the obsessive preoccupations of the half-Jewish grandchild of survivors and the immigrant's consciousness of the culture of his new homeland, reflected in the curious 'Helvetisms' (or Swiss quirks in high German) that color his dreaming speech.

Roman Buxbaum

Dreams

Dream of September 9, 1995, Ljublin

I am the follower of a dictator, a short, stocky, agile man. His
strength comes from castrating other men. A big turtle comes and
bites off my testicles, which hurts a great deal. The turtle resembles
a stone sculpture that I have seen that same day during a visit to the
Majdanek concentration camp. An inmate at Majdanek made it in
order to give form to the survival principle in the camp: 'Work
slowly!'

Dream of September 25, 1995

I am walking through the barracks in Auschwitz-Birkenau. They
are residential barracks of the stall type, like the women's barracks
in Birkenau II, with three bunks, one above the other, and ten
women per bunk. It smells unmistakably of Auschwitz: of dust, of
burning, of mold, and of carbolineum. A sticky brown coating of
dirt covers everything. At this I am seized by naked terror: 'If I don't
get out of here in a hurry, something awful will happen to me!' I run
away in the direction of the exit, but around every corner I find only
more barracks rooms. I awake in a panic.

Dream of October 20, 1995

I am a young captive and am marching in a group to a transport to
Auschwitz. We are walking over a bridge, and below us, just at that
moment, a train is passing by. Without hesitating, we jump onto

the moving train and escape. Then I turn into a fleeing woman, a Frenchwoman, who is protecting her small child. I feel great sadness and fear. Everything will end in death. I entrust myself to a native woman and beg her to hide me and my child. I awake in tears.

Dream of Spring 1996

On the edge of a river there has been a small landslide. The river has undermined its banks and a section of the grass-covered bank has slipped down into the river. Lower levels of the bank have now been laid bare. I see something glittering in the earth. I bend down and see that it is gold teeth that are glowing there. Hundreds of white human teeth with gold fillings. I am quite excited and run off to get photographic equipment. The discovery is to be photographed before the gold teeth are archaeologically excavated.

Dream of Spring 1996

I am in Auschwitz. In the dream, Auschwitz is a big, clean, many storied factory. It is bright and tidy—very Helvetic. All the people around me are adept and hard working; no mildew, no stink, no torture, and no dead, but cold, quiet hunger. I lose my tin pot for soup and am desperate. I am hungry.

But then I get an easy task: as an archaeologist, I am clearing off a mosaic with a little brush. Brush stroke by brush stroke I am wiping the dust from the mosaic tiles. The picture is slowly becoming visible.

Dream of April 27, 1996

I am in a transport of blind people. We are to be gassed in Birkenau. We are led through a basement room to Crematorium II. There we find operational prisoners (Funktionshäftlinge) sitting on the floor by heaps of coal, ashes, and Jewish belongings. In an unattended moment, I separate myself from the group of blind people and attach myself to this Special Commando. I salute the passing Kapos loudly.

Then I flee up a staircase to freedom, into a park. I hide behind trees and bushes. It is winter and night is drawing near. There are guards everywhere, and I consider whether I should dig myself into the snow until it gets dark.

Dream of May 30, 1996

I am inspecting Buchenwald. The pathology building at Buchenwald is a stone building, immediately to the left after the entrance to the camp. It reminds me of sports halls from the turn of the century. The entrance is in the form of a niche and has two solid wooden doors with glass windows. The door to the right leads into the general pathology chamber. Here is where the inmate doctors dissected the corpses of their fellow inmates. A tin stretcher can be pulled out of a device on the wall, on which the corpses could be laid out for storage in a cold room. The door to the left leads into the private dissection chamber of the SS. A dissection table there too.

I open two locked doors with a key and make my way to freedom. I observe, 'Aha, so with one single key one could get through both doors and straight into the dissection chamber. . . ' I become aware that my companion, the man I am speaking with, is Josef Mengele. In the dream Mengele is a friendly, black-haired man in his mid-thirties. On the floor in front of the dissection chamber there lies a death mask made from his face. It is stone and dented in the middle. It reminds the visitors of Mengele. Mengele looks at the mask and says, 'A shame that I am not dead.' That moves me to the most profound sadness. I lean my head on his shoulder and weep bitterly and deeply. Mengele consoles me. A friend in need.

Dream of 1996

Hitler is a good-looking, outspokenly friendly manager. He is wearing a suit and has a full black beard. He is holding a workshop, a sort of psycho-group or team coaching. We are about thirty people and are sitting in a circle. I am on Hitler's right and I admire him very much. I realize a contradictory feeling in myself—something cannot be right. Shyly I pose a question regarding the murdered Jews, instinctively, however, without putting Hitler's person in question in any way. It is as if I were putting myself in question with the question.

Dream of September 18, 1996

A large tree, already grown, is being planted by means of a giant machine. The supports cut deep wounds into both its main branches close to the trunk. But the workers applaud; they are satisfied. A boy helps adroitly to turn off the giant machine. I stuff myself full of bread and honey.

Dream of 1996

I am visiting Auschwitz with Father. We come to the ruins of a bunker, wildly overgrown with plants. In hindsight it reminds me of the destroyed Crematorium II in Birkenau. I go for a walk by myself—Father has vanished—through the ruins that are to be found under the earth, wet and cold; light streams in through holes in the ceiling. Next to a parking lot there is a kiosk where I ask for a map of Auschwitz. My path leads me through a park with avenues lined with tall poplars, and I arrive at a Wilhelminian hospital building of the type of the Charité in Berlin. There I meet Professor Charcot, the Paris neurologist from the turn of the century who showed Sigmund Freud the way to the psychic origin of hysteria.

Dream of October 21, 1996, Dunajovice

I am in the cellar of an old lady's house. There I find objects from Auschwitz: shoes, containers, mess kits, a leather shoulder bag. The objects have the air of a reliquary and are very different from the other objects in the cellar. A little number tag has been hung around each Auschwitz object, the way it's done in a museum archive. I want to take one of the objects in my hand, but the owner cries out immediately that one may not touch them, otherwise they will lose their aura. At a later point in the dream I am carrying the old gray-haired lady like a baby in my arms.

Dream of November 6, 1996

I am an SS man in Auschwitz. At the entrance to a ruined barracks in Birkenau III I find an interesting installation of green and brown bottles. I go in and find booklets by the inmates stacked up in piles. I pull out a large brown booklet. It has the name Daniel Buxheimer written on it. It contains artful drawings of male and female figures—wonderfully beautiful watercolors in the expressionist and cubist style. It is the lifework of a man who has been exterminated. I become very sad and weep in my dream. I weigh in my mind whether I can save the booklets.

Dream of January 11, 1997, Phuket

I find myself in a courtyard enclosed by a high wall. I am preparing myself in a great frenzy for a deportation. I put on two dark gray wool coats, like the ones my father used to wear. On my right breast I am wearing a Star of David, which seems in the dream white gray rather than yellow. I am afraid and consider feverishly how I might escape the deportation. I am able to hide in the courtyard and then to go undercover as a U-boat. At first I drive around in an old Tatra with fat, round mudguards. I am denounced and flee farther. Later on I find shelter in an agricultural business working as a potato peeler, and in the end I am lying hidden in the dropped ceiling of a stall, and am liberated, together with other Jews, by the British army.

Dream of January 18, 1997

It is the end of the war. I already have several years of captivity behind me and have now been deployed in a work detail to build the fortifications along the shore of Lake Constance. Big cement pillars are set up, and upon them are mounted the iron locking mechanisms for the artillery pieces. One evening I return from a special project with a small group of captives, and we find that all of the members of the work detail are dead. They have been shot, out in the woods. Their corpses are lying strewn about in the foliage among the trees. There are around sixty men lying there like that. Some distance away we can still hear voices. It is already dark. We stretch out on the ground and pretend to be dead. After a while it is quiet. I creep away. I pack a blue work jacket I have found on the construction site and follow the road along the lake to the city. I am politely greeted by a small detachment of soldiers; I greet them back. I find a nun helping refugees in a small store. I want to cross the lake, but she advises against it and organizes an escape guide to lead me over the mountains into Switzerland. The trip lasts three days.

Dream of February 13, 1997

I am a concentration camp inmate and am wearing the typical striped inmate's clothing. It is the end of the war, and we are marching from one place to another. I dream two events on this march: I am able to hide in my sleeve a file that has been sharpened to a point and that I could use as a weapon should the need arise.

In a rural area we walk through a village. I am hungry and beg the villagers for something to eat. At first they are afraid and draw back, because I am so emaciated and dirty. Then a woman thrusts two pieces of bread upon me, which I immediately cause to vanish into my jacket.

Dream of April 23, 1997

I am a figure of note in a concentration camp. I am sharing a room in a fortification with other such figures. We have a refrigerator and enough to eat, all of which we have brought along ourselves or organized. We even have French cheese. I am worried about thieves, and I look for a hiding place for nonperishable goods, like bread and salami, in the tower of the fortification.

Dream of May 11, 1997

Hitler is conversing with two boys of about four years of age. He is kind to them, bends down and speaks to them in such a way as to overcome their shyness. One of the boys draws a little piece of paper out of his sack and reads aloud to Hitler, 'We are members of the Zionist, antifascist resistance organization of France!' Hitler turns away in irritation.

Dream of May 29, 1997

I have inherited a phylactery from my grandfather Buxbaum. I bind it around my left arm and show someone how the thong provides support. It is very pleasant to wear it. The phylactery is made of cheap artificial leather, of the composition of those with which I played as a child in my great-grandfather's workshop. At the front the phylactery has a sling into which I loop my middle finger, as if into the hole of the sleeve of my 'inmate's jacket' during the performance at the Vienna Festival.

Dream of June 30, 1997

I am invited to dinner at Adolf Hitler's house. There are about forty guests around the table. We are all sitting at a table decked with a white tablecloth. I come disguised as a blonde, with a stiff, straw-blond, back-combed wig, the way they were worn in the sixties and seventies, the way they have come back into fashion today. I am wearing a short jacket, like a torero, that is open in front and strongly emphasizes my large breasts—which seem to be genuine.

Dream of July 7, 1997

In 'Sharewood Forest' or 'Shadewood Forest' there lie three hundred tons of gold plundered by the British. The British have taken it

from the Nazis and hidden it again. I am one of the discoverers of
the cache of gold. It is a dark forest, quiet and remote—a secretive,
somber mood.

Dream of July 22, 1997

I am visiting a cemetery in Buchenwald. We are in a great spacious
tower structure and enjoy from there a comfortable and generous
view. The cemetery is a black, bare field without gravestones or
vegetation. The death field stretches to the horizon without its
borders becoming visible. In the front section, an area of the graveyard the size of a soccer field has liquefied. The mass graves here
have melted into a breast-deep mud pond. Some of the markers of
white sandstone are lying there, wet, in the mud. With the director
of Buchenwald I discuss what sort of protective suit I should put on
in order to wade through there.

Dream of July 24, 1997

I have cured a depressive and psychically disturbed patient. I have
implanted a piece of gold—like a gold filling—from outside into his
left cheek. The man immediately becomes lively and cheerful.

Dream of December 3, 1997

A black rose has grown overnight in my garden. It is sturdy, as
broad and tall as a person and crowned with a single, full, velvet-
gleaming black blossom. The rose glows dark and mysterious in
the dream. Now I look on the ground. In the middle of the otherwise green stretch of lawn in my garden there is a circular piece
of burned earth on which the rose is growing. I kneel and gaze
at the charred pieces of wood that are sticking out of the earth
around its root. The black rose has grown up in the middle of the
fire's focus.

Dream of December 11, 1997

My family and I are among the first to be sent to Theresienstadt. I am a boy of about six years of age. While the adults are taken away, we children have remained behind, unattended, in a cellar. I am able to unscrew some bars in the floor. I flee with my sister, who is somewhat younger. At first through the ghetto's back allies, then through the wonderfully beautiful northern Bohemian fields. It is a late summer evening, and the sun is sinking far off on the horizon. We two children are happy and free; we run and run along the dusty street toward the sun.

Dream of January 6, 1998, Kandy, Sri Lanka

It is nearing the end of the war. I am an inmate in a concentration camp in the east. The Germans are loading us into a freight wagon bound for the west. We stop for a long time at a train station. Several trains stand before us. There are rumors that inmates are being murdered in the station up ahead. Night falls and I am able to escape with a group of my companions from the now badly guarded wagon. I set off alone in the direction of the east, where I light upon Czech partisans who turn out, however, to my amazement, to be boys between the ages of four and five. Even though they are handling dynamite, their activities seem like a game.

Dream of January 13, 1998, Wadduwa, Sri Lanka

I am with my father in Kyjov, in the courtyard of our house, the house of our forebears. Two Holocaust survivors come into the courtyard. They are both good-looking men of about fifty. Both have shaved, sunburnt heads. On the back of the head and on the nape of the neck, each has a tattooed image. On the back of the first's head there is the famous photograph of the inmate's column in Dachau concentration camp: sturdy, strong men arrayed in rows on the roll call grounds. The other man, whose face clearly shows scars and marks of abuse, bears on the back of his head the tattooed photograph of the Nuremberg tribunal. The chief defendants, Goering and Hoess, are standing among others in the bench, in bad suits and with dark sunglasses hiding their eyes.

Both of the arrivees seem familiar to me. I greet them warmly, as if I had been awaiting them a long time. We examine characters and Yiddish inscriptions on a wall of the courtyard. Ever more Jewish relatives keep appearing in the courtyard. Suddenly I discover that there is an old Jewish graveyard under the ground of the courtyard. Using my hands, I lift up one cement slab after another and lay bare grave upon grave. In one of the graves there comes to light a gold-embroidered robe from the year 1734. We breathe in relief—it is good that we have finally found the graves of our ancestors.

Dream of August 10, 1998

We are fleeing from a concentration camp. We tear boards out of the back wall of a shithouse and escape into liberty. The road leads to a vineyard.

Marta Rubinstein

Marta Rubinstein was born to Russian-Jewish parents in 1936 in Argentina. She attended English boarding school and emigrated, first to Israel, and then, in 1972, to Switzerland, where she has lived in Zurich ever since. She worked as a teacher of English and music and as a tour guide in Israel before founding a publishing house, edition eden, with her husband, the painter Dan Rubinstein. The two have collaborated on numerous works, including a chronicle of the Yehudi Menuhin Festival in Gstaad and a study of local customs in a remote Swiss mountain community. In the tale that follows, her own English original of the title story from her collection Der Schneider (1990), Rubinstein creates a Chagal-like illumination of recent Jewish history, using the motif of the sewing machine to symbolize both the travails and the endurance of the Jewish people.

Marta Rubinstein

The Shneyder

A tailor is a tailor, isn't he? Well, not quite. Say it in Yiddish—*der shneyder*—and, hocus pocus, you will find yourself in a *shtetl* inside a cold, bare room, and before you there will be this haggard-looking man, bent over his old sewing machine. He is sewing a bar mitzvah suit, or maybe a wedding gown, which will have been paid for with promises of payment. Heaven knows when. A smell of fatty food will seep through the cracked, crooked door in the back. Fat, because it is cheap and fills you up.

Here and there the man will cough and we know that he will die of consumption. That is, if a pogrom doesn't get him first.

At sundown, our *schneyder* will interrupt his work in order to say his evening prayers, following which he will slurp that faintly colored water his wife calls tea. His days will be what they were for generations: deprived of everything but the most essential to survival. And his nights will give him children, who will enrich his heart, yet make his burden heavier. With the years his eyes will get dimmer yet at the same time brighter, for he knows that soon, very soon, Mashiach—the Messiah—will come. Very soon. . . .

A pogrom snatched him away from the grip of consumption. Not only him, but also his wife and five of his six children. His eldest son Yankl—called Hayim Yankl since his miraculous escape from certain death—was on the way home, having ended years of study in a distant town. His only consolation upon realizing what had befallen his family was the conviction that now, now indeed, Mashiach was on his way. He could arrive any minute. And because he wished to receive Mashiach in a clean, white robe, he at once sat at his father's old sewing machine which, incredibly but fortunately, had survived the onslaught. He worked frantically, because he knew that the moment he had finished the robe, Mashiach would appear. And having finished, he leaned back in ecstatic expectation.

A young woman came in. Shy yet insistent, she asked if she could use his machine, the only one left in the whole *shtetl*. The other one, she said, had belonged to her mother, but the Cossacks had disposed of both the mother and the machine. Fighting back her tears and her pride, she said the only way she could survive was to take in some sewing. She wouldn't dream of taking away his clientele, God forbid! And there and then, the new *shneyder* asked her to be his wife.

Raisl and Hayim Yankl—the newlyweds—took turns at the sewing machine. They worked very hard. They were clever, imaginative, and full of ideas. Success stuck to them. Within five years they had become the proud proprietors of a store carrying clothes and accessories, and the happy parents of four children: a boy and a girl, a boy and a girl. In that order. An appropriate teacher was brought in from a town renowned for its scholars, and the children grew up in an atmosphere of dedication to the study of the Law, and to the interests of the family. In that order.

When the eldest son became bar mitzvah, the family had already moved into a large house with three stories. The ground floor comprised the store. There they sold material, accessories, shoes, hats, and, of course, clothes. Behind the store was the small office. The second floor was the workshop. There Raisl ruled, with a sure hand and a far-sighted eye. Her eldest daughter did the basting with other young employees. In the next room, two seamstresses worked full-time using two new sewing machines. Hayim Yankl's kingdom was a small back room. Somewhat prematurely bent, he continued to work at his late father's old heirloom. To use a new machine was for him something akin to treason. The old machine was the link between the past and the future, between his roots and Mashiach. Although now that life had turned so much better Mashiach could bide his time, he would come. For that day, Hayim Yankl would again sew himself a clean, white robe. Only his old machine would be capable of doing the job, because that machine had a feeling for godliness, a feeling no new machine could ever possibly have.

There came the day when Raisl said it was time to move into a big city. Warsaw. For an instant, Hayim Yankl's heart stood still. But his wife was right. Warsaw would offer his children better study opportunities as well as better marriage chances. Following a short scouting trip, the couple returned with a contract. They had rented a house in a fashionable street in the Jewish quarter where a *schneyder* was very much in demand.

The family moved to Warsaw and success followed them. The small workshop had become a large and fashionable atelier, which eventually became a cottage industry, which was about to turn into a proper factory.

Then the wind turned. There was pest in the air. Satan's whip cracked down upon God's Chosen People. And as the *schneyder*'s family were confronted with the Ghetto walls and searched about with burning eyes for an answer to their hopeless, desperate 'why?!' Hayim Yankl suddenly laughed gently. 'Why despair?' he said. 'It is time to rejoice! Mashiach will be here, any minute.' And he sat down to sew a new robe. Only this time he had to sew by hand, since he had not been allowed to take his old sewing machine with him. His work did not progress as fast as then, many years ago. For some strange reason, Hayim Yankl worked very, very slowly. As though by postponing the end of his work he would postpone the human catastrophe which would bring about the coming of Mashiach. But slow as he might be, the catastrophe would not be kept back. Inexorable, merciless, it came down in fire, thunder, and brimstone over them. 'Fee, fie, fo, fum,/I smell the blood of a Jewish man!/Be he alive or be he dead,/I'll grind his bones to make my bread.' Thus sang the brown giants in chorus, while they trampled with their heavy boots on God's Chosen People.

When the smoke lifted and the ashes of the dead became one with the earth, Hayim Yankl came back to himself and looked around. He found himself in a large, bare room. Friendly voices were speaking to him. Something was being said about Eretz Yisroel—the Land of Israel.

'Who are you?' he asked.

'We are Jews. From Palestine,' was the answer, pronounced in a raw, guttural Yiddish. 'We are here to take you home.'

'Home? Home? To Raisl? To the children?'

'Home, to the Land of Israel,' someone said.

'With Raisl? With the children? Where are they?'

The answer, brought on the wings of a stifling silence, hit him with such force that a shrill cry tore through his throat. He rent his garment and shook his fist. 'Mashiach, where are you? Where are you?! You are a lie! A miserable lie! I shall never again sew a robe to greet you. Never, do you hear?! Never! You are a lie. A miserable, blatant lie.' And he fell back on his chair like a sack, depleted, defeated.

No one spoke. No one moved. Hayim Yankl began to weep. Tears rolled down his cheeks. 'It was all a lie,' he sobbed quietly. 'There is no Mashiach. It was all a lie.'

A young woman kneeled down next to him. She looked up and, almost whispering, said, 'Mashiach will come. In Eretz Yisroel. We are building a Jewish country where we can all live as Jews, proud and free from fear. Like in the days of the Prophets. That is our home. We are taking you home. Home to Eretz Yisroel.'

Hayim Yankl's sobbing stopped. 'Mashiach will come, to Eretz Yisroel.' These words stroked gently over the chords of his heart, as King David's fingers had once stroked over the chords of his lyre. Of course! How could Mashiach have come to Auschwitz! Or to Warsaw! To Eretz Yisroel, Mashiach would come. To Jerusalem.

'I need my sewing machine,' he said softly.

Hayim Yankl went in search of his sewing machine. Nothing else mattered. The notion of Eretz Yisroel as Homeland gave his heart a new impulse. But only the recovery of his old heirloom, his old sewing machine, would afford him the sap of life.

The daily activity with the young Jews from Palestine wrought a subtle spiritual change in him, a change he hardly noticed, but which was clear to others around him. Unwittingly he began to imitate their decisive, self-assured attitude, their carriage and their speech, the bright look in the eyes of these Palestinian Jews. These were Jews of another mettle! He felt attracted to them.

He reached Warsaw toward evening and directed his steps toward his factory, which stood outside the Ghetto walls. Somebody seemed to live there. His heart beat furiously. He was intent upon rescuing his sewing machine, come what may. He felt the strength of a lion grow within him. He quickened his steps and stretched out his hand in order to open the door. It was locked. He rang the bell impatiently and pounded with his fist upon the door. Somebody opened, protesting angrily. Hayim Yankl, his eyes dark with rage, looked through the man, pushed the door wide open, and stepped inside. His feet took him into the back room, his room, where the sewing machine was meant to be. There was room for nothing else in his mind. He kicked the door open—and roared like a wounded lion. A bed stood there, where his sewing machine should have stood. He turned to face the man, who stood there shocked, grabbed him by the collar, and literally lifted him off the floor.

'My sewing machine! Where is my sewing machine?!' Hayim Yankl felt ready to kill the man. He would kill him, if he did not produce his sewing machine, instantly. For this sewing machine was the depository of all his pains and all his hopes, all his dreams, his happiness, and all the sorrows of God's Chosen People. The agony of all that plundering, the degradation, the murder. The murder, and murder and murder. The humiliation and murder.

Hayim Yankl was ready to erase all those memories, represented now by this short, rough man who had taken over his possessions, convinced that he, the Jew, had gone up in smoke. But he hadn't gone up in smoke. He was there. And he wanted his sewing machine back.

'They're— they're — they're all here. Here, sir. Please. All here,' blubbered the man, who seemed to be hanging in the air, his eyes wide with fear. 'All here. All your appliances.'

'To hell with the appliances! I want my machine! My old machine! Where is it? Give me my machine or I'll kill you! I swear I'll kill you!'

'Please! Please, sir: all the machines are here. Please— here, all of them.'

'My machine! In this room. My machine!'

The man searched in his disconcerted brain. Then it struck him. 'Yes, oh, yes! Please, sir, let me show you. Here, sir, here,' he said, pointing at a corner of the room. There, under a mountain of rags, covered with its scratched wooden lid, stood the heirloom. At the sight of his treasured sewing machine, Hayim Yankl stood in awe. It was an overwhelming feeling, it pushed everything else away, out of his sight. The crushed impertinence of the whimpering man, the room, the factory, everything. Only his sewing machine, this old, faithful sewing machine, this all-encompassing, momentarily missing link in the heavy chain of his life, stood before him.

Many years later, Hayim Yankl would remember this as the decisive moment in his life. He would vividly remember how he had to decide within a fraction of a second between two lives. On the one hand, he could give in to his overflowing emotions and return to the unrealities of Mashiach. On the other hand, he could suppress those feelings, face the cruel reality, and take a stand. And within that fraction of a second he made his decision. Away from barbaric Europe! He would be a proud Palestinian Jew, would learn how to work the land, would join a kibbutz, would help to restore to his people their dignity and honor. His sewing machine, that and nothing else, he would take with him, even if he never got to sew again.

The moment Hayim Yankl set his foot on the Land of Israel, he knew that here he would live life in its fullness. Here he would be master of his destiny, he would participate in the rebuilding of the Land of his Forefathers. Then he realized that he had turned forty, that very day. His life would begin at the age of forty. He felt this to be very significant. From now on, he decided, his name would be simply Hayim: Life. Because from now on, it would be Life.

Hayim never made it to a kibbutz. On this wet night on the Mediterranean coast he was suddenly picked up, covered in blankets, and driven off between cases of citrus fruit. After a very bumpy half-hour's drive he was ushered quietly into a house. No sooner was he inside than he was hushed with a gesture. Everybody was listening attentively. A car was heard approaching. One of the men opened a cupboard, pulled out a shelf full of clothes, opened an inner door, and shoved Hayim into a hollow space. Within seconds, Hayim found himself crouching inside the dark damp wall, cut off from the world.

Later he was told that the search had lasted over an hour. The British soldiers had kept fumbling into every possible nook and cranny. The family members had had to refrain from any sign of impatience, otherwise the soldiers would have stayed longer. And once they left, it was necessary to wait a while, lest one of the soldiers had been left behind, hiding, so as to suddenly surprise them. That was why Hayim had had to spend a good two hours crouching in that hole.

He had great difficulty in getting out. His joints hurt terribly. The family did not yet dare to turn on the light. Anyhow, just the light of the moon and stars was enough to hurt Hayim's eyes. He took a few steps, then sat in an armchair. They spoke in whispers. He was told he was to stay with them until the British had calmed down. Then they could take him to a kibbutz. Right now the roads were being closely watched, every vehicle thoroughly checked; it would be tempting the devil to travel that night. And Hayim was appalled to hear of the many refugees who had been interned in camps, or sent back, or even drowned at sea.

'Creator of the Universe!' his heart cried out. 'What have we done to you? Why all this? Why all this? Why. . . .'

Hayim was led to a bathtub full of warm water. He was given clean clothes and by the time he was finished, breakfast had been served. As the sun rose, the room became flooded with light. And now he saw the faces, he saw the table, the house. Through the window he could see the fields. And again the faces. They were smiling at him. Now he knew he had reached home. He just couldn't help it. He began to cry.

After breakfast, the family insisted he get some sleep. But how could he? He was too excited. This day was far too important. It should be recorded in the Book of Chronicles.

He wanted to help. He wanted to work. They asked him what he could do. He was a *schneyder*, he said, but he was ready to do any work they would give him. 'A *schneyder*?' It was a big surprise and a stroke of luck, because the family ran a textile business, and so was in urgent need of a tailor.

Thus it came to pass that Hayim became the best tailor in the Lapids' employ. And Gila and Arieh were delighted. In the evenings they taught him Hebrew and English, and during the day he did his sewing in the house. Hayim would have preferred to use his own sewing machine, but he had no idea what had happened to it in the confusion of the arrival. Gila and Arieh promised to do everything possible to find it. Arieh also wanted to get him legal papers so that he could make Hayim his head tailor. Hayim was pleased.

On a certain Friday morning Gila became very excited. Her eldest daughter, Orit, would be coming to spend the Sabbath with them. She lived in Jerusalem, and traveling the road between Jerusalem and Tel Aviv was very risky. It was over a year now since that fateful day when Orit and her husband had been caught in an ambush.

Her husband had been killed, and Orit herself severely wounded. Her coming, therefore, was the cause of much joy, but also of justifiable fear.

She arrived an hour earlier than expected. Her parents were out, visiting a sick neighbor. Hayim was alone in the house when she arrived. Six months later they married and settled in Tel Aviv. Hayim became a citizen of the British Mandate, and a partner in the Lapids' business.

Their first child was a son whom they named Issi, short for Israel, because he was born at the very moment when David Ben-Gurion proclaimed the State of Israel. Orit listened to the news while giving birth. Hayim felt as though someone were blowing up a balloon within his chest to the point of bursting. Again his heart cried out. 'Creator of the Universe! You threw me into the deepest recesses of Hell, and now you lift me to Heavenly heights. How can I thank you when so much happiness rests on so much suffering? Why do you play with us so?' And he thought that Orit and her parents were probably right. God is not a Being of whom one may demand this or that. God is—Life. Me and you and all of us. Therefore, do not pray. Do. Work. Take your destiny in your own hands. Don't waste your time asking. Do it yourself!

'Yes,' said Hayim to himself. 'That was our mistake then.'

Drora—which means Freedom—was born during the signing of the Armistice. Hayim returned from his military reserve duty a few hours after her birth. A week later Arieh announced his retirement from business in order to enjoy whatever life had in store for him. He left his share to Hayim.

Orit had no sewing talents, but she had a good head for business. The firm opened a branch in Haifa and another one in the new part of Jerusalem. Hayim had long stopped sewing. He dedicated himself to designing and supervising the work. There was nothing about him to remind one of the Hayim Yankl of the shtetl, or even of Warsaw. In those days, he had worn a long beard, temple locks, and a yarmulke. This Hayim now was clean-shaven, and his head rebeled against the religious dictates. It was almost impossible to recognize in him the Jew of the Old Country.

His inner conviction of the coming of Mashiach had not been cast off, but it had taken on a new significance. The coming of the

Messiah meant to him now the return of the People of Israel to the Land of their Forefathers, to the Land of Israel. For each Jew who returned to his Land, the Messiah had come. His personal Messiah. The other one, the Messiah for all, would come the day when all the Jews lived in their Land. Because the fact of all the Jews living in Israel, that in itself was Mashiach.

There were times when the curtain protecting him from his memories would rise, disclosing Raisl and the children. Hayim would then let the curtain drop at once, letting Raisl and the children disappear behind it. The first time this happened was shortly after Issi's birth. Hayim would then lie awake through the night, filled with unbearable pain. Did he have a right to discard Raisl and the children from his memory? Had not Raisl been his beloved wife, the mother of his children and his partner in the business? Then he would turn to Orit, sleeping next to him. He would think of Issi, his first born. And then he would remember Mottl, his *first* first born. They had named him Mottl after his father. All these memories would then flow out of the vessel of his memories, his heart would shrink with pain, and he would curse his destiny for letting him survive. But when Orit moved in her sleep next to him, he realized that he had finally to bury the past. In the Old Country they had tried with all their might to keep the past alive in the present. That had been their mistake. The past should remain the past. Dead and buried.

The years went by, the children grew, business prospered. The Sinai War came and went. It brought an end to the constant terrorist activities by infiltrators who had made the roads unsafe. But for Hayim it meant that he had not understood the meaning of the expression 'God's Chosen People.' He had firmly believed that the War of Independence had opened a totally new chapter in the history of the People of Israel: the beginning of Redemption. Yet the very fact that the Sinai War had taken place, its background and implications pointed exactly in the opposite direction. 'Yes,' he thought. 'God has obviously chosen us in order to beat us. We are his favorite toy.'

The bitterness that the Sinai War deposited in his soul was diluted by his daily affairs. Life at home and in the business followed its course. The children lived up to their parents' expectations, and sometimes even beyond them.

The time arrived when Issi had to join the army, while Drora still had two years of school ahead of her. She was an excellent student, just as Issi had been and would continue to be once he finished his army service.

With the years, economic stagnation paralysed the country. Immigration dwindled, building almost came to a halt, unemployment prevailed. The spring brought with it a real economic crisis. Worse than that, the neighboring countries seemed to be preparing for war. Sometimes, when listening to the news, Hayim had a vision of ravens hovering above dying animals. And then he would recall those thoughts he'd had about God's Chosen People. He came to the conclusion that God had an unending amount of humor. Black humor.

Just like everyone else in Israel, Orit and Hayim followed their instructions. They took mirrors and pictures off the walls, covered the window panes with tape, bought enough black cardboard for the blackout, kept baskets filled with victuals ready by the door together with a first-aid kit; they even organized a first-aid course for the personnel in the business in which they themselves participated. And just like everyone else in the country, they were deeply worried.

It was a Monday, June 5, 1967, at eight o'clock in the morning. Hayim was crossing the street toward the bus stop when the first siren sounded. It was a clear, warm morning. The streets were empty. Hayim had just noted that the street lights were functioning for an empty street. And while the siren drew a deep, invisible trough in the sky, Hayim raised his head and asked, 'Are you really capable of this? The love that went into building this land, the work, the sweat, the tears, the blood, but above all the love. Are you really capable of destroying it all? Is this what you chose us for?' Then he turned quietly home to join Orit in the bomb shelter.

The overwhelming outcome of the Six Day War changed Hayim's attitude toward his Creator. It was no longer to a God reveling in black humor that he offered his gratitude for the safe homecoming of his son. And as for the reunification of Jerusalem: his newly recovered religious fervor told him this was indeed the antechamber to Mashiach! 'During two thousand years our forefathers have kept our faith alive and have called again and again: Next year in

Jerusalem. And we now, Mother, and you, Issi, and you, Drora, and all of us alive this day, we are privileged to be free in Jerusalem, after two thousand years! Do you realize what this means?' Hayim was drunk, but not on wine.

Issi was unable to share his father's enthusiasm. He could not see the antechamber to Mashiach. He only saw Yossi, his best friend, bleeding to death. He saw Shmulik, who would remain a cripple for the rest of his life because a bullet had entered his spine. He saw the tank going up in flames just a few steps away from him.

'Do you realize what this means?!' asked his father.

'No, I don't,' answered Issi in a dull voice

Hayim's euphoria vanished. He looked at his son.

'Really, Father, I just don't get it. Or perhaps I do. To me it means that my friend Yossi is dead and that well over six hundred families are now in mourning.'

Hayim gasped. And like lightning they came back to him, one after the other. Raisl, Mottl, Mireleh, Berl, Chavaleh. He couldn't breathe. He looked at his son, and he realized deep in his heart how much this second first-born son meant to him. If Issi had not returned. . . .

Hayim sunk into a chair, suddenly aged, his eyes desperately trying to escape beyond the horizon of his thoughts.

'What a price to pay!' he whispered. 'What a price.'

Hardly over, the war was given yet another name: the War for Peace. Because, under the circumstances, nothing but unconditional surrender was conceivable. And Israel's only condition was contained in one short word: peace. Peace for land. Simply peace. And if the terribly high price paid for this war brought the highest possible reward, peace, then it had indeed been the War for Peace. Some even called it the Last War. From now on, peace would reign over the region, over all the neighbors near and far, all would profit from it, all would live happily ever after, the wolf would abide by the lamb, and the swords would turn to ploughshares.

But it was not to be. Through one of those fortuitous circumstances in which God's Chosen People constantly found itself, and to the great disappointment of that people, the war had to be reduced to its first name. The other two denominations lost their meaning. Since the vanquished set their course on the 'no peace' road, one couldn't very well talk of the War for Peace. And there being no peace, there was no guarantee that this had been the Last War.

Hayim thought it best to concentrate on his work and nothing else. Issi, his military service completed, settled down as a medical student. Drora served her country by teaching in border settlements. Later she took up studies in economics. Both Issi and Drora excelled in their studies. Their parents were happy and proud of their children. And in spite of the political confusion, the country appeared to have secured its future.

Issi was one of the first casualties of the Yom Kippur War. Hayim was alone in his house when the military rabbi came. Hayim opened the door and, seeing the uniformed man with a *yarmulke* on his head, he knew at once what had happened. For years to come, the rabbi was to remember the expression of dismay and grief imprinted on Hayim's face.

That very night Hayim suffered a heart attack and had to be taken to hospital. There were no ambulances available, so that Orit and Drora had to undertake the difficult task of driving him through the blackout, crushed by pain and fear. The hospital was overfilled with the wounded. The two women were not allowed to remain. Chain smoking, Orit suggested they drive to grandmother's. It was a very dark night, but they knew the road by heart. They could have driven blindfolded. Off they went into the silent darkness. Drora offered to drive, but Orit shook her head in a determined 'No.'

Upon reaching the coastal road, Orit accelerated. She needed the fresh air against her face, she said, turning toward her daughter. In so doing, she missed the curve. The car crashed down the cliff and burst into flames. By the time help arrived, little was left of the two women.

The hospitals needed every single bed for the wounded soldiers, so Hayim would have to have home care. Gila and Arieh, bent with age and pain, took Hayim to their home. It was months before he was able to move freely again. He had turned skinny and gray and had let his beard grow, at first as a sign of mourning, and then out of inertia.

One morning after breakfast Hayim announced he was going to the flea market in Jaffa. He had never been there yet and felt it was about time he went. Gila and Arieh tried to dissuade him, arguing that he was not yet strong enough. He should wait a couple of weeks. What was the hurry? The flea market would always be there. But Hayim smiled, promised to take care, and called for a taxi.

It was very early. The market was just coming to life. Hayim thought it strange that in all those years he had never thought of coming to the flea market. There was an amazing assortment of things, starting with heavy furniture and going all the way to rags and broken old tidbits. Old and new lay side by side. There were new things made to look old and old things made to look new, and it was not always easy to make out which was which. Now that old sewing machine there, for example, seemed really old. That old thing seemed—.

Hayim held his breath. He didn't dare breathe. He walked toward the machine, his hand outstretched, his eyes closed, for he couldn't trust them. He had to touch it, that rickety old thing, feel where the varnish had cracked, feel where Mottl as a little boy had barged into it with his toy and left a mark. Yes, it was it.

'That is a good machine, sir, a very good machine. It is old, I know, but still very reliable. You can have it for twenty dollars, sir, because you are my first client today. Twenty dollars, sir. What can you buy today for that?'

'Twenty dollars?!' Hayim asked, enraged. 'I don't have the money to pay what this machine is worth!' And so saying, he emptied his wallet on the counter. 'Here is my address. See to it that the machine gets there before noon.'

The next day Hayim took a taxi to Jerusalem. Most uncharacteristically, he put on a hat, and under the hat a yarmulke. He asked the driver to bring him to the religious quarter, gave him a generous tip, and set off to wander through the narrow streets. About a half hour later he felt suddenly tired, found a run-down tearoom, entered, and ordered a glass of tea and some cheesecake.

While slurping his tea he asked himself what on earth he was looking for there. He felt very tired. From time to time he would look out the window. He saw women carrying heavy shopping bags walking by, here and there a car, every few minutes a bus. He saw men with their long temple locks swishing by on their bicycles and more women with their shopping bags fully laden. It was Thursday.

On this day the women did their cooking and baking for the Sabbath, just as in the *shtetl*. Somehow, that street reminded him of his *shtetl*.

That sign on the dilapidated house across the street intrigued him. He tried to make out the writing, but it was too far for his weak eyesight. He summoned the waiter, paid, and walked over. After all, there was nothing in particular that he wanted to do, so why not go over and read the sign? Small shop to let, it said. Stung by curiosity, Hayim rang the bell. An elderly man opened the door.

'I would like to see the shop,' said Hayim. The man showed him in. It was very small indeed. It reminded him of his father's workroom. But this one had an extra room in the back, as well as a tiny, primitive bathroom and a cooking niche.

'How much?' asked Hayim.

'A hundred dollars a month. In advance,' was the surly answer.

Hayim took out his checkbook. He handed the man a check for fifteen hundred dollars. 'Here is a year in advance and a little extra for *shabbas*. Clean the place up. I'll move in next week. Here is my card.'

The man couldn't believe his eyes. Those were very difficult times. He had never dreamt of renting the place that fast, and on such terms.

'Do you know somebody who makes good signs around here?' asked Hayim.

'Signs? Oh, of course, of course. . . . My son-in-law, he does beautiful work. His shop is just round the corner.'

Hayim found the son-in-law without any difficulty. He seemed to do very good work.

'Let me write down what I want you to paint on a large wooden sign to be set above the door,' said Hayim to the young man; then he wrote: 'Hayim Yankl, *Schneyder*.'

Hayim Yankl became famous in no time. His reputation he owed to two unique qualities: in the first place, he was an exceptionally good tailor, certainly the best near and far. And in the second place, his fame was due to the pace at which he worked: he was slow, very slow. Nobody had ever worked so slowly. But this was not due to the old sewing machine, oh no! His slow work resulted from all that Hayim Yankl put into every stitch.

'God, you God of our Forefathers,' he would say while sewing, 'remember what you did to your Chosen People! Let me remind you, lest you forget! Here is a stitch for the blood we shed. And a stitch for the slavery we had to endure. A stitch for the plunder of our earthly goods, not to mention the others! A stitch for the insults bestowed upon us by those who do not have the privilege to be chosen by you. A stitch to remind you of the humiliations suffered by your people, because it kept its covenant with you. A stitch for the destruction of synagogues and houses of learning. A stitch for the murder of those who put their trust in you. A stitch for the awe in which we stand before you. A stitch for the hope we always carry in our hearts. A stitch for the coming of the Mashiach. And a stitch to ask you: Why?'

At this point, Hayim Yankl would stop stitching. He would stroke the cloth lovingly; then he would search the distance with his eyes and ask: 'Why do you hammer on us again and again? Aren't you afraid we might break some day? Ten plagues you have sent to the land of the Pharaohs, but to your Chosen People you have sent ten times ten plagues. Why? Creator of the Universe, give me a sign! Tell me that there is a reason, a purpose! Tell me that. You are the smith and we are the iron. And life is the fire over which you strike us with your hammer again and again, because you want to shape us, give us a form conceived by you and known only to you. Give me a sign. Let me know that it is not wantonness. Help me believe that you have a purpose. But until then, let me remind you, lest you forget.'

Again Hayim Yankl would press the cast-iron pedal of his sewing machine and would recite while sewing: 'A stitch for blood, a stitch for slavery, a stitch for plunder, a stitch for insults, a stitch for humiliations, a stitch for destruction, a stitch for murder. A stitch for the awe in which we stand before your throne, Creator of the Universe. A stitch for the hope in our hearts, and a stitch for Mashiach.'

Luc Bondy

Luc Bondy was born in 1948 in Zurich, son of the Berlin-born scholar and journalist François Bondy and grandson of the Prague-born director, writer, translator, and radio personality Fritz Bondy, who brought his young family to Switzerland between the world wars. Luc Bondy, who lives in Paris and Vienna, is well known throughout the French- and German-speaking worlds as a theater director and is currently the head of the prestigious Wiener Fest-wochen. The selection that follows, 'Elsa, or Where Was I?' is from his memoir-cum-short-story-collection *Wo war ich?* (Where was I, 1998) and lyrically recalls his youth with refugee grandparents in postwar Zurich.

Luc Bondy

Elsa, or Where Was I?

Elsa Blumenstein, that's what my grandmother was called. And when I saw her for the first time I asked her:

'Are you the woman, the Omi?'

I spent the first years of my childhood in her apartment, Seminarstrasse 6. She was soft, tender, fragile, ironic, small, and hated all quarreling. Quarreling seemed to her like a cool and powerful draft:

'Quick, quick, close the window!'

Elsa often leaned against the heater in her living room. Her husband, Grand-père, would spend the whole time staring at his little radio set, the way he had probably done during the war in his hiding place when he had wanted to tune in London. The little set that kept the free world informed. Now it was the sounds of Glenn Miller, news from Switzerland, and so on.

'When are we eating?' he asked hoarsely.

'In half an hour, Joseph!'

'What are we having?'

'Calf's liver and salad.'

'Calf's liver and salad?'

'Yes. That's what you asked for.'

'I did? Me?'

'Yes.'

'And when are we eating, Elsa?'

'In half an hour, Joseph!'

'Who is this boy?'

'Your grandson, Joseph.'

'Mine? Lilianne's son?'

'Yes.'

'No. . . . How do you like that. . . .'

Joseph Blumenstein got up out of his deep green armchair and took a single turn around the living room. Elsa was smoking, one elbow propped against the heater. She blew the smoke out lightly between her lips, and the effect was irony. . . . The irony that she was in this little Zurich living room subsisting on relatively modest reparations payments, with a husband who no longer had any idea about *now*, who only remembered the far distant past.

At lunchtime we sat at a black, gleaming table. The room opened onto a hill down which we would go sledding in the winter when it was covered with snow. On a green meadow behind the hill lay the big playground. On a branch of the lime tree hung the swing on which, standing, I would often soar giddily up into the clouds. . . .

'Higher! Farther! I want to go up to the sky,' I shouted to my older sister, who was pushing me on the swing with energy.

During lunchtime the playground was empty and the swing motionless. Like a stork during its midday nap.

My grandparents' world had weight. The tragedy of the Second World War hadn't swallowed them up, perhaps, but it had made them hesitant, shy, and skeptical.

Blumenstein spat out grape skins onto his plate, for he had no teeth and couldn't eat with his dentures in.

Omi hardly looked at him anymore. Just as his memory was fading, her relationship with him was fading too. He would get up after the meal to sit down before his radio: every moment was new to him. . . . A hundred times he learned of the erection of the Berlin Wall, and that it would not rain in Zurich the next day.

'We're going to go play canasta!'

I ran to the little card table by the window, opened the drawer, and took out the big bundle of cards.

Omi, who with this idea had saved the afternoon once again, followed me with a cup of tea. I see Omi with her heater and her cup of tea. She burned her tongue every time; I can see it still.

'Elsa. . . . The Communists have put up a wall in Berlin!'

'Joseph, they did that two weeks ago already!'

'Well, but now it's standing, the wall.'

Joseph Blumenstein had been a manufacturer of jute in Mannheim. Before the accession to power he had heard Herr Hitler's first speeches and known that he and his family would have to leave his beloved Germany, for which he had fought proudly in the First World War. His parents were dead, and he had taken over responsibility for his ten or twelve siblings.

Elsa's parents were the Blochs; they owned one of the biggest bakeries in Flanders. That's where they hid the Blumensteins. . . .

Oh, how little I know about my mother's past, for until recently she had no wish to talk about it, to tell stories. That's why I made up my own. Once, I think, the Gestapo came to get my grandfather in the hospital (where? in what year and in which immigrant land?). He saw the gentlemen coming up the hospital steps, and he went to meet them:

'You're looking for the Jew Blumenstein, I presume?'

'Precisely!'

'Top floor, room 33: that's where his bed is.'

And while they hurried up, Joseph got away.

I'll know more about the time my mother spent in Marseilles, soon. When my mother gets older, then she'll be able to tell stories better.

Omi's death was slow, calm, the way death comes to elderly people. She lay on her bed, eyes up, toward heaven. My paternal grandfather also looked upward a long while, as if to bid heaven call him to itself. . . . Her eyes were watery, and she hardly spoke. Except Oh God, oh God. . . . Then she would drift off for a few hours. For my part, I thought of this as her slumbering-off-into-death, her getting used to death. Reconnaissance visits to the beyond.

Her face and hair became one in their silver-gray color. She grew ever more fragile, ever more. Elderly people become in age either more deeply etched than they have been, or their faces begin to swim in uncertainty, as if their features were being drawn within.

On one of the last occasions I stood by her bed I thought of something from an earlier time. How Omi had taken me for a walk in the woods behind Bucheggplatz. She was talking to me about my refusal to eat anything for breakfast, lunch, or dinner. That was our conversation. Not the way adults call a child to attention at the table and scream Eat! No, it was a topic for discussion, the way the rabbi in the synagogue or the priest in the church chooses a topic for his congregation. We went up through the meadow to where a fence runs along the track. And that's when my grandmother said to me: *Then you'll get as thin as Struwwelpeter and slip through these bars. . . .*

She was lying on my parents' bed, waiting for her end, and she was so thin—just as thin as one of those fenceposts, my grandmother.

'Are you the woman, the *Omi*?'

I never visited her grave. I wanted to see her still leaning on her heater, tender, diaphanous, forever avoiding death. I don't know where I was when she died. Where was I?

Gabriele Markus

Gabriele Markus was born in 1939 in Bern, the daughter of German-Jewish immigrants. After an education in pedagogy, she studied to become a singer, both in Switzerland and abroad. She has given concerts and recitals of classical *Lieder* in Switzerland, Germany, and Israel. She lives today as a writer and singing teacher in Zurich. She has published several volumes of poetry, including *Urlandschaften* (1985), *Unverzichtbar* (1986), and *Ohr am Boden* (1997), and has contributed works to journals and anthologies. She has won literary prizes from the cities of Graz, Vienna, and Zurich, and is currently at work on a novel of her childhood, tentatively entitled *Zugvögel, wir: Eine Kindheit* (We birds of a season: A childhood). In the poems here translated, her range, both topical and stylistic, is evident: Jewish mysticism, contemporary Zionist politics, the poetry of exile, and her own history as the child and grandchild of survivors and victims—all provide the material for songs and incantations of a spare and lovely vitality.

Gabriele Markus

Selected Poems

Exile

Homesickness grows
my body is my ghetto
I am in exile.

In my dreams
of fire and snow
I am a stranger
trackless traveler

but where to
when Jerusalem is burning
and the prophets
are hiding their faces?

Indispensable

The dream
of a life lived

your breath
Jerusalem
blows upon us

we dance
on the graves of kings
until we drop

until you take us
up
into your lap.

In the Ruins of Warsaw

From a photograph by Werner Bischof

The little stone angel
—a child—
seems dreaming
with half-closed eyes
he goes
over a rubblefield
his arm
as if in defense
before his face

But doesn't he know
that there is nothing more here
to avert
and that he is the only
angel
far and wide?

Grandmother

When they took my grandmother
to Theresienstadt
she walked with her head held high

she was accustomed
to giving orders

'I'll make it hard for them'
she is supposed to have said

soon afterward she died
in the camp

from—as they said—
natural causes

I hope
her proud backbone
remained upright.

Jerusalem

A psalm

I will build me a fortress
of reddish stone
my house will stand in the city of the kings.
A scent of orange petals
over our gardens
and the smell of salt borne up
out of the deep
from the feverish breath of the desert.
Impious Sodom
kingdom of the dead under the seas
heavy as lead hangs silence
over you.
Still staring
Lot's godless wife
will never see the blossoming
all around her.

Dark house
monument
on the hill over there
why don't you shatter
from the outcry
of a thousand thousand voices
tortured
cremated
risen again out of gas ovens—
over Jerusalem's flaming heaven
they weep no longer
they sing.

Your temple walls
Jerusalem
keen-eared
heavy with prayer
heavier with the lamenting
of your people
teartracks
have furrowed you
ancient stony face.

Soldiers watch
archangels
cut from the midday glare
their trumpets ready
but the time of judgment
has not yet come
Wait—

Jerusalem
Lofty city
from early on your streets were
my ways
I must walk them to the end.
It will not be hard for me
light is your air
and no sky can be brighter
than your heaven
Jerusalem.

Birthplace: Czernowitz

For Rose Ausländer and Paul Celan

She the windborne
high over Czernowitz' walls
unmistakably light
in billowing shawl
still vulnerable above the towers of mourning

high in the bells
she sings wonder
upon wonder

He the other, the dark one,
in gaping chasm
between moss and stone
to the wounded
roots of the earth away
sleeps the sleep of lizards

his ear attentive:
unceasing birth.

Emigrated

Emigrated
into the word

One foot before the other
still frightened blind
feeling along the border

fear's border cry
your eternal doom
Ahasuerus

you have escaped
here you may rest
and settle down

perhaps at the source
put down roots

wanderer, scion
of David's tribe
here build your house
make yourself at home
within the word

be trusting
but be wary, who knows
that you might not have to
emigrate again

wanderer
stranger
who knows.

Sylviane Roche

Sylviane Roche was born in 1949 in Paris, where she grew up in a family of Alsatian Jews in the Marais. She studied literature in Paris and Baltimore, where she worked with René Girard at Johns Hopkins. Since 1969 she has resided in Switzerland with her Swiss husband and family; she took a degree at the University of Lausanne and now teaches high school there. Since 1986 she has co-directed the journal *Ecriture*. Her books include *Les Passantes* (1987) and *Le Salon Pompadour* (1990), which draws upon her own roots to evoke Jewish life in Paris during the Dreyfus period and which won the Prix de la Commission de Littérature Française du Canton de Berne and has been translated into Albanian, German, and Romanian. *Le Temps des cerises* (Cherry-blossom time, 1998), from which the following chapters are excerpted, reviews the history of communism in the latter part of the twentieth century through the eyes of Joseph Blumenthal, Polish emigrant to France, veteran *résistant*, former concentration camp inmate, and staunch party member who nevertheless yearns for more than a few fragments of memory of his parents' bygone *shtetl* world. The book was awarded both the Prix des Auditeurs and the Prix Franco-Européen for 1998.

Sylviane Roche

EXCERPTS FROM Cherry-Blossom Time

Monday, May 16, 1994

Last Tuesday I turned seventy-five. . . . It's not particularly amusing, but that's life, it seems. Yesterday was Sunday; my children took me out to a restaurant and presented me with a device for listening to compact disks, as well as a few disks to go with it. It's a little flat box, not much bigger than a camembert. It connects to an amp, quite extraordinary. I'm not a big music listener, but I have to admit that it's a nice piece of engineering! There was also a new silver mechanical pencil with my name and the date engraved on it, with which I am writing at this moment. They were very happy to be giving me so much pleasure. That's what family is, and it isn't all that bad after all. I used to think quite badly of families, when I was young (I almost wrote when I was younger!). I even used to say as much. Everyone reacts according to his abilities: me, I defended myself. And then I came back to it, back to the family. The children, the grandchildren, soon the great grandchildren too. I'm not unhappy; I'm even pretty proud, as if there were a reason for my being here. In the end, the party yesterday did me good; the children were right to insist. At the beginning I protested, Oh no, no party, it's idiotic, it's no fun turning seventy-five. And Nina replied, in a queer voice, a little aggressively, 'Well, it's better than not being seventy-five at all,' and I thought I was hearing her mother. I said, 'I haven't asked after your mother yet, Nina.'

'Mother?' she replied, questioningly. 'Oh, she's very well. She told me to give you a kiss on your seventy-fifth.'

So then something made up my mind for me, and I said okay to the party. But I didn't dare tell Nina to invite Anna. Didn't dare. Nevertheless, I think I would have liked her to be there. And maybe she would have liked it too? What was I risking by asking Nina, anyway? We always got along well, Anna and I, especially since we stopped living together. But I didn't dare. At my age!

Well anyway, it was a swell party in the end, as they say. After the restaurant we all went to Nina's, and there was cake. I felt all loosey-goosey, like I had become a kid again. A cake! It's been a good sixty years since I had a birthday cake. Right when it happened, I felt a bit irritated, almost ashamed. I've never liked being in the middle of a cliché. And then a cake with candles, seven big ones and five small ones, and me blowing them out! For a moment I thought, 'Put on your bomber jacket, Joseph, roll out your motorbike, blow this dream; you're not really seventy-five, old man, and your buddies are waiting. . . .' And then Marie whispered into my ear, 'Hey, Grandpa, are you sleeping?' and I blew out the candles and there was applause. Yes indeed. And it made me pretty happy. We took pictures. Nina had invited David and his family for the cake, and they all came. All of them! That really blew me away, like the candles on the cake. Not just David and Léa, but their two children, too, Patrick and Thierry, with their families. All of them. There were a lot of people, in the end. . . . 'You see,' I said to David, 'we came out of it all right in the end!' And he smiled. My brother doesn't smile often, and, if for no other reason, that made it worth it.

In the end, and I've only just now figured it out, what we celebrated yesterday was a tremendous victory. And what's more, I don't think anyone realized it, and it's just as well. Because it's been a long time since any of us has turned seventy-five.

This mechanical pencil is going to end up giving me ideas. It's heavy and shiny; it fits my hand well. The lead is quite thick and soft; you don't need to press very hard in order to write. It's even pleasant.

Often of a morning, when I rise, I'm not in a particularly good mood. I have an aching back. My face in the mirror is awful, that rough beard all white in the wrinkles on my cheeks; I can hardly imagine that it's me. I make myself a coffee, I listen to the radio, and that doesn't do much for my mood. I get washed, I shave, I get dressed . . . I drag my feet. I have never liked the morning, even when it was the beginning of a day full of projects and expectations. And now . . . I look at my hands as I butter my bread. Those spots, those veins, those hard nails! And still, inside, this is certainly me, no mistake; I recognize the contents, if not the envelope. I reject the envelope, and yet, being against your own face is like being against the weather, or like that fool I met the other day who told me he was *against* computers. So I give myself a shake and try to limit the damage. I've turned into something of a clotheshorse in my old age. I change my shirt, I put on scarves. . . . It makes Nina laugh. She should be crying, though, but she is still too young to understand, and that's good!

It isn't just my old man's face that meets my eyes when I get up in the morning. There's also the day stretching out ahead, twelve hours at the very least, to fill, to furnish, to try to prove that it's all good for something, at seventy-five, to still have a will to live. I go and get my mail and the newopaper. That is a high point. With the letters from the bank, the notices of deposit of my pension, the various associations of veterans of this and friends of that, there's always mail in the box. I go back up. I read through it. I scan L'Huma. It's been a while now since I did any more than scan it, especially during the week, because in the Sunday edition there's a magazine section with some very interesting features. That's what I'm always telling David when he asks. He nods and changes the subject. At any rate, it's something that I don't care to discuss with anyone, and certainly not with Jérôme when he gets on my back about it. I answer my mail immediately, if it's necessary. And it's often after that that the problems begin. Well, not every day. There's the shopping, visits to sick buddies; there's more and more of those. On Fridays I'm on duty at the local party headquarters from two o'clock on; I might almost say it's the best time of the week. Sometimes I go by to say hello to David, but never just like that; Léa doesn't like it. I telephone first and I can hear in his voice whether it suits him or not. I also go to the cinema a lot, to the six o'clock show, in order to take advantage of the senior rate. And then I stay at home and read; I like that, too, as a matter of fact. Historical novels, political biographies recommended by my children, especially Nina. I just read something on the war in Spain, and also *Anna Karenina*, by Tolstoy, but I found that a bit long. I had never read it when I was young. Nobody I knew was a reader. At Buchenwald there were comrades who recounted books to each other, who passed each other poems on scraps of paper they had collected God

knows where. Who recited them under their breath in the evening. I
will never forget a copy of 'Les Yeux d'Elsa' that made the rounds of
the camp in August of 1944. I never knew how it got there. There
were at least five thousand of us Frenchmen in the camp in those
days, and in the end everyone had heard tell of it. We copied out the
poems; we learned them by heart. We didn't know the name of the
author, or at least I didn't know it. But I learned 'Le Pont de C' by
heart and would recite it to myself as I marched along on work
detail (I still know it). It wasn't until after '45 that I learned who it
was by and, anyway, I had never heard of Aragon before. Apart from
school (but school and me, we were always like oil and water), that
was my first contact with literature. At Buchenwald! You know, it's
funny; I never looked at it like that before. I had never thought
about it in that way. It's this silver mechanical pencil; you start to
write and it goes by itself. Maybe I'll write down my memoirs for my
grandchildren! They wouldn't be any more stupid than anybody
else's, for that matter, or any more irritating to read. It's not as if I
have nothing to tell! *Joseph Blumenthal, Memoirs of an Old. . . .* An old
what? An old activist? An old fool? An old Polish Jew? An old man,
short and simple? Memoirs of the brilliant inventor of the individual circular knitting machine? Yes, I could write a whole chapter
explaining how I got the idea of knitting in the round on little
machines with perforated cards, and how we became the kings of
the seamless hem. And even after 1970 and the invention of the
computerized loom, they still needed my invention. Okay, this is
not the right moment to go into the subject at length, but it's
something I would really like to talk about. My invention. My pat-
ent. And how we've been living off it for thirty years now, me, the
children, and the wives, too, to some extent. Is that what I am most
proud of? No. But it's what I would have the least trouble talking
about. What would come the easiest. . . .

Right. So it's decided; I'm going to go and get paper. It's funny,
I'm as excited as a kid. And then I'll get my mail on the way back up.

Friday, May 20, 1994

I was off like a shot, and then, of course, I haven't written a line in
four days. Still, I bought a pad of Clairefontaine paper that re-

minded me of when Nina was a kid, after '57, when she would
return home on Saturdays with her backpack. She would get out her
workbook: 'I still have some exercises for Monday; Mama said you
would correct them for me.' I always had the feeling that Anna was
trying to get my goat. Later on, it was Mathilde who would help
them, because school really wasn't my forte.

Here I am, writing in no particular order, just the way things
occur to me as I go along. It might not be the best way to pro-
ceed. It's astonishing how ideas come, and how the present and the
past get mixed up. Must be this Clairefontaine paper. Nina had a
checked apron with flouncy shoulder straps. They crossed in the
back, and she couldn't do it up by herself. Who would ever have
said that I would keep something like that in my head? I said to
myself, 'Writing will keep you busy,' and now I wonder whether I'm
going to be happy about that. If it caused too many things to come
back to me.

On Monday, when I went out to get this pad, I found a death
notice for Friedman in my mail. It's mostly because of that that I
didn't start writing immediately. That really did something to me,
even if we hadn't seen each other for years. He was seventy-eight,
that is, my age. I telephoned David, and he said right away, 'Oh,
but he was much older than you.' David can never hide what he's
thinking.

Friedman was a fool. It's odd to write that about a dead person; I
hesitated. I'm learning. The second time it's easier: Friedman was a
fool. The war made something of him, a bit, but it wasn't really his
doing. If he had been named Dupont, he wouldn't have lifted a
finger, if only perhaps to clap for the Marshal. . . . I knew a lot of
them, actually, guys like him, but it took us a long time to realize it.
A guy you knew at Buchenwald, whom you had taken for dead like a
hundred others, whom you met again by chance in a hospital in '45,
it takes you years to notice that he's a fool. And still, it's only now
that he's dead that you dare to really think it, to write it, even, now
that he's dead and it doesn't matter anymore. I could have avoided
thinking it; what could it do for me, what good is it, now that he's
dead? Between '45 and '47 we saw each other every day, Friedman
and I. Anna didn't like him much, but she wasn't to touch him,
wasn't to touch Albert. In '48 we started seeing each other less; it

was normal, he had got underway with his schemes, fixing cars, making money, and with Nina's birth it was less easy to have time for buddies; you get a bit older, the war is over, we all retreat more or less into normal life, almost thirty, a wife, a kid. . . . *The war is over*, precisely; Albert used to say it more and more often, and it irritated me even though I didn't know why. *The war is over.* That meant that, from now on, we had the right to be just as big sons-of-bitches, just as stupid, just as bourgeois and cowardly as they were before. As if the war could pass like winter, and then it's spring, the birds are singing, and you don't have to think about it anymore—until the next one, of course. *The war is over*, we were lucky, we got away, good riddance to bad rubbish. As for Friedman, he bought up repair shops and tossed out the union workers. 'Stop fooling around, Joe, it's not the Russkies who are going to rebuild France. The war is over, old man.'

Anyway, it still irritates me to this day. *The war is over, grandpa*, which means leave us in peace, goddamnit, with your ancient history, with your old dreams. I say Stalingrad—they reply Budapest, Prague, Berlin. . . . I say the Party of the Martyrs, the bread smuggled in, of an evening in Buchenwald, come from who-knows-where, *from the comrades*—and they say that the war is over. And what can I answer them? That Léa hasn't been able to sleep without pills since '45? We aren't talking about the same thing, in any case. The other day on the TV, there was a guy, a historian, who was explaining that the recent opening of the KGB archives in Moscow suggested that the Party had given up Gabriel Péri. Or Manouchian. Or both, for all that it matters nowadays. Next Friday, while I was on duty, there was a big discussion with the young people.

'Do you believe it, Joseph, that the Party gave up Manouchian?'

'I don't know, my son, but I remember 'L'Affiche rouge,' by Aragon, and those posters of the people the Nazis had caught and executed, so what can I tell you?'

I can't take part in discussions. And I don't want to, even if all of this is coming to mind now in connection with Friedman's death. And by the way, I can't believe that he's dead, even if I went to his burial yesterday. A rabbi and the whole works, and his sister there from Israel. And as it happens, it was over Israel that we had our first big fight. After '48 he became a fanatic. Not me, to say the least. He wound up calling me a *bad Jew*. I said, 'Well, that's better than a *dirty Jew*,' and we almost came to blows. That was in '50, '51. I had just met Solange, and I was angry at the whole world for not understanding what was happening to me. Albert had reacted like everyone else, with reproaches; old man, I don't understand you, your woman, your little girl. And by the way, if I had become a bad Jew, not even a Zionist, wasn't that after all the influence of. . . . He had stepped over the threshold. And then we saw each other again, of course, and we made up. No matter what they say, the war doesn't end as quickly as all that.

It's like a great ball full of lots of little wires passing through it. Albert Friedman . . . I pull on it. Nina's workbook, I pull on it. I like it, and it passes the time. It's almost time for the news on TV and I haven't even heated up the soup yet.

Heat up the soup. . . . When my father and my mother used to argue, my father would wind up banging on the table, or on his knee, or on the arm of his armchair, anyway, banging his fist and saying, 'You would do better to go and heat up the soup!' And my mother, reminded of her duties, would hurry into the kitchen, wiping her hands. He would say it in Yiddish: *Gay shoyn besser kokhen di zuppe*. I can still hear it. Here I am now, talking about my parents! But perhaps that's where I should start after all?

Sunday, June 5, 1994

I was goofing off pretty good at the beginning of the thirties, and my teacher advised me to sign up at the state youth organization, Thursdays in the rue Julien Lacroix. I liked it fine. We learned songs, we went to the woods at Vincennes. At the youth organization there were all kinds, Jews, non-Jews, emigrants, French, all the kids all mixed up together. And at that time no one had any problem with it. At school and at the organization, they talked to us about France, about the Republic, that was what mattered. Recently I've been thinking about my teachers a lot. There was one of them, Monsieur Remond; he was the one who got me to sign up at the organization. I was eleven or twelve. He had been wounded in the First World War, he had a stiff leg; sometimes he told us about the trenches. We admired him. He taught us civics, the rights of man, the laws we had to respect, the French Revolution, fraternity. . . . In Belleville in those days, in some schools, half the class was the children of emigrants. Monsieur Remond made no distinction, French or emigrant, there were those who worked well and those who worked badly, that's all. And every morning, on the blackboard, for our lesson in writing, there would be a phrase or a moral to copy down and learn. Like for example, I can still remember, *The Republic is like a mother; she loves all her children*. We read *Le Tour de France par deux enfants*. And we all loved France and the Republic. We taught it to our parents, who had come to France looking for freedom or the right not to die of hunger. That was what school used to be like. Liberty, equality, fraternity. Now that's all over. Sure, Aurélien would be right to call it old-fashioned, but it meant something, and it was with those ideas, because of those ideas, that we joined the Résistance during the war, completely naturally.

In Belleville there were Italians: we called them Macaronis, but we didn't mean it badly. There were Armenians, Greeks, and Jews from everywhere, but especially from Central Europe. We all got along pretty well when I was a kid. And then, toward the mid-thirties, you started to get called Jewboy or kike. Not systematically, but once or twice was enough. It was the beginning of the extreme right-wing groups. In February of 1934 we even discussed it at home, although my parents never talked politics in front of us. The Action Française was organizing raids down the rue des Rosiers to attack the Jews, to pull their beards as they came out of synagogue. A friend of my father's had witnessed a scene like that and had spoken of it at home, in front of my mother, who had refused to believe it. We discussed it at the youth organization. A lot of the counselors were in the Jeunesses Communistes, the youth wing of the Communist Party. I remember Robert in particular. He explained to me that the Communists were against racism and anti-Semitism. And besides, it was clear who had stood up to the fascists in '34. Hitler came up more and more. In '35 he started with the persecution of Jews and Communists. The way Robert told it, the Party meant happiness for everyone, fraternity. The Soviet Union was the ideal of the republic our teachers had talked about. All of that had its own logic, obviously. In '35 I joined the Jeunesses

Communistes. My father was on the whole okay with it, by the way. He was starting to think about things too. A better life, an ideal. And then came the Front Populaire, Blum was president, and for my parents and their friends, this proved that France was paradise on earth.

When the strikes hit in '36, I lost my job. The workshop where I was working closed. It wasn't going much better for my father at the shoemaker's, either. In August of 1937, with two buddies from the J. C., I left for Spain. It had been bothering me for some months, since Guernica in April. I was eighteen years old. It was the first time since our arrival in Paris that I had left France, that I had gone farther south than Fontainebleau, where we used to go sometimes with the youth organization. I was dazzled, aroused, transported, horrified too. By Spain, even if we never got any farther than Barcelona, by the war, the Brigades, the comrades, everything Robert had been telling me about at the organization and that had so suddenly become real.

Barcelona fell at the end of January, Madrid held out until March; it was a slaughter. Millions of refugees on the roads. I was able to get back into France in a pretty frazzled condition, physically and morally. I was to see worse some years later, but at that moment I thought I was at death's door. I spent some time at a hospital near Collioure, and I went up to Paris just before war was declared in August. I was twenty, but at that time I wasn't French yet. So I wasn't called up. There was the Non-Aggression Pact. A pretty bad shock for some. I didn't think about it too much myself; I believed what people told me; I thought it was a maneuver on Stalin's part, and, in '41, I saw, sure enough, that I was right. Those of us who were returning from Spain, it was like we had haloes over our heads.

My parents stayed in Paris during the Exodus. They had nowhere to go, no family, no money, no car. The Party had sent me into the hinterland to Châteauroux, to try and make a bit of order out of the chaos. The Exodus, when you think of it, that was complete madness, too, all those people on the roads, and the Germans sniping at them. We were a load of young Communists; we were taking care of the refugees. In July of 1940, I went back to Paris. I was put in contact with Pierre Georges, Colonel Fabien. But I didn't see him much. Two or three times in all, perhaps. Afterward, there was another guy, from the nineteenth arrondissement. He was called Tondelier; we called him Le Tondu, or 'Skinhead.' He was my contact with the direction. I was the runner in the neighborhoods I knew well, Belleville, Ménilmontant, Pelleport, Charonne. At the beginning we organized groups of local kids, fifteen, sixteen years old, almost all Jews, as it happens. We handed out pamphlets in the street, in the cinemas. At the Ménilmonant Palace, at the Phénix. For a while I was teamed up with a guy called André Burty, who got shot. I had contact with Commander Dumont, shot too. One after another, they got themselves taken. They were kids playing war, at the beginning in any case. One evening in '41 we managed to hang a red flag on an electrical wire above a wasteland between the rue des Panoyaux and the rue des Cendriers. The next day the firemen had to come get it down. People watched, smiling to themselves, and the firemen took their time. It seems simple today, but in the context of the period! You could get yourself killed for less. That little Belleville group fell during the roundups of August 1941; actually it was just after the flag incident. I had incredible luck; I got through it. I wouldn't go home anymore; I would sleep where I could. But the group had been decimated. Of the whole twentieth arrondissement in those days we must have been only four or five who made it. I was twenty-two and among the oldest. They gave their lives for France, for France and the Rights of Man, and for the Party. Because it was the same thing to us. That's what young people today can't understand. The enemy of everything they had taught me to love, to respect, was fascism. And against fascism there was Stalin and the Red Army; there was just no getting around that, as far as I was concerned. After the war they called us the Party of the Martyrs. And that does mean something, after all!

After '41 I joined up with the Jewish groups and the Main-d'Œuvre Immigrée, the immigrants' union that had gone over to the Résistance. I stayed with them until the end, until my arrest in January of 1944. It's unbelievable the luck I had. Until '44 I got through everything. In '42, when they took away my parents and Roseleh, I didn't even realize it right away. I was on a mission in Lyon. We learned about the big roundup of the Vel' d'Hiv' the next day, of course. But right then I didn't think it could concern my family. I didn't know until several weeks later, when I had returned. Since then I've often thought that if I'd been in Paris then, I would have been warned, and I could have got them to safety. I knew quite a few people. But we didn't have families anymore, no ties, nothing. We followed orders, we risked our lives. There were comrades disappearing every day. In March of 1943 the Gestapo managed to get its hands on some of us. I always thought that we were ratted on. I was in the eleventh arrondissement at the time. In a few weeks we lost thirty-six comrades. We took a nosedive. And then, in January of 1944, my turn came. And even then I could almost say I was lucky. So many of us were shot or tortured to death! I had proper documents, in the name of Joseph Bourrelier; some things just can't be explained. I was deported to Buchenwald with hardly a scratch on me. They must have needed the workers.

Once inside, it was again thanks to the comrades that I held up. And when I returned in '45, in what a state, I won't go into it; everyone has seen the films, the photos; those aren't things I need to talk about, even if I am making an effort to say *everything*, to explain, even if I believe, today, that the children should know. When I got to the Lutétia, no one, I had no idea, there was no one; the Red Cross, the Swiss nurses, the Swedish nurses, well-fed girls who were trying not to let on just how disgusting they found us. The hospital. The nightmares. I had tried to have them telephone the shoemaker's where my father worked. There was never any answer, of course. Afterward I found out that the boss and his family had been arrested the same night as my parents. As soon as I got out of the hospital, I ran to the rue Julien Lacroix. I have already mentioned the bashed-in door, the ransacked apartment. The next thing I knew I was back outside on the sidewalk.

If it hadn't been for the comrades. . . . That's how your life gets put together for you. You don't really choose; things push you. So many people gave their lives. And so many others had them torn away. It couldn't have been for nothing. I have often wondered, then and since, why I got through it all, why I didn't get shot, like André, why I didn't die of typhus eight days before the camp was liberated, like Lucien, Anna's brother. I wonder if there was any meaning to it all. And I have thought that it was me, us, who would give a meaning to all this unimaginable misfortune. And that it was

for that that I had to go on. So I went on. That's all. And they want
me to be sorry for it, to ask for pardon, to *acknowledge our errors!* Our
errors! What errors had Roseleh committed? And my mother, who
said that the French would protect her, that the Jews had nothing
to fear in France? The error of being born, the error of trusting,
of believing in the goodness of men? In the name of God, here I
am getting angry again, all by myself. Some angers will never be
calmed, and I realize this every time. That's why I have avoided
speaking about it all for so long. But it hasn't changed anything.
Hasn't settled anything. It's there. All I have to do is raise the lid for
it to come to the surface. And now I know that it will always be this
way. Angry to the very end, Joseph Blumenthal. Never calm, never
resigned.

You have to understand this, too, my children: there are some
angers that will never be extinguished.

Saturday, September 17, 1994

I'm in a nice room with a view of the park. I asked them to put my
desk in front of the window, and I've taken up my pad again at last,
after two months. Of course it stayed there on my table in Vaudeurs,
and I had to ask Jérôme to bring it to me. I wonder if it occurred to
him to glance at it. He didn't say anything to me about it, at any
rate. Anyway, it wouldn't be so bad, because I wrote it for him, too.

The place where I am is called the Domaine de la Renardière,
Foxfarm Estate; it's a rest home. I'm doing very well here; I'm
tranquil, well cared for; the residents aren't too much of a pain in
the ass, though I hardly spend much time with them. Apart from
illness, what we have in common here would actually be money. A
stay at Foxfarm Estate really takes it out of my knitting machines!
But I still don't feel like I come from the same world as they do;
their conversations make me laugh (or rather the opposite, they
drive me crazy), and the *Figaro* is passed from hand to hand. For my
part, it's been years since I read *L'Huma* with so much attention,
preferably in the lounge after lunch, when they serve us this ersatz
even worse than in the old days and try to make us believe it's
coffee. Because, as for coffee, I think it's over, definitively. Tobacco,
too, even lites.

I almost bought it there.

On July 15, after lunch, I was out on the lawn, under my linden tree. The children wanted to play wolf. I had been feeling off my game all day, I had slept badly, Mathilde had pointed out that I looked awful. I more or less sent her packing; she has a way of making observations full of silent reproaches that just exasperates me. Clélia was calling out that she wanted me to be the wolf. We had played *Wolf are you there? Do you hear me?* often that week, and they would run away screaming, as if they were really afraid. They loved it. But at that point I said no, I was too tired. She insisted, and I was starting to have a ringing in my ears. I heard Mathilde telling her to leave me in peace; a hand gripped me around the chest, a pain like a stab with a knife, and I woke up I don't know how much later, in the hospital, with tubes everywhere. I had had a heart attack.

They operated on me, a triple bypass, and I spent three weeks in the hospital. I had trouble recovering. I'm still having trouble. It's more than a month now that I've been at Foxfarm, and I'm going to be staying on a while longer. I'm well off here, even if I want to get back home. In reality I'm a bit divided; I'd like to go back to rue Malher, and at the same time I'm a little afraid. The doctor says it's not a good idea to live alone right now. But I'm divided about that, too.

When I woke up and learned what had happened to me, I felt a sort of regret. If I had died, I wouldn't have noticed anything; I wouldn't have had the time to ask myself any questions. I sort of feel I missed my chance to die the best possible death. And then, when I saw them all around me, the children, Anna and Mathilde, the little ones, David and Léa, old comrades with chocolates and sorry looks, I told myself that it is the love of others that makes life precious. You can't wish to die when there are so many people who love you. Or at least, you have to do all you can to hold on.

David came every day; he stayed for hours, sometimes almost the whole day. We talked an enormous amount, just as soon as I could. He interrogated me about our childhood, mostly about his own, and even about Ruda Pabianicka, but the truth is I don't remember anything; all I could tell him were certain things that Mama used to say and that have stayed with me, like, 'Winters in Ruda you would sink into the snow up to your ankles,' or, when we were eating that braided bread she would often buy for Friday evenings, 'This is nothing compared to my grandmother's *challahs*, on *shabbas*, when I was young, in Ruda.' He also wanted me to talk about her, about our mother: 'Sometimes I have such trouble remembering her.' And we even burst out laughing more than once, like when we recalled how she would sometimes cut Papa off when he started making like he was going to get involved in politics, or when he brought up the unions. *Shister! Blaybe bay dayne meloueheu*, she would say: 'Cobbler, stick to your last.' He talked to me about Léa, and about his life, like never before. About our sister Roseleh. I understood that Léa was for him like another Roseleh, one that he had been able to save, and that that was why he loved her so much and had been so faithful to her. He didn't say it like that, but that's what I gathered. Maybe I would never have talked about all of that with my brother if I hadn't had this heart attack. Actually I'm even pretty sure of it.

And that's why I say I'm divided: me, who always felt ashamed for surviving, now I tell myself that it's not that difficult to die, especially at my age, and that it's maybe even harder to be the one left behind. Jérôme says that if I don't make a fool of myself, I'll be good for another ten years. It's very nice of him, and it's his job to say it, but I hope that he's wrong. Ten years is too long. I think one day sooner or later I'll have another heart attack, and that'll be it, for good. But it doesn't worry me anymore, as long as I have the time to make up for all the stupid things I've done to the people I love all throughout my life. And that's why I would still like a little more time. And that is why, now that I'm doing better and getting stronger, I asked Jérôme to bring me my blue folder, the one in which I keep my pad of Clairefontaine paper. But I don't much care to continue. I want to stop now. To finish up. I think I've said the essential things, and I have enough to do just looking after myself. But it's crazy how quickly I get tired. I will try to finish today.

Sunday, September 18, 1994

I read through everything I'd written while I was at Vaudeurs, just before my attack: I complain about my aches and pains and whine about the past. A real old fool. And yet, that's me, no doubt about it, I recognize myself. I have become that old man. And all of a sudden it confirms me in what I was saying yesterday: writing isn't fun any longer. What else could I tell? Haven't I said the essential things? What are they made of, after all, the years I would still have left to describe?

I earned money, I bought the apartments on rue Malher, and I knocked down the walls. Result: I've never lived so well. I've lived here since 1978. I lived with Anna, Nina, and David in 42 square meters in the rue Payenne, and now, in my 150 square meters, I live alone. Do I really want to go through all of that?

The buddies on their way out, the widening gaps, the springs crapping out, my heart calling it quits in its turn, the world becoming more and more alien, more and more complex. Does all of that really interest me still? I turn on the TV, the news show: Rwanda, Bosnia, Mafia in the USSR, anti-Semitism in Poland, Le Pen in France. But what did we do, in the name of God, with our hopes, with our victory, with our youth?

'We were well and truly had,' David would say.

'You really asked for it,' Jérôme would reply.

But what does he know? What business does he have with an opinion, the little ass, born the year Castro took power in Cuba? Could we have acted differently? At what point did we take the wrong turning?

I think of Lucien in Buchenwald, Lucien who entrusted Anna to me before he died. What I promised him! And what we said about what we would do afterward! Result: I drove Anna crazy, and she wound up throwing me out. And the world! What we did with the world that thousands of comrades left in our trust when they died! Often, at night, I think back through the years, and I try to understand. I run the film again. And sometimes I wonder whether we weren't mistaken from the beginning, whether the error wasn't in believing that we could change something, change people, change life.

I can still hear my father saying, with a shrug of his shoulders when I was getting all worked up, *Tumet zayn raych un urem:* 'There will always be rich and poor.' And that would really drive me into one of my furies! He didn't understand the striking workers in '36, and even his admiration for Blum couldn't convince him. *Tumet zayn raych un urem.*

And what if it's a curse? If there really were nothing to be done? It's been almost sixty years now that I've been struggling, swimming like a fool, and the shore keeps getting farther away. I'll never reach it. What is my life today? I wanted to contribute to human happiness, and I wasn't even able to make my own family happy, my wives, my children. And what if I hadn't left Solange? And if I had told myself that no good would come of those who prevent people from loving each other in peace? And if I had chosen love? The worst is that I thought I was choosing it, choosing love. A greater love, a more worthy love, total, universal. The love of peoples and of comrades. And what I find around me is hatred. They tell me that we were liars, criminals, even worse than the Nazis. That we closed our eyes to the suffering of millions of men. I don't know any longer. Did I close my eyes? Did I deliberately not see, not hear? I had so many other horrors in my eyes and in my ears, from Barcelona to Buchenwald, from the Vel' d'Hiv' to Drancy; it's true, maybe I haven't thought of anything else for too long, my whole life long. One day the world was cut in two. In the middle, in the gulf, my universe disappeared, all of the people I loved. And I stayed here.

Perhaps they are right, after all. Perhaps wars do end, and then others begin, and the whip changes hands. Yes, perhaps it is true, and I didn't know how to see it, or didn't want to. Perhaps.

But criminals? Assassins? No. The pendulum swings, and one day it will swing back in the other direction, and then the young people will give us our due. I won't be around to see it, but I'm sure of it.

At any rate, it's too late for me; you don't change at my age. And then, even if your dreams keep falling on their faces, even if your luck isn't just around the corner yet, even if the road we've taken is the wrong one, I *know* that there is a right one, and that others will find it.

I know that there will always be men who will seek, and who will believe, and that they will get humanity onto the right path in the end.

You must never give up hope.

Sergueï Hazanov

Sergueï Hazanov was born in Moscow, where he studied science and literature at Lomonosov University. *Lettres russes* (Russian letters, 1997), from which the following excerpts come, is a Swiss-Jewish updating of Montaigne's *Lettres Persanes*, the outsider's view of a familiar culture that reveals its contradictions and curiosities. Hazanov is also the author of *En déshérence* (Unclaimed, 2000).

Sergueï Hazanov

EXCERPTS FROM Russian Letters

Letter I: Yuri to Igor

Geneva, May 1989

So, my good fellow, you want to know how to put down roots in Switzerland, do you? Without a proper residence permit, of course, because with the permit you're not interested, and, since you ask the question in the first place, you must have more than half a brain. Right, then, without a permit, but entirely legal: you know very well that I have a religious respect for all institutions and established powers, the United Nations, the League of Sexual Reform, the penal code. . . . All you have to do is skim the code, as a certain celebrated Nazarene once said, as he walked on the water. I, for example, know at least three hundred and twenty-six ingenious ways, all relatively honest and legal. Once I even made a list, and I could publish a manual: *If You Haven't Yet Got Settled in Switzerland, Do It Now.*

To get properly established, you have to demand political asylum. And to demand political asylum you have to be hunted, preferably by Interpol. Of course, you can also marry a Swiss woman. Unfortunately, you're already hitched for life, and your partner, alas, is the jealous kind, suspicious to the point of indecency. She would never let you leave her behind, even if it were only provisionally and for a noble cause. But console yourself: as far as women go, you're not missing much. Swiss women are too masculine, too emancipated, too uncultured; they think only of cash and clothes and they're real inflated dolls, although, alas, they're not inflatable. And to top it off, they are often skeletal, endowed with an ugly complexion, from my point of view, of course; but you know well that you can trust your old master in matters of feminine aesthetics.

Just think, they are so cold that you absolutely cannot approach them in the street or on the bus. You can smile at them until you unhinge your jaw, flash them the most ardent looks; they won't even notice you. And this takes on the dimensions of a national tragedy, what's more, for Swiss men are reduced to seeking their better halves all over the place, in Latin America, in Thailand, in Mauritius, and, not long ago, in Russia. Yes, just think, female Russian citizens are highly valued here: completely European and yet, contrary to Swiss women, tender, fleshy, and well brought up and cultivated to boot. They answer the Biblical requirements: 'Women, be submissive to your husbands if you want to keep them under control.' So there's no chance for you in the sex department, but maybe, if things go badly, I could think up a solution for your old lady.

Well then, it's decided; there's nothing left for us to do but consider asylum. The easiest thing, if destiny has smiled on you, is to be a poor Negro hung up on a branch by the KKK in Louisiana; or a miserable Tamil, persecuted on all sides, and where? In a paradise on earth. Another possibility: be the descendant of great conquistadors, or of the noble and unlucky Incas, by some miracle escaped from the claws of Pinochet's or Allende's secret police; or better still, be both at once. Of course, I'm not even mentioning the unlooked-for luck of having been born in Iran, in Cambodia, in Africa, or in Siberia. In other words, outside of Switzerland you have every chance of being persecuted, humiliated, hunted, and, by consequence, welcomed into this little alpine island. Even for us Russians it's doable. On the condition, of course, that the candidate say nothing of his three years in prison for attempted gang rape, nor of his deportation to the north as a result of chronic alcoholism; they think big here, but there are limits, and a misunderstanding is always possible. You would do better to look among your ancestors for a forebear with Jewish blood, or Armenian, or German, for a Baptist or a dissident. If your genealogy is one hundred percent pure, look for one of your relations whose misfortunes have made you suffer, at least psychologically.

Now, let us suppose that you do find the grounds to give Switzerland the pleasure of your arriving here. There's still getting in. How? Good question, as Hamlet said. He too dreamed of emigration, and what did he get? For the so-called miserable Africans, Latin Americans, and Asiatics, nothing could be simpler: they procure for themselves (each in his own manner) the money for a plane ticket to Geneva or Zurich, where they are met with open arms. But in our country, which has acquired for itself the reputation of being the most progressive place in the solar system, in our Kingdom of Absurdia, in our rotting anthill where the *perestroïkis*, the stagnation, and the hypocrisy are veritable beauty marks, the trivial business of buying a plane ticket is threatening to become as complicated as Einstein's theory.

Till my next missive, I am

Yours, Yuri

Letter VII: Yuri to Igor

Geneva, September 1989

Dear disciple, joy of my soul, your list of questions is truly inexhaustible. Even before budging a toe you want to know everything. You put me in mind of certain chess fanatics who spend years studying the theory of the game but who have no desire to move a pawn in a match against a real adversary. That would be a waste of time for them. But the criterion of truth is practice, as our prophet Vladimir Ulyanov said, leaving little Switzerland for great wild Russia and accepting money from the enemy of his fatherland, Kaiser Wilhelm, in order to make a revolution there. And do not forget, either, that a fool can ask so many questions that even a hundred sages would never be able to answer them. But I will try; I am no sage, just a man of a certain age, and with some experience.

Let us begin with the history and the geography—that is to say, with the country itself. As you can guess, Helvetia, or Switzerland, is to be found at the heart of Europe, nibbling a little on Germany, France, Austria, and Italy. A nice state of affairs, wouldn't you say? It is a federation of twenty-six republics, here known as cantons, autonomous in all things save the post, the army, the railway, and a slew of other portfolios being gradually wrested from them by the central state, under the guise of simplification. They have no idea that they are following in the footsteps of Papa Stalin. Sounds like our Union of Soviet Socialist Republics, no? Does this mean that these skiers, these bankers, these shepherds and clockmakers have stolen our Marxist-Leninist ideas? That may be too glib a claim, for you will recall that Switzerland was, after all, born a little earlier than the USSR, that is, about seven hundred years ago. But it is in the process of adopting the Jacobin way at a speed that commands admiration, while its neighbors to the west are (at last) assessing the damage of centralism, all without knowing how to remedy it.

Do the Swiss represent a people, a nation? Let me give three hearty guffaws. Why three? Because there are three official languages—and-a-half. The best part of the population speaks French, as in Russia during the czars; the rest, German, Italian, and a tiny number Romansch. What a Russian salad! Of course, their mutual aversion is profound, but their fear of foreigners prevails. Whence the solidity of their confederation and their neutrality. But while the Romandy Swiss and the Ticinese speak basically classic versions of their respective tongues (if a little provincialized), the first and most numerous folk, the 'Alemannic' Swiss (*those-deprived-of-Lac-Léman?*) speak their own dialect, *Schwyzerdütsch*, which changes from one household to the next.

Here they believe that these are old Germanic dialects, although to my ear they sound more like Yiddish, which I had ample opportunity to hear at the clandestine Jewish school for *refuseniks* that Your Humble Servant directed in Moscow during the 1970s. To the indiscreet inquiries into my activities posed by the authorities during this period I would answer that I was doing research on the field of 'expreszionism,' while in my own mind this vivid term would evoke the image of a train stuffed full of Herzlites: 'All *aboard the Zionism Express!*' And later on it did arise that many of these expresses left for the Promised Land, but at the beginning there was nothing more than my tiny school.

Naturally we were supposed to teach Hebrew, but where in Moscow could you scare up a professor of Hebrew in those days? I tried the capital's official rabbis, of course, but they could only recite the statutes of the KGB and a couple of old Jewish jokes. I invited a patriarch whose mother tongue was Hebrew, because he had emigrated from Israel to the USSR in order to become an Orthodox Christian. But like all converts, he had gone a bit extremist and

would fill his courses with anti-Israel propaganda. This provoked
discontent among the students, who were, after all, dreaming day
and night of their ancestral land, where the milk and honey flow.
Happily, my old codisciple Shmuel knew Yiddish. After considering
the problem, I accepted this subterfuge: for me, the uncircumcised,
Hebrew or Yiddish were all of a piece, and for our students, it was
better than nothing. In their eyes this dialect of their grandparents
could pass for Hebrew because the characters were the same. And
everyone was happy: Shalom Aleichem is a much better read than
the Talmud, which is in Aramaic anyway, as anyone can tell you.
Later on I learned that my students, thanks to their perfect Yiddish,
had all gone on to become Hasidic Jews, which gave me a solid
reputation in the Holy Land.

Well then, are *Schwyzerdütsch* and Yiddish cognate tongues? *That is
the question.* It's nothing but a linguistic hypothesis, a parlor game,
but imagine that it's true, and that the German Swiss turn out to be
a lost Jewish tribe! Do you think they would immediately rush off to
Israel to fight against Yasser Arafat? I rather fear the opposite: the
noble descendants of Abraham, Isaac, and Jacob would invade the
hills and dales of the land of William Tell.

After Arafat, let's get right back to our Romandy Swiss. The
Alemannic Swiss burn with the desire to distinguish themselves
from their huge northern neighbor by means of some sort of Great
Wall of China, or of Berlin, for they wouldn't want to be identified
with the provincial Germans for anything on earth. That's why they
will always be against the Confederation's entry into the European
Community. The relations of the Romandy Swiss with their neighbor, France, are different and rather ambiguous. Among their Ger-
manophone brethren they put on a great show and play at being the
representatives of French Culture, but in private they are mostly
concerned that the French not make jokes about how they are tire-
some bumpkins, slow, uncouth, and materialistic. In revenge, the
Swiss mock the French disorder, their superficiality, their vanity.
Once, in the Canton of Valais, I watched with my own eyes as
the Swiss took to the streets following the televised showing of a
France–England soccer match to serenade and celebrate the French
defeat as if it were a national victory.

But the important thing is that the Alemannic Swiss put up with all these Romandy pretensions to intellectual superiority, and that they do it without so much as a complaint. Little Romandy has more universities, theaters, conservatories, museums, and libraries than big Alemannic Switzerland. And this although it is the Germanics, for the most part, who nourish the country, toil in its industries, do its business, and direct its biggest banks.

There's nothing left for the Romandy Swiss but *montagnard* activities, the hospitality sector, and diplomacy. These are the typical relations of a man with a spoiled prima donna, of a grandfather with his capricious grandson. In fact, the ecological movement is much more pronounced in the Alemannic part, with all its factories and population, than in Romandy, where some people spit on the landscape, both figuratively and in the proper sense of the word (if you will!). As for the Italian part of the country, like every minority, it entertains a disproportionate self-conception.

The lesson in Swiss ethnography is now finished. Farewell. *Auf widerluege. Do svidania.*

Your tutor,

Yuri Nikolayevich Arkadiev

Letter XII: Yuri to Igor

Geneva, January 1990
Oh my my! And there I was, treating you like a real disciple and thinking that you had learned something from all my lessons! Too bad, we'll have to start all over again. What have you come up with now, my boy? What deadline, what cooperative, what trade in arms and toiletries? Now listen to me. First off, all your Kalashnikovs and Migs have been rusted for ages and will explode at the first opportunity: that is, as soon as your clients, valiant but backward, press them into use. Why? Because weapons have to be cared for, caressed, oiled. And this just as often as the taking of nourishment and its inverse. And what is regularly to be found these days in your army? Political debates, perhaps, but certainly not oil. And when these explosions occur, who will go up in the air? You and your public toilets, and all their contents, of course. Bravo.

No, my very dear fellow, exit this dubious 'paradise' at once, before it becomes a hell. And stop with the drugs, the arms, the houses of ill repute. Avoid duties, skim the code, give advice; that doesn't oblige you to do anything, but stop compromising. Do like me and you will be successfully touching down before long on these seductive alpine pastures. Understood? Right, now back to the Khazars.

Dear Igor, it is no great surprise that you have had difficulty getting any information in Moscow concerning this poor nation. The Slavs have never been able to forget that, thanks to the Khazars, they were only inches away from converting to Judaism. Imagine the millions of Shmuels, Sarahs, and Nathans, all blond and snub-nosed. That is why, during Stalin's time, with its stirring up of Russian nationalism, enormous dams were planned, right there where the Khazar ruins are to be found. Because it was a very good pretext for getting rid of the western archaeologists, who had for the longest time been burning with desire to carry out excavations there. And just what sort of contradiction of official doctrine would they bring to light? No, thank you; let's not take any risks; the water was going to cover up all the traces and all the anxieties. Out of sight, out of mind, as the Soviet diplomats said at press conferences in those days, answering questions on the violation of human rights in the Socialist Paradise.

Nevertheless, the Khazars did not disappear from History, as against the example of the Canaanites, the Amalekites, the Aegeans, and the Babylonians. They survived; they muddled through despite their persecutions, naturally less severe than those inflicted upon the Jews. Nowadays one finds their little communities all over the place: in Provence and in Quebec, in Beijing and in Tananarive. Little communities, but quite powerful, because over the centuries the Khazars have changed, and, contrary to the obstinate Jews, have even modified their religion, creating a sort of symbiosis among Judaism, Christianity, Islam, and atheism, which has drawn not a few liberal and relaxed spirits their way, among whose ranks I hope to see you too one day. In Geneva they have established their moscathedrasynagotheque in a luxurious building, nestled in among the most celebrated banks and consortiums, in order to recruit their members from these brilliant circles. They seduce them without surcease from dawn to dusk. It's a good example for the other sects.

Their sacred day is neither Friday, nor Saturday, nor Sunday, as it is with normal people, but all three days together, as well as Monday, which makes the flock happy. In Khazar temples you will find no icons, but they will oblige you to don gloves at the entrance and to put up with a lot of music during the service—classical, jazz, and funk, played on organs, tam-tams, and your nerves. For the armless and those without a musical ear, this poses . . . yes, problems; I write against my will, for, like an old bear always swimming against the current, I try wherever possible to avoid the word 'problem,' which has become a cliché of appalling vulgarity.

One might also remark in this regard upon the equality of the sexes, which is already manifest in the diversity of the priests; on the use during offices of modern audiovisual equipment and of Sanskrit as the lingua franca; and on the installation of a wet bar in each corner of the prayer room. And, what is truly moving, their priests are known as cherubim. Not bad, eh? Imagine a forty-seven-year-old cherub with a scruffy beard, an obese belly, and wings on his back. But the name has stuck. In other words, there are so many astonishing and amusing things that I suggest you take it in yourself. Careful: in their great wisdom, the Khazars will welcome their poor brother from the East, that is, you, into their bosoms and offer him aid. Charity, fraternity, maternity, and, above all, intelligence: they understand perfectly well that a hundred franks invested in you will be repaid ten times by the publicity they receive for their generosity.

But even this little community suffers from internecine political battles. In Geneva alone there are four principal Khazar sects, each one with its own cherub: the Archaists, the Avant-Gardists, the Snobs, and the Carpet Salesmen. The aim of the first two is completely clear: change nothing, and change everything. The Snobs are the descendants of the Khazars who left for the north after the fall of their empire and settled in Europe. As for the ancestors of the Carpet Salesmen, they set off in their caravans for the south during that same tragic period and spent centuries in Asia and North Africa. Luckily for this tribe, the many admirers of Jesus and Mohammed wasted their energy battling with the Jews, and the Khazars were forgotten for a certain time. But during the truce they were able to become almost unrecognizable. My Khazar mentor, of whom I've spoken to you, told me that his father's last words on his deathbed were, 'Protect the Jews!' 'Why?' asked his son, astonished. 'Because as soon as they're done massacring them, it'll be our turn!'

There is one thing about your situation that bothers me: the Swiss, thinking that all the Khazars left Russia a long time ago and for good, have imposed a quota. Their certitude is founded on the advice of their experts. But European experts, with all their science, are just theorists, while the Russians, with all their troubles, are the real thing. If it is necessary, half the Russian population will declare itself Khazar, Tutankhamun, or what-have-you, and they will have irrefutable papers to prove it.

This is why I fear that the quota will be filled instantly and that, once again, you will be left high and dry. What's more, I have been having some disturbing forebodings about Eastern Europe, and particularly about Germany. I have even been losing sleep over it. There's something in the air over there. Perestroïka breaks down walls, but without walls there are no houses. And who is going to rebuild them?

Your master, Yuri

Letter LV: Yuri to Igor

Geneva, December 1992

It's a curious thing: the trail of Russian settlement in Switzerland was blazed, once again, by Jews. Beginning at the end of the nineteenth century, the youth of this chosen and unlucky people, deprived of all rights in the Russian Empire, including that of education, made a beeline for the universities of this alpine land, where conditions of admission were much more liberal. Of course, after finishing their studies, a large number of these young and brilliant doctors, lawyers, and engineers linked their future to this land of glaciers and banks. They married local Israelites, and, when that meager reserve was used up, threw themselves upon those Christian women of Basel, Bern, and the Vaud whom no one wanted but who were quite ready to furnish them with the Helvetian passport. Full of energy, they hoped to integrate as quickly as possible, just like their coreligionaries from the countries of Central Europe. But, alas, the year 1933 was soon to show that these were nothing but pretty dreams: for, despite its efforts at assimilation, this unfortunate nation always distinguishes itself, which often leads to regrettable consequences.

The fate of these new emigrants in Switzerland was more pleasant, and most of them assimilated without causing a stir. But their grandchildren have now suddenly taken an interest in Judaism (will the circle be unbroken) and are rushing off to Israel after finishing their studies to work for several years on a kibbutz, or even to serve in the army. It's a compensation for the lack of romanticism in their comfortable daily lives. Their move reminds me of how young people in the USSR used to search for meaning in their lives by going to build factories on the *taiga*. The difference is that, for the former, their goals and achievements are more real: you will find among the Helvetian Israelites neither drugs, nor AIDS, nor other effects of progress.

The Russian Jews, or, rather, the Reds who came to the Land of Tell after the Second World War, are not numerous, nor do they bear comparison with their ex-diplomat and dissident compatriots. But you do meet some tasty types in this little group, like the Putzky family. A good Jewish name, if a little daring. In fact, the Putzkys are a real tribe, some hundred souls in all. More than the house of Jacob when they went down to Egypt.

How did they enter Switzerland? At the beginning of the century, a member of the family, Rachel Putzky, of Vilnius, married a Swiss merchant and followed him to Fribourg. The Bolshevik Revolution brought down the walls of the ghetto, and, at the same time, put up a Curtain that was even more difficult to breach.

For fifty years Rachel's brothers and sisters, in deadly fear, didn't want to know anything about their capitalist relative. They refused her letters and mentioned her name nowhere in their papers. But at the end of the sixties they received a message from her lawyer, informing them Mrs. Duschnock-Putzky, a rich widow without issue, and eighty years of age, was gravely ill. Man is a mysterious structure, and sometimes his actions are unpredictable. The same can be said of the Putzky family: familial sentiment for their poor dear aunt was suddenly roused, like the water gushing forth under Moses' staff. The second generation, the four Putzky cousins, already retired and thus relatively at liberty, instantly burned with the desire to spare nothing to go and care for their unfortunate aunt, all the more so as the Soviet borders were starting to creak open.

Mrs. Duschnock-Putzky accepted these acts of charity, and the cousins began to prepare themselves for the journey. And, as the irony of fate would have it, these four harpies, who had been ruthless with each other all their lives long, now, when they had the chance for the first time to show a little largesse of spirit, would have to fall into squabbling again. This holy rivalry brought with it a conflict among the Putzkys like to those of certain royal families, or to mafiosi. The peace conference was held in Tallinn, where all the representatives of the clan arrived, from Leningrad, from Vilnius, from Moscow. And what do you want, these are serious people, much more so than the Corsicans, who are sort of vindictive 'lite.' Following feverish negotiations, a deal was struck: their dear aunt's precious time was to be shared in seasons, one per cousin. They would serve 'by quarters,' like Louis XIV's gentleman-in-waiting.

And then the visits to Fribourg commenced. Each cousin, seeking to ingratiate herself with the powerful Rachel, boasted to her of her own children and grandchildren, explained how much they loved and respected their Fribourg aunt, and how they were suffering in the USSR, of anti-Semitism and above all of the fact that she, Rachel, was so far away. Even the rich are sentimental on occasion, especially as they get older, and the elderly lady, quite overcome, decided to save her poor Russian family by inviting them to move to Switzerland as part of the Family Reunification Program announced and supported by the Red Cross. The Putzkys got to Switzerland just in time: after the Moscow Olympics, the little door in the Iron Curtain closed with a bang. And, what's more, old Rachel died shortly thereafter, certainly of the pleasure of having finally encountered her nearest and dearest.

She shared her bequest among her four nieces, just like in a fairy tale: one got her apartment, another her car, the third her cottage in the mountains, and the fourth her collection of paintings. Contrary to the local Israelites, preoccupied above all by their carpet sales, their children, and their kosher kitchens, the newly arrived manifested much more energy and ambition.

Your correspondence course leader,
Yuri

Letter LVII: Yuri to Igor

Geneva, February 1993

Whether you like it or not, here I am again, sonny, and there's nothing anyone can do about it.

In my last letter we spoke ill of the Putzky clan. That's right, my boy, because your silence is a sign of approbation, and we are now linked in calumny like partners in crime. And that's not all; the subject (unlike you) is not yet exhausted. There are still two picturesque fellows to be described, the representatives of the third generation, the sisters Dina and Khinina. Their moving tale deserves to be not only told, but even attended to. These two creatures, allegedly engineers, lived the life of sybarites in the USSR; pardon me, they worked (if one may express it thus) in a consultant's office in Vilnius, rather like your Academy of the Palisades. And, in the brief intervals between tea and knitting, they made up amusing stories, some of which were even published.

There are many famous duos in the annals of literature: the Goncourt brothers, Ilf and Petrov, you and me. But a feminine duo is something new. The Putzky sisters quickly found appropriate employment in Switzerland: one was able to install herself at the cantonal highway board, the other with the natural protection agency, the very post I was keeping for you in the old days. But you are far away and the lucky duck is already here, gorging herself on your dish.

Their roughly equal passion for work allowed them to balance each other out, so that neither the civil engineering branch nor the protection of nature was any the worse for it. Now, no one who has once flown in heaven will ever be happy again on earth. This (Fri)bourgeois life did not satisfy the sisters' artistic temperament— for it was as comfortable and tranquil as in a hospital—and they took to writing again. I understand them; otherwise why do you think I would waste my time and energy in these epistolary games, as wordy as they are unproductive?

It soon became clear to Dina and Khinina that no one was lamenting their humorous stories. At the time, the early eighties, Russian dissident journals only published articles on religious subjects and commercial advertisements. And for the Soviet press, émigré literati did not exist. The solution, like everything in Switzerland, came quite logically: our women of letters (if I may be permitted this sexist neologism) resolved to bring out their material in translation into foreign tongues, above all in French and German, for Fribourg is situated right on the frontier of the two linguistic zones.

Every scribbler has his own circle of readers, when it is not limited to his immediate family. My heroines chose to address themselves to their coreligionaries, in their desire to fill the niche left vacant by the death of Shalom Aleichem. What is more, they hoped that their enchanted readers would help them with the translation: for their knowledge of the languages of Voltaire and Goethe is about on a par with your own. In this laudable aim they turned their old stories into Jewish novelties, everywhere inserting old Russian jokes, and changing the names of the protagonists from Ivan to Moishele, and from Dunya to Shulamit.

It worked like a charm. The Jews of Switzerland were extremely moved to witness the appearance in their consumer society of two writers, and sisters, too, what's more, with the exotic name of Putzky, which, as I have already told you, demands not a little courage from its unlucky bearers, on account of its anatomical significance in Yiddish. Soon reliable translators had been found, and the works of the Putzky sisters had begun to inundate the bookstores of Paris, Berlin, and, of course, Switzerland. Books by the sisters Putzky are better known in Europe than those of Bulgakov or Gogol. They certainly deserve it, but I cannot help a vague feeling of envy.

As for you, as usual, you have nothing better to do in Moscow in 1993 than to await with impatience my next message. And soon it will be your pupils who are awaiting your letters, and covering you with compliments, although feigned.

That is what I wish for you with all my heart. . . .

Your Yuri

Amsel

Amsel is the pseudonym of a writer and photographer who lives and works in Zurich and Paris, has studied psychology and German literature at the University of Zurich, has apprenticed as a photographer, and has published and exhibited widely. The following story, which has been variously distinguished in Zurich literary circles, sketches a vivid erotics of second-generation relations between a surfeit of memory and the seductions of oblivion.

Amsel

In the Tower

To the memory of Selma Meerbaum-Eisinger

Kiki and I hadn't seen one another for a long time, but we continued our conversation right where we had left off. Kiki is one of the few people I have felt an understanding for from the very first. After just a couple of sentences, a couple of gestures, I had the feeling I had known her for years; perhaps it was her voice, or her way of moving her hands as she spoke, or maybe it was our little stories and experiences, which had shaped and molded us in such similar ways despite our considerable differences. We laughed at ourselves together, asked ourselves the same senseless questions, suffered from the same hypochondriacal fear of sudden death; and we hungered, both of us, for ever more life.

The tower stands just behind the dunes, a former lighthouse that serves today as a residential tower. From its highest platform you have an incomparable view over the ocean to the west and the forests to the east, and the border between sea and land describes a seemingly endless line from north to south. The wind blows day and night here, unceasingly altering the order of the clouds in the sky. I've been living in this tower since my birth, and each time I look out the window, the sky presents me with a different picture. These innumerable celestial images have taught me that everything occurs only once. But whatever does occur, even just that one time, is

observed somewhere, and what is observed is
stored away, and what is stored away will one day
be recounted.

Kiki is at least as unconventional as I am. We
have never cared the slightest what other people
thought about us, how they judged us or discussed us—at least, that's what we believed until
recently, until our reunion, which made us, reluctantly, think again. We were sitting in the round
room in the tower; I had poured us dry sherry in
two tiny glasses, and it was beginning to loosen
our tongues more than ever in the past. I don't
know if it was the sherry or the rising wind from
the south that was whistling through the tower's
cracks, or just my delight in Kiki's company. Kiki
is older than I am, but in the flickering glow of
the two candles I had lighted, as was my custom
on Friday evenings, she looked like a girl. Small,
delicate, with her red hair in bangs and a generous mouth that opened to reveal a gap between
her incisors à la Jane Birkin. After about two
hours we had reported to each other on the most
important events of the recent years.

'Better other people don't know too much about
you,' my mother used to lecture us. 'There is only
one God, and we don't believe in him,' my father
often said. 'Everything that happens finds its way
sooner or later into the affairs of human beings,'
my grandfather taught me, and he was one to
know. Every Friday evening at sundown Mother
lit two candles. I never asked her why, and after
my parents' deaths I simply continued this tradition. I have stayed on to live in the tower with my
children; their fathers visit us regularly, and then
I cook a great feast for everyone, a bouillabaisse,
perch filets, salmon trout with orange sauce. Our
favorite thing to eat is seafood, because we want
to be reincarnated as fish. Every Friday evening at

sundown I light two candles, and every weekend
one of the fathers sleeps with me in the tower.
Then he has to go again.

'I've fallen in love,' Kiki was saying. 'Such a man,'
she went on, and raised her hands in the air like a
Catholic priest making the blessing over the host.
*This is the body of Christ, which he gave to atone for our
sins.* 'A body I tell you, a dream, and strength, I
tell you, real power.' She laughed, and I thought
that she would run straight to him if she could.
'He's younger than I am, and he still lives with
his mother.' Kiki wasn't laughing anymore: 'I'm
always falling in love with unattainable men.
Maybe it's because my father left me when I was
still so small. . . . It's good to understand the
reasons,' Kiki went on, 'to know why something
happens or doesn't happen, even if you suspect
that things are quite different from the way you
perceive them, or want to perceive them; but at
the moment, since a particular reason seems
plausible, it very likely did happen just that
way. Events become comprehensible, and less
overwhelming, and lose their power to make us
afraid. Explanations are chains forged of words
and can cast a spell.' I say nothing.

I think of the young man singing a song against
forgetting, not long ago, on the street. A head
taller than I, skinny, long-boned and curled up on
himself. I stopped and listened to him, to his
words, which reminded me of the things my parents kept quiet about. *How glad am I that no one
knows/That Rumpelstiltskin is my name.* He was
wearing red plaid twister pants and a woolen cap.
'I'm a homeboy,' he said later. A boy from home?
A kid who hangs out in the living room, or what?
'I'm a towerwoman,' I responded. 'Why are you
singing against forgetting?' I asked him. His
gaze was soft, but he was unreachable, uncom-

fortable in conversation and not given to any ex-
pressions of emotion. It was in at the moment to
sing against forgetting, and you had to be in so
as not to be forgotten yourself. A stranger, a
boy at that, a homeboy who was perhaps actually
a homelessboy, even if he still lived with his
mother; someone who dreamed of fame and
smoked up too much on the weekend. 'Do you
want to come visit me in my tower?' I asked him.
He smiled vaguely in response and shrugged his
shoulders. After a pause in which neither of us
said anything, although I sensed that, just as between me and Kiki, there was a secret understanding in the air, I went on. 'Maybe we'll run
into each other again,' I called back to him a bit
helplessly. 'Who knows?' he called back.
'We would meet twice a month,' Kiki was telling
me. 'I bought myself embroidered underwear,
black silk with red frills, look!' She giggled and
unbuttoned her blouse. Her skin was white, and
her small breasts looked inviting in the new bra. I
would have liked to touch them. I have never
touched a woman's breasts, apart from my own,
but that isn't the same. Kiki and I hadn't seen
each other or spoken at all for a long time, but we
were as close and as familiar as if only a few days
had passed since our last meeting—but not so
close that I would have dared to ask her if I could
touch her breasts. 'He was great at making love,'
Kiki said. 'Not one of those who gives you a couple of nipple-twists and then sticks his finger in
your hole, I tell you he was a real artist of love. I
will never be able to settle with a less talented
man now.' Kiki sighed audibly. Her father had
also been an artist of love, her mother had always
told her; he had loved women for what they were,
and all of the women who had fallen into his
clutches had remained alone after his passing. It

was better, her mother had always firmly believed, to nurture an excellent memory than to
lose it by way of mediocre substitutes.

My parents moved into the tower by the sea soon
after their wedding. Grandfather had bought it
cheap back then. 'We can't live in a townhouse,
we're strangers in a strange land, the neighbors
would want to know where we come from. It's
better if no one knows that we fled from a smoke-
stack. It's better to keep quiet about who we are,
because in silence dwells not being-there, and
what isn't there cannot be removed.' My grandfather could think logically. 'What makes us vulnerable is what ties us down, words, names,
dates. We need only change the words that tie us
down, or keep them silent, that's all.' I have never
lived anywhere else but in the tower, and I think
that once someone has lived in a tower, then nowhere else will seem a desirable or even a possible residence. Tower dwellers distinguish themselves from townhouse dwellers, that's why there
isn't much intercourse between them, and when
they do meet somewhere, a harmless conversation grinds quickly to a halt; they turn away from
each other, perhaps a little consternated, a little at
a loss, for they don't quite understand what went
on here, or rather, what didn't go on here; they
had the best will, after all.

With Kiki it wasn't like that. We could talk for
hours, best of all about love, relationships, and
men. She lay on the sofa with her legs drawn up;
the sherry had made her cheeks red. 'He called
me yesterday and said that he had fallen in love
with someone else, a younger woman, do you
understand?' Kiki put her face in her hands. 'I'm
not like my mother; I want to forget him.' 'The
sooner you forget him, the quicker he'll be back,'
I said, because I was one to know. 'Men are hunt-

ers, above all; they eat their kill with great pleasure, but then they're off to hunt again.' *Thou
gentle kid, run for thy life, o'er field and meadow flee the
knife.* 'Down below on the street there is a homeboy sometimes, who sings against forgetting,' I
began to tell her. 'Stands on the sidewalk and
does a rap against forgetting. I wanted to touch
him, but I couldn't manage it.' 'Ah, forget him,'
said Kiki, and it sounded a bit desperate. We fell
silent and nipped at our sherries. The two candles
burned down, while outside the wind howled.

'My father was a Nazi,' Kiki said suddenly, and
her words expanded in the silence. 'He was an
overseer in Auschwitz. He probably killed your
grandmother, and not only her.' Through a veil of
sherry I looked at my friend; she didn't look at
me; she only looked down at her hands in her lap.
'I loved him; even today I sometimes long to sit
on his lap and wrap my arms around his neck,
can you understand that?' Through the window I
watched as the wind drove herds of clouds over
the black sky. 'He confessed it to me on his deathbed; I've been carrying his killings in my soul ever
since.'

We went into my bedroom below the turret before daybreak. In the middle of the high room
stands a large bed, with a mirror leaning up
against the wall in front of it; otherwise there's
nothing there. We were trembling and we crept
together under the blanket. For the first time I lay
in bed with a woman, with my best friend; we
squeezed tightly together, and through our skin I
could feel our fear of death. In a quiet voice she
asked me, 'Do you love me?' I said, 'I love you.' I
wrapped my arm around her tender body and my
hand came to rest on her little breast, to catch the
hard beating within.

Kiki and I have never mentioned her father again

since that night. Before she left, she had begged
me to keep her murderous secret, which was now
mine, too, to myself. My whole life long. We have
also never slept in the same bed again, and I have
never again felt the desire to touch her breast.
From time to time we get together and talk about
love, relationships, and men; we giggle over a
successful seduction and sneer at lost lovers and
help each other, as much as we can, over the fear
of sudden death. Not long ago, unexpectedly, I
found the homeboy standing before my door. He
said dryly that he had come to visit me in my
tower. My heart leapt up, maybe because he sang
lyrics against forgetting, maybe because I suddenly found it wonderful to know nothing about
him, maybe because he was so young, too young
for too long a story.

We are all the same race, the homeboy rapped under
the sky on the highest platform of the tower and
explained to me that a rapper must move his body
like a boxer in the ring. I sat on a weathered
chair and watched the way he bent his spine and
whipped his limbs like springs back and forth.
The wind altered the order of the clouds in the
sky unceasingly. Before the homeboy left, I asked
him why he had come. 'Oh, I had a bad conscience, of course,' he said, and gave me a grin,
cool. 'Better that other people don't know too
much about you,' I mumbled, more to myself, as
I walked down the stairs behind him and accom-
panied him to the door. I stopped on the threshold; he turned lightning fast and his lips brushed
against my ear, and without another word he
went off. I watched him go for a long time,
the way he disappeared in the distance with his
gangly stride.

Shelley Kästner

Shelley Kästner was born in 1961 in Zurich. She was trained in psychology in Zurich and as an actress in Zurich, Munich, and New York. She has worked in film, television, and theater for the last two decades and has been variously distinguished. Her poetry has appeared in a collection of writing by women in German Switzerland. 'Antisemitismus, oder die Lust, gemein zu sein' (Anti-Semitism, or the pleasure of cruelty) was first produced on June 9, 1997, at the Theater Neumarkt in Zurich; it has since been mounted elsewhere in Switzerland, as well as being revived in 1998 in Zurich with an added roundtable discussion by historians and specialists on Swiss-Jewish relations. The piece, a carefully orchestrated pastiche of actual letters to the editor culled from Swiss periodicals during the mid-1990s, the period of the most heightened confrontations of the Swiss with their country's past and claims made upon it by international organizations, is a slow crescendo of resistance and hatred that suggests the dangerous affinities of philo-Semitism and anti-Semitism.

Shelley Kästner

Anti-Semitism, or
The Pleasure of Cruelty

WOMAN

Sir:

Since fall of '96 we have been following with mounting shame the discussion of dormant Jewish accounts in Swiss banks. We are Swiss citizens, a fact of which we are not proud, but for which we are grateful. Grateful that we have been and continue to be so fortunate in comparison with other, far less privileged people in other lands. This gratitude means, at the same time, a duty and a responsibility to be open to the problems and needs of others. We take great care, too, to be open to other ways of life and opinions, without denying our own culture and views.

MAN 1

We are made speechless by the misanthropic and cowardly policies of cover-up and stonewalling that have clearly been followed without interruption by whole sectors of our government, administration, and banks. And that this behavior should also be approved by a majority of the population embitters us immeasurably. We are made very ashamed both by the refugee policies of the era and, still more, by the dissembling and dishonesty that have attended the critical study of this pitch black topic. We can excuse ourselves in these pages neither for what happened then, nor for the current outrageous events and the insolent comments of Mr. Delamuraz, but we can certainly in no wise approve of that which occurred and is now occurring. And we can with greater engagement and conviction bestir ourselves in our personal lives in the cause of a symbiosis among peoples of various races and religions. A symbiosis marked by knowledge, mutual comprehension, esteem, and respect.

With best wishes,

Hans K. and Brigitta B., Z.

MAN 1

I have worked for several decades with Jewish businesspeople the world over and prized their high intelligence.

Hugo M., Sulgen

WOMAN

We Christians have more than enough on our charge sheet: bloody Crusades, a bloodier Inquisition, and, as the crown of all inhumanities, lethal gas factories. It would certainly behoove us, and it is high time indeed, finally to accept the Jews as human beings of equal value. They are human beings like us, with defects and weaknesses.

MAN 1

Since the Middle Ages Jews have been associated with rapaciousness and money. This musty, vague anti-Semitism has been evident for quite some time, in fact, at all levels of the population and in many countries. Intellectuals of all people have tolerated—and continue to tolerate—this stupid myth. Anti-Semitism has never been 'the problem' of a specific class of people, and that among other things is precisely what makes it so dangerous.

A.B. of C.

WOMAN

I note with shock that anti-Semitism is very widespread in my generation, those around thirty, whether among left-wing, Green-voting friends or casual acquaintances, all of whom are given to disparaging remarks about the Orthodox Jews (costume, size of family) and who at the same time say that one cannot do anything about it, unfortunately, because the Jews have the feeling that they have suffered so much injustice. I have even heard colleagues make speeches on the character of the Jews (whatever that might be) and on their lust for money. And these are not, let it be noted, uneducated or simpleminded creatures, but often enough people with university degrees and experience abroad, who enjoy reading Kaminski or Roth.

Esther G.

MAN 1

Joke

A Mercedes 220 SE Cabriolet is cruising down the road. A VW tries to overtake it. Each time it's about to, the driver of the Mercedes taps on his gas pedal and zips away. This goes on about ten times, until finally the VW is able to slip by at an intersection. He cuts the Mercedes off, climbs out and asks, 'Excuse me, are you Jewish?'

'No.'

'Then come on out, you bastard!'

MAN 2

Whoever thinks himself capable of choosing his ethnicity at will should be no more surprised than the bigamist when one side or the other rebels. From this point of view it is understandable when the member of one single ethnic group or country finds it somehow not correct if 'others' are constantly proclaiming their simultaneous belonging to another group. Accusing such protesters of anti-Semitism goes too far, I believe. The Biblical rules of conduct have stood the test of time as general precepts; only the business of loving thy neighbor was probably badly formulated from the beginning, for you can't order love. Do such opinions make me an anti-Semite?

WOMAN

Dear Letters-to-the-Editor Team:

First— and in retrospect—thank you very much indeed for the new year's wishes, which I am pleased to reciprocate. Here's to further successful collaboration. Now my point: it is hardly a surprise that the Jews in Switzerland should have more and more to be afraid of. After all, it is them we must thank for this impossible antiracism law, which is used at every opportunity and with gusto against decent Swiss. This displeases many citizens—and they needn't be extremists.

Sincerely

MAN 2

I am in solidarity with those who are calling for an accounting and an apology in favor of the victims. But there is one thing about which we must all be clear: the way in which this process is being carried out is of no particular benefit to Semitism, to which the reticence of the Swiss Jews bears evident witness.

MAN 1

Up to now I had belonged to the ranks of those Swiss citizens who defended the Jews. Since these last few days I am forced, however, to alter my opinion radically. Federal Councilor Delamuraz was not correct in every regard, but his remarks to the effect that the Jews' demands amount to extortion are unfortunately quite to the point. And the behavior of the Jews following this comment by the Federal Councilor is yet another extortion. So take your whole Jew-pack and go to America, or better still, to Moscow. Anti-Semitism is now at the boiling point. Countless citizens of this country feel an indescribable anger at the cursed Jews, and wish them where they belong.

P.S.: I'm looking forward to the antiracism suit!

MAN 2

As an engaged defender of animals, I am an anti-Semite because the Jews cannot refrain from the gruesome torture of animals through slaughter without anaesthetic. The Jews simply have other ideals. A central concern is, indeed, money.

Karl S., architect HTL

WOMAN

When will the demands of the Palestinians finally be met by the Jews? The Jews' behavior with regard to the rest of the world can surely only promote hatred of Jews.

MAN 2

It is a dirty trick to bring up the politics of the contemporary state of Israel to justify one's anti-Semitic remarks. Swiss Jews and the Likud's settlement policies in Israel have nothing at all to do with each other.

WOMAN

Why was our Federal Councilor Cotti wearing a Jewish cap during the wreath-laying for Holocaust victims in Jerusalem? An alpine dairyman's cap with the Swiss crest, a white cross on a field of red, would really have looked better, for one mustn't deny one's identity for all one's tolerance of suffering people from other cultures, morals, and religions. As Christians who consider our Lord Jesus Christ to be the resurrected son of God, we should hold our crest of the cross, recalling his cruel death, always and everywhere in honor, something one might well expect from a representative of the country.

MAN 2

Are you a Jew? Two thousand years ago your ancestors cried, *The cross for him, the cross for him, crucify him!* You killed our Lord Jesus Christ, murdered him, an outrage that could have been committed only by bandits devoid of conscience. Now we call, *Out with them, throw them out of Switzerland, these Jews, out with these criminals, they have no right to live in this beautiful land any longer.* You have been warned now; pack your things and go.

Signed: Union of the Righteous

MAN 1

Joke

Little Ilse: 'I mayn't play with you, Moishele; Mama says your people crucified Christ.'

Little Moishele: 'That can't have been us; it must have been the Cohns from next door.'

MAN 2

While historians and theologians concern themselves with anti-Semitism in Swiss history, real Judeophobia is raising its head with increasing audacity. A consideration of letters to the editor on this topic reveals that they begin in a plaintive, self-righteous tone, but then become ever more daring and aggressive. Thus there has appeared in the newspaper, for example, mention of 'Jewish marauding,' and the maestro of this orchestra, Christoph Blocher, has no problem speaking of 'extortion' in his position paper on the Solidarity Foundation. When Federal Councilor Delamuraz used this expression in his turn, there was still a cry of outrage to be heard in the press and among a part of the population. Today one has grown accustomed to the fact that the sluices have been opened up again for the stinking flood of racism.

WOMAN

I am a Swiss expatriate. On March 1, 1997, I went to hear a speech by the SVP politician Christoph Blocher. There were more than one thousand people in attendance. Mr. Blocher spoke for two hours. These two hours consisted entirely of Swiss self-aggrandizement. I have never before felt so ashamed and depressed. Christoph Blocher is evidently a populist who plays upon the lowest common denominator. He is a clown and a revisionist of Swiss history during the Second World War. He makes cheap jokes at the expense of others: critics, Jews. All of this was met with applause and laughter from the audience. I heard not a single voice of protest during those two hours. I studied the faces. What I saw alarmed me, and what I heard as I left the hotel was ugly, very ugly: a crowd that dripped of self-aggrandizement and in which anti-Jewish remarks were common currency. I had to bear witness to the fact that these people had learned nothing in the last fifty or sixty years.

MAN 1

Extortion! Repulsive & mean. Little Switzerland at war. Enclosed by a hostile world. We had a heart and saved persecuted Jews. Much more than any other country. We do not ask for praise. But we reject the extortion of guilt. Secure future and freedom. Swiss People's Party of the Canton of Zurich. The SVP, the party of the center.

MAN 2

Hundreds of thousands of Swiss soldiers had to spend thousands upon thousands of days of duty on the border—for the protection, among others, of the Jewish refugees in Switzerland! The soldiers thus no doubt made more of a sacrifice—a material sacrifice, too!— than the sacrifice of money that was demanded of Jewish circles for their refugees. We were never compensated for this, nor did we ever seek to be. Members of my family were also among those who made great sacrifices, material and immaterial, and they certainly do not deserve to be treated today as nothing more than scapegoats. Not demands, but words of gratitude were to be expected.

MAN 1

Holocaust specialist Raul Hilberg said in his lecture at the Zurich Polytechnic that he is convinced that even in Switzerland much was known about the extermination camps during the Second World War. In which regard the following anecdote from the time of active service: in December 1942 our cook told us that there had existed in Germany for some time so-called death camps, where Jews, Gypsies, Communists, and even the mentally handicapped were being gassed, ground into body parts, and processed into soap. That we as ignorant listeners did not take such horror stories seriously was perhaps understandable. But that jokes should be made on the subject was pretty macabre. The next day, when the army rations of corned beef were being served, I heard for the very first time from a soldier the expression 'corned Jew hash.' I am afraid I can testify that throughout my active service this horrible term became standard parlance in the army. Toward the end of the war I was nevertheless to witness the efforts of our then commandant, who wanted to ban the term from our unit under pain of penalty. But the expression can still be heard to this day in the ranks. Now that we are working on our history, it is really high time that this expression vanish from the Swiss colloquial language.

MAN 2

The debates over the role of Switzerland in the Holocaust and toward its victims comes late, but not too late. Those who ask today what all the fuss is about fifty years down the line come mostly from those circles that have consistently hindered a critical study of the contemporary politics of our country. The debates over the 'full boat' policies, the J-stamp, the plundered gold, or the ownerless accounts have tended sooner or later to awaken the realization in most people that the climate of the period was nationalist, egoistical, and hard-hearted. One seldom encounters questions of the following sort, however: Didn't all the official, army, bank, and church authorities behave in this way because they were themselves hostile to the Jews? Is there not a link to be drawn, for example, between Philipp Etters's hindering of a Red Cross protest against the Holocaust and his anti-Semitic pronouncements during the '20s and '30s? Such troublesome questions today hang in the air and explain at least in part the mood of general uncertainty. They must be brought into contact with the precepts of the political debate.

Josef L., historian, politician

MAN 1

It wasn't 'the Swiss' who turned the refugees away at the border; it wasn't 'the Swiss' who bought gold from the Nazis. It was in every case men of rank and name who made the decisions on their own authority. If the banks took money from the refugees during that period, then they should give it back to its rightful owners, along with interest and compound interest. But why a Solidarity Foundation deploying tax money? I received no share in the industries' war profits, nor a gold chain or commemorative coin from the banks' dubious gold dealings, nor a single franc of the Holocaust moneys.

MAN 2

It is unfortunately common wisdom that financial rewards could be interpreted as a recognition of guilt. Thus the Swiss get the impression that they are to pay with their own hard-earned money for a deed of which they are not guilty. This is a distraction from the real topic, namely, that we must at last recognize, openly and without reservation, that our prosperity represents the counterpart of the horrendous material damage that the people around us suffered during two world wars, and which they are continuing to suffer in large parts of the world. And above all: that it is not only 'the banks' and 'industry' that profit by this state of affairs, but also the state's coffers, through taxes, and in the end every one of us, through high salaries and quality of life. It is this admission that we owe the world above all! And if deeds follow this insight—for example, the Solidarity Foundation proposed by the Federal Council—then that is only to be welcomed; but such a foundation has certainly nothing to do with an admission of guilt. If we continue to believe, however, that we are better than the rest of the world, then we do indeed make ourselves guilty. Not in the eyes of the world, but in the first place in our own eyes and in those of our children.

MAN 1

The very criticism of the mismanagement of the crisis gives me pause for thought. Too often do I hear that we could have gotten away cheaper with a prompt payment. Not a word about the horror or the human tragedies behind the moneys.

MAN 2

It is a false assumption that valuables and gold teeth were taken from the victims of the Holocaust and melted down directly into gold bars by the Nazis. The bars from the German Reichsbank that Switzerland received are of fine gold (at that time 24 karat). The gold from the dead people consisted of alloys of gold with silver, copper, and nickel, with a grade between 14 and 20 karats. In order to make up the quality of the Reichsbank's gold bars and to achieve the fine grade of 24 karats, this gold would have had to have been separated from the alloyed metals by a goldsmith. Without such a procedure, melted gold teeth would have been delivered to German dental laboratories or passed on to goldsmiths for further processing. In the absence of precise knowledge of these processes and without clear evidence, the reproaches being made against Switzerland must be returned to sender.

A dentist

MAN 1

A human soul with the cabalistic number 613 in the year TDOJ
Dear Sir,

I congratulate you and the Jewish circles on having yourselves finally broken the spell. The spell that only you yourselves could break. Now destiny can take its course with regard to the ownerless fortunes, the Nazi fortunes, the Holocaust victim fortunes, accounts or moneys, reparations fund, Solidarity Fund, fund for the victims of the Nazis, for the victims of the Holocaust. Life is a game, as the saying goes. Now you're on top, now it's someone else. Most top players only lose because they have overlooked their own traps. Many of those who play along with them have developed their own laws. They and Judaism are now making their final move. The current tragedy is that every single human being is playing along with the game but knows neither the rules nor the strategies.

A small number guess at the rules. Fewer still know them quite well. They know above all the tricks and the dodges. These players, as is well known, are at the moment you Jews. Of course, there are souls on the other side of the playing field who know their way around, too. They are more numerous than you suspect. The above-mentioned spell that you have undone with your actions is now ringing in the year TDOJ. TDOJ means The Downfall Of Judaism. No, not the way you think: that perhaps now all those lies you have spent centuries and millennia spreading about—but especially in the last fifty years—are now going to be realized. You and I know that they are primitive lies, and that the fabricated Holocaust is only supposed to distract attention from those Holocausts that you Jews have on your conscience, that is, those carried out against the Russian peasants, or the Indians, in the Crusades, in the countless wars. Despite the countless Nobel Prizes, the scientists, and the other title bearers, you are too dumb. You are not capable because you are blinded by hatred. You have even invented this so-called anti-Semitism in order to keep the lamentable remnants of the world united in confused belief. You yourselves know what crimes you Jews have on your conscience. You got the whole misery going in the first place with the slave trade between whites and blacks. It was your Robert Lewis who dropped the atom bomb on innocent civilians. A stolen bomb, by the way, for your scientists would not even have been capable of that. You are corrupting the young people with your New Age craziness; you are veritably flourishing in the pornography business; you are dismantling the family, destroying our food sources, manipulating nature. It was because of the Jews that National Socialism was born. I know no hatred of you. I overcame my hatred years ago, which does not, however, stop me from naming facts by name.

P.S. You are of course welcome to interpret these lines as anti-Semitic, although there are no greater anti-Semites, no more brutal race haters, and no sneakier destroyers than you Jews.

WOMAN

Dear Journalists and Historians, if you understood the mentality of the Jews properly, you would know that the majority of the Jewish moneys was deposited with other Jews, with trustees or agents, and scarcely in banks, unless they were private banks run by Jews. The

Jews control the media and possess colossal fortunes and still it's never enough for them; now they are taking whole countries hostage. Jewish materialism has managed to convert their dead into cash. From now on the dead are being entered in the Jewish ledgers under expense and yield, and mostly under 'yield.' It wasn't only Jews who died in Hitler's concentration camps. The first to be killed were the Germans opposed to Hitler. Hitler, who in reality was named Alois Schickelgruber, was himself a Jew, though they hardly boast of this fact in Jewish financial circles or at the Jewish World Congress. Did the Jews fail to take Hitler's warnings seriously at first because Hitler was by his biological father himself a Jew? Not only did this Jewish father not recognize his child, he even chased away his pregnant mother, whom he had employed as a serving maid. One certainly understands the bitterness of little Adolf-Alois, who became 'Adolf Hitler' at the age of five. Trotsky, a Jew, and Lenin, another, are responsible for so many deaths. . . . But the Jewish World Congress isn't boasting about that, either. When will the Christians finally seek justice and reparations from the Jewish World Congress? Dear Journalists and Historians, do you know who defended Switzerland against the Germans during the last world war? It was Swiss women. That deserves to be said this evening.

Madame X.Y., teacher

MAN 1

To the Supreme Fanatic:

Just so it's clear: the press, radio, and television, all purchased by you, have absolutely no effect on us citizens, because we are accustomed to thinking for ourselves! We know that you wish to destroy us economically and financially with the help of America. That's where Jewish high finance has long since risen to power! But we will take you down with us. You can play the victim again afterward, when you've destroyed a whole country with the help of America. Have never had anything against a Jew in my whole life. But what you are now doing, with the Nazi money as a pretext, has fundamentally changed my position. For me you are no longer Swiss. For me you are traitors who are delivering us over to your ideological allies so that you can take over here too.

Signed, 'Without Any Respect'

MAN 2

My demands as a Christian Swiss: 1) Isolation of all Jews living in our land in concentration camps. Unpaid labor for Aryan Swiss. 2) Expropriation of all Jews. 3) Marking of all Jews with the Star of David. 4) Boycott of all Jewish businesses. 5) Should the need arise: deportation of all Jews to their promised land, where the Arabs will one day drive you into the sea. Jews—you are and remain alien bodies. Piss off. Too bad Adolf was not permitted to finish his work. But: Adolf lives—among us. Soon there will be a *Reichskristallnacht* in Switzerland, too. Then you Jews are in for it. You are the chief evil in this world—you only want power and money, money, money, money, money, money. You are insatiable, but you are condemned to extinction.

Anonymous

WOMAN

Hello Joseph—you miserable fat Jewish bastard. Your mere outward appearance is revolting: big old greasy paunch, like a safari swine ready for slaughter, soon to be done away with forever. Your time has been up for a while now. And your slimy pop-eyes, too, full of hypocrisy with regard to your long since well-known mentality, that of a son of a bitch, as a result of constant cheating. You've been utterly disqualified on the professional level for a long time now— Jewish idling in the cultivation of unadulterated species department, completely asshole style—total loser on the railway siding. And as I've already mentioned: your liquidation is only a matter of time, as an Orthodox Jew bastard you have been a real public nuisance for a long time now already. Your term is up—soon you will be delivered.

MAN 1

Six million Jews are supposed to have been gased in the Third Reich?

WOMAN

Since the world began the Jews have been disturbing world peace.

MAN 2

Now, at the very latest, everyone should be absolutely clear who runs the world.

MAN 1

The Holocaust is history, finished; we have other problems today.

MAN 1

Greed clearly has no limits.

MAN 1

You want to wangle yourselves a perpetual pension out of the Holocaust, and it makes us sick.

WOMAN

Jews, you are international bloodsuckers.

WOMAN

There are eighteen thousand too many Jews in Switzerland.

MAN 2

We're back. Heil Hitler!

Short pause of three beats.

MAN 1

Joke

Two doctors meet. One gives the full-armed Hitler salute. Says the other: 'You know, I've been having the same problem with my arm lately.' Says the first: 'Yes, there's a lot of it going around.'

Short pause of four beats.

MAN 2

Recently I received a letter, naturally anonymous, with the following contents: 'Who made Zurich Jew-free? Rudolf Brun. Who made Tennessee Jew-free? Ulysses S. Grant. Who will make Switzerland

Jew-free? The law on health insurance + the state old age pension. Dreipussy is cheating and conning us all! Jewfuss doesn't belong in the Federal Parliament; she belongs in the gas chamber! Switzerland, awake!' What must I do against this cheap harassment? What can I do? What can we do?

Michael Guggenheimer

Michael Guggenheimer was born in 1946 in Tel Aviv, where he attended primary school. Further schooling followed in Amsterdam and Switzerland, where he studied modern history and social psychology. He lives in Zurich, where he works for the national cultural funding agency Pro Helvetia. He has published widely, essays as well as photographs. In his 1999 volume *Personal*, from which the following piece is excerpted, he uses text and color photographs (the innovatively designed book appeared in alternate wrappers, to be hung up as posters) to define and explore his various habitats, both spatial and temporal. 'Adler' develops the sticky, veritably closeted atmosphere of silence and denial in which secular Jewish life is often lived in Switzerland.

Michael Guggenheimer

Adler

During his very first tour of the company he asked himself this question.

One hour after he had taken up his new position, the head of personnel was leading him through the building. They went from office to office, and she introduced him to the secretaries and the departmental specialists. As they were walking up from the first floor to the second, he realized that he would not be able to retain the names of his new colleagues. Should he ask the head of personnel for a sheet of paper in order to write down their names and functions? He couldn't decide; he felt inhibited in this woman's presence. There was one name, however, that he was able to remember. And when they were introduced, he thought he detected the other's locking onto him, his testing him, his scrutinizing him from top to bottom. Was the other just as uncertain as he was? Was Adler one too?

In the following days they saw each other often in the company cafeteria, and at the second meeting of department heads at which he was present, they even sat across from each other. He had the impression that the other wanted to undress him with his eyes, as if he wanted to determine whether he were circumcised or not. All the while he studied the other carefully, trying to tell whether his nose, his lips, or his gestures offered a clue as to his descent. He decided that Adler could not be a Jew. Adler was too self-assured in his presentation. He looked at him from the side. No, Adler did not have a curved nose. At the same time, he knew that a curved nose was not necessarily evidence of Jewish descent. He recalled how a gay acquaintance had told him that gays could spot one another at any time. And he remembered reading that drug addicts recognize each other even when they meet in an environment and in circumstances in which drugs are being neither consumed nor offered for sale.

That this should happen to him. Ordinarily he could recognize other Jews any time. With the Orthodox it was the easiest. But he could spot even American Jews, who wore neither caftans nor temple locks. Actually, he didn't especially like this department head. But if he was one like him, if he should be a Jew too, then they would belong together. He thought of the story of the two men who both came from the Balkans, one from Romania, the other from Bulgaria. Two men who had gotten to know one another in Berlin, who didn't like each other particularly, but who needed each other as evidence of an existence that had once been but that had long since ceased. Did one simply need each other as fellow strangers when far from home? He thought of the associations of foreigners: the Catalans, who met regularly, the Sudeten Germans, or the Piedmontese, all with their clubs. He wasn't the type for groups, he wasn't even a member of the Jewish community, hadn't taken part in a Jewish service since his thirteenth birthday, knew only a few synagogues, which he had furthermore visited more out of art historical interest.

The other's name was noncommittal. Adler was not necessarily a Jewish name, although the psychologist Alfred Adler had been a Jew. He thought of the name Rosenberg, which had been the name of Hitler's party ideologue. He himself knew a tailor named Rosenberg, a Pole by birth, an emigrant Jew. How happy he himself had been to have the noncommittal name Klein. Who knew that Klein could be a Jewish name? Given that there were indeed non-Jewish Kleins. If only the other had a more telling first name, he thought. Anyone can be called Andreas; why isn't the man named Saul, or David? If only he were called Christian or Christoph, everything would be clear. He looked at him and wondered how he could find a sign of Adler's Jewishness.

Days later, the two of them fell to talking again during a coffee break. But neither Adler's birthplace nor the schools he had gone to nor Adler's previous workplaces nor anything else gave Klein a clue as to the question that so preoccupied him. He couldn't even explain to himself why the subject would not leave him in peace. He was here to work, not to enter into new relationships, and certainly not to find out whether a colleague was a Jew or not. He asked himself what possible relevance Adler's potential Jewishness could have for his work.

It went on in this fashion until one meeting at which they were once again sitting side by side, and the other said to him, quite casually, shortly before the meeting began, 'So, now another new year is beginning.' He heard the other's remark and did not react, did not even watch how Andreas Adler's gaze left him. It was only after the meeting, as he was seated once more at his desk, that he suddenly realized what the other could have meant. It was September, the end of September. How could he have forgotten that it was during these days that the Jewish new year began? He went to Adler's office, knocked, and tried to speak to Adler, which was, however, not possible, since he was in a meeting and was not to be disturbed. The next day he passed him in the stairwell and took up the subject again—somewhat helplessly, it's true—by saying that Adler had surely wanted to say something to him the day before. Adler did not take him up on this, however, because in the meantime the sentence that had preoccupied him the day before was over and done with. 'You know,' he said rather awkwardly to Adler, 'I believe we two have something in common.' He didn't get any further than this, as Adler answered him, contemptuously, that they both worked in the same firm, didn't they? 'No, I mean we have something more in common.' He could not pronounce the word 'Jewish.' He seemed to himself no Jew at all, at any rate a person who did not dare use this word, out of fear of hurting the other.

Since then the two of them know of each other that they are Jewish. What connects them is the fact that their ancestors came at some point out of the Orient to Europe. But they have not grown any closer. Adler gets along better with the other department heads than with Klein. And they have never once met privately, outside of the company. Adler sometimes goes out with the other colleagues. And Klein has invited several of the department heads over.

Something connects the two of them. But they do not feel connected to each other in the least. Sometimes Adler reacts with special irritation at Klein's proposals at meetings of the department head. And Klein has often made fun of Adler before their colleagues. And yet it has happened to Klein that when he is on vacation and thinks of the firm and of work, he thinks of Adler first.

Regine Mehmann Schafer

Regine Mehmann Schafer was born in Vienna and has lived since 1960 in Switzerland. She was educated as a teacher for children with special needs at the University of Fribourg. She has published poems and short prose in various anthologies and journals. Her 1996 novel, *Geometrie des Wahnsinns* (The geometry of madness), treats in phantasmagorical fashion the experiences of German nationals, both Jewish and non-Jewish, in Pomerania and elsewhere, before, during, and after the Holocaust, and thus attempts a coming-to-terms with her own family's involvement in the Holocaust, about which she learned late in life. Her new book, *Jeremias Himmelstösser*, is a biographical novel 'concerning an unknown young Jewish writer who was reluctant to be a Jew.' In the previously unpublished short story that follows, she stages the encounter of a Jewish woman with her non-Jewish Swiss in-laws as a play on the notions of ritual purity and religious prescription.

Regine Mehmann Schafer

Trayf and Kosher

Only your own cooking will fatten you up; only your own pots can guarantee purity.

They are sitting on Malka's halfway successful cushions as if they were rotten eggs.

Malka is aware of her own degeneracy, as a housewife and otherwise. In the eyes of her guests, she and her husband are hygienic and culinary primitives.

Her husband refuses the food. Not Malka. On the contrary. She blows soap bubbles of praise over it. Truly, sometimes Jewish people could just eat up that Christian love-thy-neighbor stuff with a spoon.

Malka invited them; her husband was against it. He knows why: they are his relatives.

And they have brought pots and pans with them, and full, too. They eat their homemade beans and potatoes cooked with bacon, spoon and fork them out of their own dishes, and shower themselves with praise, so that you can't drown it out.

They do not touch anything that Malka, their hostess, has touched, let alone what she has cooked.

Moses has nothing to do with it. The relatives are Catholic. Not very. Almost faded.

After the meal Malka dares to offer her own coffee. Maybe it will find takers. Just a nip at the rim of the cup would be confirmation that the disgust on their faces is only show, a sort of mask behind which hides the purest, most superb modesty.

Wrong.

Her sister-in-law conjures her own coffee out of her shopping bag, lays out her own cups and saucers and cutlery, and pours the coffee with her own hand.

Malka vanishes swiftly into the kitchen with her full pot.

She has compassion for the rejected coffee, sets it on a little tray, and drinks half the pot. The rest she pours down the sink. Gone is gone. Not a drop should remain to bear witness that she, the *trayf* Jew, is incapable of serving an appropriate dinner to the kosher non-Jews.

As she returns to the porch with a beating heart, her sister-in-law is putting her Argovian kosher carrot cake on the table.

Needless to say, Malka leaves her own *trayfediges* in the icebox. Her brother-in-law cuts the cake. The knife is sharp, and no wonder; he sharpened it himself, on his own whetstone, of course. He stresses this.

And her sister-in-law serves the slices with her own hand.

Malka's husband pushes away the piece he has involuntarily received. Not Malka. She eats and blows new soap bubbles of praise upon the heads of these truly un-*trayf* paragons of *kashrut*.

The table is empty.

Not for long.

Her sister-in-law serves up a conversation topic: the death of their mother-in-law.

It is soon clear that this is the perfect topic for knocking one another's teeth down one another's throats.

Her sister-in-law is in her element.

She cared for Momma selflessly, bathed her, put her to bed, rubbed her down, powdered her, brushed her, talked to her, scolded her, watched over her, took her for walks, threatened her with a wagging finger, and encouraged her with her words: Momma, Momma, these medications will be the end of you! (Momma wanted to shorten her pain and her life. Of all the . . . !) Truly, death and her sister-in-law hung lovingly, side by side, over Momma's bed.

Malka understands. Her husband is deaf to it.

Her sister-in-law accuses him of not having cared: If you knew what I went through for Momma!

Right. . . .

You left me all alone with the trouble, with the work. . . .

What? That's how you wanted it! I would barely have set foot in

Mother's room before you appeared and started making yourself busy in every corner. You liked being a heroine and a martyr. And you didn't do it for nothing!

What? I don't believe these accusations!

She throws herself, weeping, into her husband's arms.

Malka's husband answers, Crocodile tears!

Her sister-in-law responds, sobbing: No one cared for Momma except me!

Malka sits and is silent.

But she is not still.

She is working on her Swiss floor. She wants the boards without gaps, Helvetian. But her effort only results in patchwork, faulty knitting, to be unraveled anytime, like an unfinished cardigan.

Her brother-in-law consoles his wife. For Malka's husband this only proves his stupidity: Your wife is playacting!

Now Malka's opinion is added to the family quarrel. Luckily it is not even heard over the noise of the battle.

Malka doesn't hear it herself.

But she knows that she has just called out to the warring parties, Be happy that Mother died in bed; in my own family things were different.

Thank God it didn't get through; it was completely beside the point. She is ashamed of herself. But she has an easier time with forced death in gas chambers than with natural death in bed.

She is arrogant with regard to this difference. But it's because she cannot find her way in to a normal death: for instance, to that of her mother-in law.

There she sits now and has said something.

The two brothers are still crossing swords over Momma's dead body.

The sister-in-law is sobbing in her husband's arms; this gesture has nothing to do with Malka. It is foreign to her, overly normal.

She makes herself scarce. Sits down in the kitchen again.

Outside the brothers fight on unperturbed, with the miserable sobbing in the background.

Malka's husband finally tells his relatives to go to hell.

They leave, glowing with rage, like wet poodles, laden with pots and pans, leftover beans and meat and potatoes, dishes and cutlery. They've even mistakenly taken the tablecloth, which belongs to Malka. They didn't notice that they were eating from it, *trayf*; how angry they'll be when they realize it! But they can't very well send it back.

Malka knows that these two, with their hygienic, culinary *kashrut*, won't be setting foot in this *trayf* household again. The separation is official. No one has been murdered, except for their relationship. But it probably didn't exist before either.

Whatever that means.

Marianne Weissberg

Marianne Weissberg was born in 1952 in Zurich and grew up in Winterthur and Zurich, where she studied history and English literature. She worked as a cook, a waitress, a concierge, a telephone operator, a writer and a talk-show host for radio, and an editor at various newspapers before becoming a freelance journalist and columnist in 1987 and a full-time writer in 1993. She has written for Swiss periodicals such as the *Weltwoche*, *du*, the *Neue Zürcher Zeitung*, and *annabelle*, as well as for *Cosmopolitan*, *marie claire*, and *Stern*. Her books include *Das letzte Zipfelchen der Macht* (1993), a collection of cultural-critical satires, and *Meine Chaos Küche* (1997), a cookbook-cum autobiographical-novel. The chapter translated here is from a novel-in-progress, 'Männerjagd oder Lili und die Schmocks' (The manhunt, or Lili and the schmucks), in which the madcap escapades of a Swiss-Jewish food columnist in a city closely resembling Zurich are used to illustrate the often tragicomic intersections in a modern society of ethnicity, family, friendship, and sex. Lili and her friends are engaged in a project of recording and exposing the scandalous behavior of their male partners, Jewish and non-Jewish alike, but have run up against some murderous resistance to their scheme. As the chapter opens, we find her on a fact-finding mission-cum-romantic weekend with her erstwhile beau, Freddie Schweizer.

Marianne Weissberg

EXCERPT FROM The Manhunt, or
Lili and the Schmucks

It was 10:30 A.M., we were driving on the highway, and I was in an astonishingly good mood. Freddie was whistling under his breath next to me and studying a roadmap. I would take my eyes off the road from time to time and give my ex a sidelong look. What a difference a few days apart had made! My spirits had lifted considerably since he was no longer living right on top of me. Nor had our little manhunt played an inconsiderable part in all of this. Well, if I must work, then at least I would do something that amused me: I was, after all, a former JEP, a Jewish European Princess.

And spying on all those schmucks was certainly a lot more exciting than lifting old Jewish recipes from Grandmother Helene's cookbooks and modifying them to suit the local palate, staunchly Protestant as it was. I could do without all this scribbling anyway, because when my new story was published I was going to be appointed, a new Martha Gellhorn, to the staff of an unbelievably prestigious magazine. Which would bring with it a huge expense account; and before long, the editor-in-chief, as witty and as Jewish, of course, as Woody Allen, would be throwing himself at my freshly lifted, wrinkle-free neck. And soon I would be bowing to the wishes of his mother, that salt of the earth, who would rejoice to see her yingeleh so well married in the end; I would be setting up a kosher household and, the very picture of the Queen of Sabbath, having company in to feast at a table laden with the creations of our brilliant cook.

Freddie was pretty sexy, in fact. I licked a bit of lipstick off my lips. I could, very tentatively, suggest a modern long-distance love affair. Maybe what the two of us needed was really just a bit of time apart, to fall in love all over again and pull ourselves together. In short, I found myself in the midst of a postmenstrual hormonal surge: I was viewing the putz next to me through rose-colored glasses.

We were bumping our way to our goal over a little local road and, finally, just a breakneck gravel path. I was a bit skeptical: a grandiose backdrop of mountains, a shimmering alpine lake decorated with tiny houses far below, and dense stands of fir (albeit rather thinned out by the recent record hurricane), but otherwise not a trace of civilization.

'All right, Lili,' Freddie announced in a portentous voice. 'Close your eyes and don't open them until I say so! And don't worry, I'll just count to three: one, two, three, open your eyes!'

I had driven a shaky fifty meters with my fingers wrapped tightly around the steering wheel; now I was staring straight at Freddie's chalet. It must have had a past life as a mobile home, but now, deprived of its wheels, it had been planted firmly in the ground. It rested on a concrete slab, and on top there were the beginnings of a potential penthouse, obstructed by the wobbly scaffolding that surrounded it. An oversized lock decorated the solid oak door (what else had I expected from the Schweizer mishpocheh?), and on the ledges to left and right stood cement windowboxes full of great, fat, hanging geraniums. Garden gnomes, rabbits, and deer peeped out here and there. The door also sported a cross, from which hung a rather naked Jesus. Like the geraniums, he was made of weatherproof plastic. There was no evidence of any view, however: giant pine trees grew up on all sides around this Swiss monster home.

'Voilà, our chalet, "The Belvedere," ' Freddie announced gleefully. He flung the door open. The furniture was, luckily, all made of wood: the buffet in the kitchen, the dining table, the couple of chairs, the wood oven in the corner, and, in the other room, a tall, romantic bed of unfinished pine, a wonderful match for the pretty, red-checked curtains.

'Just something simple, you know; we've been wanting to get modern furniture for a while now, but what with the renovations we haven't got around to it.' Freddie plumped the pillows busily. I kept my eyes on him, nodded graciously, and bit into a bright red apple. 'Doesn't matter, a little roughing it will do this city girl a world of good.'

While Freddie brought in the groceries and unloaded an ominous looking giant box from the car, I got myself set up. I was planning to type the weekend's bounty, which I hoped would be abundant, directly into my Notebook. Freddie himself, he had told me, intended to work on enlarging his garden gnome kingdom. But I was tired; I lay down on the soft bed and fell fast asleep.

'Lili, wake up!' Freddie was shaking me by the shoulder. He gently brushed his lips against my cheek and invited me to the loveliest restaurant on either side of the Alps. Besides, he added, he had already reserved. The moon glowed, full of secrets, bathing the clearing in a shimmering nocturnal light.

Well, why should I deny it· the fare at the mountain restaurant was simply delicious, and the local after-dinner drink had me floating above my chair. It was the first time in a long while that I had properly relaxed, and I was, of course, a little touched by the fact that Freddie was being every bit as charming as he had been at the wedding where we were first set up by Stella and Danielle, my fancy Chutzpah Lady friends. Over dessert, wild berries with *crème fraîche*, he made a little speech. He apologized (with a cough) for his *slimy lord-of-the-manor behavior*, and for perhaps being a bad influence on my mercurial son Bernie, none of which could in any way be reconciled with his bid to become this year's Mr. City Cop. Although that was no longer so all-fire important, he was quick to add. His darling Lili was now his top priority, and he was prepared to dedicate himself to me exclusively and to respect my needs and boundaries.

These admittedly beautiful sentiments, music to the ears of any woman who still cherishes the slimmest belief in a love already given up for lost, and in the malleability of even the dumbest schmuck, and who is unwilling to hold it against him that he hasn't the faintest idea just how gifted her precious offspring is and who has already gotten powerfully tipsy on a single glass of schnapps; these admittedly beautiful sentiments of his were, however, peppered with concepts that bore a suspicious likeness to those contained in the self-help bestseller to be found in our john. But maybe this New Freddie who sat before me had a naturally psychological vein, finally discovered now thanks to the pain of his near loss. Perhaps he had already enrolled for Hebrew courses, the better to delve into my Jewish soul. That would have been a mistake, however. I only paid attention at Sunday school when our teacher, the adorable Duwidl Neumann, had us build *chanukkiyot* out of nut shells. Hebrew was and remains all Greek to me. But what about Yiddish, closer to home? Wouldn't the Abrahams on the ground floor be amazed to see me, deep in discussion with my *frummer* Freddie, hastening to the next Jewish Community Center for our lessons in Yiddish! I smiled dreamily.

Freddie dug around in his leather jacket, drew a little package out of his pocket, and had me unwrap it. I discovered, to my surprise, a truly pretty ring with little colored stones. Freddie put it on my finger, declaring, 'To a wonderful friendship—and, who knows, to forever after.' I didn't protest. I have never been able to understand those women in books and movies who throw jewels away just because of some allegedly false note in the guy's pitch. Mama would have been proud of me, even if she might also have found the stone a bit measly. As I did myself.

Back at the dwarves' cottage, Freddie drew me tenderly down into the grass and kissed me passionately. I giggled nervously at first and put up just the slightest show of resistance. But it was only for form's sake. And Freddie showed off his whole repertoire: in, out, now full of feeling, now like a bull, and, as the culmination, a bit of tongue work, while I lay on my back and kept a lookout for the man in the moon, not forgetting to groan lustily every now and again. There wasn't the slightest sign of that grubby goy in sloppy pajamas and cheesy slippers with whom I had been sharing my life for the last six months.

It wasn't until the next day that he showed his face again. A growl came from the bedroom. 'Darling, where are you?' Freddie was awake. I had been going at it hammer and tongs for two hours: cassettes, sheets of paper, jotted observations were all piled up on the table. My Notebook hummed softly. I smiled and waved dismissively as Freddie, his track pants below his navel, proposed a lavish breakfast. He scuffled off in his father's plastic beach sandals, turned up the radio in the kitchen nook to full volume (a local folk music channel), and started banging pots and pans around. Well, it was his castle, after all. I donned my headphones and attended to Stella's voice, hitting the keys industriously.

By now it was ten o'clock, time to shower and get dressed. Then I wanted to suggest a stroll, in order to begin sounding Freddie out. I felt exhilarated as I got up from my work and made for the bathroom. I was not only Lili of the Mossad, I was Mata Hari; a little spine-tingling espionage, a nice dose of sex: what more could a Chutzpah Lady ask for! Still vigorously toweling my hair, I returned from the shower to my workplace.

'It is precisely those endowed with mini-Johnsons, those who have the least to show for themselves, who are the most interested in The Longest Running Lie of All Times: it doesn't matter how long it is; all that matters is what you do with it. And it is precisely the measliest schmucks who are also the most dedicated critics of the female form.' Surely I had written that, and not Freddie, who was seated at my Notebook, scrolling plain as day through 'The Manhunt, or The Schmucks,' and reading aloud from it all the while. What's more, he had put on the headphones and was listening to Stella's report.

'It's high time masculine misbehavior was unmasked once and for all: their continual surveillance of us women, for example,' I pronounced rapid-fire from the bedroom threshold, setting my arms akimbo and thrusting out my torso. This I called my Resolute Rebbetzin posture, and it had always made a great impression on Bernie. But Freddie was a goy. They weren't afraid of their little vicar's wives; they were pale imitations of a real rebbetzin, who could strike fear into the heart of even a miracle-working rabbi. Freddie just kept gazing, unperturbed in his curiosity, at my Notebook screen.

'Wait a minute, that was Carlo and Stella. What the hell are they doing in there?' He gestured sharply at the recorder. 'Am I along for the ride in your "Manhunt" too, by any chance? If you start spreading false rumors, you'll hurt my chances of being elected Mr. City Cop!' It wouldn't have surprised me if he had wanted to run a little Gestapo interrogation, here at this wobbly table, with the lamplight shining mercilessly in my face.

'Calm down, Freddie, we're not at the precinct. Didn't you promise to respect my boundaries? Well, there's no point making a promise like that if you're going to be sticking your nose into my work all the time. When this humorous diary is finished, those concerned will be allowed to read it, and to their own advantage. Now that I've lost my job, you know, I have to keep my hand in somehow; or do you want me to apply for a job at the 'Fine and Shine' kosher bakery and spend the rest of my life baking pletzels?'

Freddie looked pensive. 'Well, all right; if it remains an internal affair, for the development of your writing skills, well, why not? And,' he added with alacrity, 'I don't think you'd feel at home in that bakery anyhow.' Mr. City Cop with a Hebrew baker's apprentice, who earned a pittance and had to feed her husband stale cinnamon buns at the end of the day, before putting up her varicose-veined legs with a sigh; that's not how he had imagined his life with me! Freddie, the passionate plate-licker, 'that *telerleker*,' as Mama was wont to call *shnorrers*; he wanted cake and cash and a regular *shabbas* fuck.

So Freddie slinked off to his unfinished upper story and started drilling. During his rare breaks, the yodlers on his radio station would penetrate clear through my earphones, around which I had wrapped a red-checked napkin. Slowly but surely, however, I was starting to boil over.

'*Cholerabsheftchoroba*, quiet down, goddamn it; what is this, a goddamned construction site?'

Freddie appeared upside down in the window. 'Sorry, darling, but I promised father I would fix up a few things around here; otherwise he would never have let us come. But fine; if you don't like it, I'll stop drilling. I'm not as inflexible as you are.' It became delightfully quiet. The birds sang. For five minutes. Then I heard Freddie outside. Hasso barked enthusiastically as a ladder was set up against the house and Freddie wheezed his way up, pushing his giant box ahead of him. There were footsteps over the roof, a screwdriver whizzed by, inches away from my head where I had long since stuck it out the window, and landed straight in the Lord Jesus' crown of thorns. And just who do you think would get the blame for that? I ran out of the house and looked up. Freddie was installing a giagntic satellite dish. I tapped my forehead. 'Schmucks.' At least Freddie would be busy for a while and not bothering me at my work, I thought. Wrong.

For, at that, Freddie climbed down from the roof, trampled into the house, and stuck the cable for the satellite dish into the socket. There was a spark and a hiss, and the computer went down with a '*wahahammm*.' Short circuit; everything had blown. Me too. I had done enough research. I just hadn't backed it up enough, unfortunately. While Freddie clambered up on the roof again with a curse, I packed my things and whistled for Hasso. My mission here was accomplished. I watched through the rear view mirror as Freddie hopped up and down on the roof and waved his arms while I drove off. This time, of course, I kept my eyes wide open on the way out.

I was still boiling when I got home. It was late and I was exhausted, but I was too wound up to sleep and decided to write up a draft of my article. What with the data I had garnered over the weekend on Freddie-putz, it would make for a fascinating study: Professor Lustenberger, the pious lecher; Constable Carlo, the willie-waggler; Editor-in-Chief Ronald, the menopausal monster; and Freddie, the pain in the ass. The stupid thing was that we had no proof of any of their misdeeds. Lusty Lustenberger, the only real criminal, would deny everything, and who cared about three old Jewish bags anyway and their problems with some completely normal goys? Well, all right, two goys and a half-goy; Ronald had a Jewish parent, after all. But he was dumb enough to be a full goy all the same.

At most, the *Jewish Gazette* would be interested in our research, provided there was nothing more exciting to print; but I had heard that it paid with coupons for 'Mammeleh's Mitzvah,' the highly questionable kosher section of a downtown discount chain. The *gefilte* fish were rumored to be a cardboard catastrophe. No sensible Jewish woman would ever drag anything home from a place like that: it was only the urban trendies who found such wretched kosher fare *très chic*, something to show off to their friends.

Besides, the *Gazette* was extremely conservative, and it would censor anything that smelled even faintly of sex. No, I wanted to publish in a big paper, so I needed to scare up some dirt on the Professor, for which I would simply need the help of Manu von Hohenfels, my therapist. This was exactly what I understood by 'concrete reparations.' And that was exactly how I was going to rub it under her nose, that archaristocratic but exceptionally cowardly Aryan. In the meantime I had more than enough on my plate, what with writing up my recent fiasco with Freddie.

Don't ask me why it took me so long, but during a break from writing I entered the keyword 'Mr. City Cop Elections' into my search engine. Freddie might have already babbled enough about the event, but a few more embarrassing details could never hurt in my characterization. And I found more than enough.

As a candidate, Freddie had been given the opportunity to set up his own homepage, which was accessible by means of the link 'Our Upstanding Candidates.' First there appeared, big and bold, the logo of a certain unspeakable group, the 'Swiss Peasants' Party,' and then, equally big and bold, the following statement: 'We sponsor the right candidates, so that our city will become and remain clean.' Then there came a blast of marching music, what else. Finally, Freddie's photo appeared, in which he could be seen grinning like a half-wit and posing in the borrowed uniform of the city's antiterror unit. 'Freddie Schweizer, a straight and narrow citizen with a good disposition,' it read, and there followed his demands: 'Our City Belongs to Its Natives!' 'Better *Röschti* than Red!' *(Please try Freddie's mini-Röschti! Click on the Schweizer recipe link!)* 'Down with Nefarious and Unpatriotic Miscegenation!' 'Sex, Fine, But Keep It Clean!'

I clicked on a little icon in the shape of a hand grenade and found myself staring at pictures of Freddie with a whole arsenal of weapons, placing his combat boot on the neck of a measly little suspect, and, as the *coup de grâce*, posing with me and Bernie, over the legend: 'Constable Freddie Schweizer with his fiancée, Liliane, and her son, Bernhard, both of Jewish descent, whom he rescued from social disaster and pressed to his generous Christian heart.' I could see on a little counter that eleven potential voters had already received this bit of news. And probably tried out the recipe, too. Which was, in fact, as I determined, a recipe Freddie had stolen from Mama's collection, one that had originally been for *latkes* and had been handed down by my grandmother, Helene Brom. Mini-Röschti! Mama would have given him one with her Golda Meir handbag for that.

So that's what my ex was. I wanted to show the printout to Bernie and then evaluate it for my research. It was too late now to wish it away: Freddie was more than just a pain in the ass. He who would have nailed me and my precious Bernie to the cross if it had made him rich and famous. He was no better than a rotten anti-Semite.

Someone opened the door. Had Bernie slipped into the house earlier without my noticing it? Was my precious boy hungry, perhaps, and had he had to slip by the Abraham *mishpocheh* with his McDonald's bag, to the sound of their compassionate sighing because his lazy *Mammeh* hadn't cooked for him? Well, I'd soon make him a nice hot chocolate; that would be better for him than showing him Freddie's garbage; little Bernie was sensitive, after all. I hoped he hadn't been out getting some little *shikseh* pregnant at the party while I was too busy with that chowderhead to keep an eye on him. As far as I knew, there hadn't been any nice Jewish girls invited.

I removed the headphones and my glasses and looked up—straight into Freddie's green eyes.

'What do you mean barging in here!' I exclaimed. 'You're behaving like the Gestapo!'

'I kept a key,' came his laconic response. Freddie's eyes narrowed to slits and metamorphosed from an injured sea green to a poisonous emerald.

'So that's what I am to you, some imbecile you can just leave stranded in the middle of the mountains. And then, Madame, sit yourself down at home as pretty as you please, with my precious ring on your finger, to do a little writing!'

'You were so all-fire keen for me to come along, what did you expect from me? That I would melt into a puddle and think all that garbage was peachy, you slimy pain in the ass, you good-for-nothing, you nebbish, you militant anti- . . . .' Just in the nick of time I realized that I shouldn't fire off all my powder at once but keep some of it dry and in stock.

Freddie wasn't listening to me anyway. 'How do you think I'll look to Carlo now? He thinks we're having a whole revivalization of our love or whatever the hell it's called, and he's probably been blabbing about it all over. Can you imagine how they'll all laugh themselves sick over me at the station?'

'It was you who told them you'd win me back in the first place!'

'You obviously didn't mind it one bit, you horny little Jewish slut!'

'Is that right?' I answered, with deliberate indifference, although I was steaming inside. 'I can't remember any longer, as a matter of fact; I have more important things to do at the moment, as you should be able to see. And by the way, give me back my key!'

As quick as a wink, Freddie had snatched the backup diskette out of my computer.

'Confiscated! Lili, you should really be thinking about your stu-

pid behavior, rather than working away nonstop on this old non-
sense that nobody cares about.' And which he would also not be
able to read, alas: the diskette he had confiscated was blank. Once
again I hadn't yet got around to saving anything on it. On the other
hand, despite his being a chowderhead, he had picked up enough
of what we had to say about him and his colleagues.

I might have been rid of Freddie, but we still had a problem: not
even the Jewish press would print my story. But wait. The Professor's photos! How could I have forgotten?

They were the key to my new brilliant career, which would begin
as soon as they were published in a major paper. With the dirty
pictures in hand, there was no need for us to get any closer to that
horror of a Professor Lustenberger. Thanks to the photos, which he
had shot of his unsuspecting former assistants, there would be a
general run on my report. I had to get to Manu, who had herself
been among the Professor's unwitting subjects. She had surely not
yet discovered the pictures, that cool and worthy Nordic lady; she
had never had much imagination. I would have to help her look. Or,
what was worse, she had already found them and was therefore in
the greatest danger, since she would not fail to wave them indig-
nantly under her boss's nose. In which case our evidence was lost
forever, since it was rumored that he had political ambitions and
was himself being wooed by the 'Swiss Peasants' Party.' So he had
everything to lose and would consequently do anything it took to
prevent their coming to light.

After a moment's hesitation I whistled for Hasso. He sprang up
happily as I was calling a cab. That would mean less of a commitment than taking my car and hunting for a parking place in front of
the Institute for Marriage and Family.

'Please wait; it'll take a while but I'll be back, and it'll be worth
it,' I instructed the driver as we drew up to the back entrance. When
the Professor had kidnapped me, I had noticed that the door on this
side was not locked, since the delivery service had used it early in
the morning. And, thank God, it was in fact open, with a stack of
cartons ready for pick up inside the entryway. With Hasso in my
wake I slipped up the stairs to the second floor. It was strange, but
the door to Manu's suite was also only ajar. Maybe she was poring
over some of her psycho lit and had forgotten the time. And most
probably the hunt for the photos, too.

'Hello, Manu, it's me, Lili,' I called out softly. Hasso whimpered. I looked into the waiting room: nobody there. The kitchen was also dark. I knocked on Manu's bedroom door, opened it gently, and saw an empty, slept-in bed. Manu could only be in her therapy room. I pushed the door open and heard myself screaming as I beheld my therapist hanging in the macramé nets by her window. Manu von Hohenfels's face was blue, the tip of her tongue protruded from her mouth, her lips were waxen, her long blond hair was loose and fell like a saint's aura around her head, and her feet, in their Black Forest health shoes, dangled above the ladder she had set up. To hang herself!

I ran for the corridor, leaving Hasso to bark at the suspended corpse. What a tactless beast. Some police dog! I hesitated a moment outside the apartment door. Should I run down to the taxi? Have the driver call the police? But what if Freddie were to roll up with his buddy Carlo? No, I would alert the Professor first. After all, he was Manu's boss. And responsible for the mess she was in.

I ran up and rattled on the door. 'Open up immediately, Manu is dead!' The light went on and a woman in curlers, obviously his wife, Klothilde, peered out sternly. Before she could say anything, I gasped, 'Get the Professor at once; Miss von Hohenfels has hanged herself in her macramé curtains!'

'Good lord, how unappetizing! But the girl was looking rather wild recently. I'm sure it was because. . . .'

'Exactly,' I snapped, 'because. . . .'

'What's going on here? And what do you mean by barging in here at this hour and harassing us!' Lustenberger had appeared, clad in a heavy silk dressing gown, and shoved Klothilde aside.

'Manu! Manu is dead, she's hanged herself in her macramé. Come on, we've got to get her down and call the police.' Tears were running down my cheeks. From below came barking, at first hectic, then gradually subsiding.

'Don't you know that dogs, peddlers, and gypsies are forbidden in this building?' Klothilde's tone was sharp.

'And Jewish women, too, probably, but you're not getting rid of me, you and your whole murderous *goyishe mishpocheh*,' I screamed in her face.

'Hold on. What in hell are you babbling about? You wait here; I'm going down alone. People like you are known to suffer from delusions and persecution complexes. Klothilde, this is none of your concern; she's a drug user, no doubt, or an illegal asylum seeker. Miss von Hohenfels was used to treating such asocial elements. And as for you, you wait right here at the door!'

The Professor steered his wife roughly back into the apartment as she gazed by turns in outrage at me and admiration at her husband and locked the door from the outside. I leaned against the wall. It really was better to wait here. It would have been too much to look into Manu's face again. Particularly since I was partly to blame for her death. The poor thing had simply had nowhere else to turn, threatened on all sides and forced into a corner. I sobbed quietly.

At least ten minutes passed. No cry of horror, no sound at all was to be heard. Then with a flash I thought of Hasso: surely he was keeping the Professor away from the corpse, and I would have to go down again after all. I crept down on tiptoe, which was ridiculous, and yet I had a dreadfully uncanny feeling.

'Hasso, where are you?' I called into the apartment. 'Here boy!'

'Hasso? Who the devil is that?' The Professor was standing in the corridor and staring at me angrily. 'There's no Hasso here, and no dead Miss von Hohenfels either. You get yourself home, and if I see you here again, I'll report you to the police.'

I was speechless, me, the chochmah. I ran into the therapy room, steeling myself for Manu's ghastly appearance. The macramé net swung gently in the draft, empty, and the stepladder stood, folded neatly against the bookcase, in its usual place.

'You've gotten rid of her, you murderer,' I screamed. 'She didn't hang herself at all; you killed her because she discovered the photos, and I must have surprised you before you could get her out of here. And now you've managed to do precisely that, while I was waiting upstairs!' I would have gladly torn open all the cupboards, looked under Manu's bed, but I didn't dare; I couldn't have faced Manu glassily staring down the dust monsters. Especially now that I no longer had a therapist to help me deal with it.

'Hasso! Seek, boy, seek,' I commanded. Not a sound. No dog.

The Professor's face became a murderous grimace as I continued to call, louder and louder. He made for me. Oy vey, now I was in for it! Why did I always have to get mixed up in everything? Let the goys beat each other to death! I turned on my heel, ran out of the apartment, down the stairs, and out the back entrance. Thank God the taxi was still there. And there was Hasso, running toward me from the street, happily wagging his tail.

'A hue and cry like in a synagogue,' muttered the driver. I wondered for a moment whether I should tell him everything so he could call the police. But what if I really did get Freddie and Carlo? I suspected that would mean jail this time for sure, or the loony bin. All the Professor had to do was call me a nutcase and a public nuisance; and, as I knew well, once you were in, you didn't get out that easily. Which would surely please Freddie.

'This is the Christian Institute for Marriage and Family, for your information. Drive us back; my friend didn't need her dog today.' With great dignity, I leashed Hasso and shoved him into the car.

We passed the city's proud memorial to one of its medieval mayors, the one who had had all the local Jews eliminated. He would not have been pleased to know that a decent Protestant had just been murdered in his lovely town and that I was still alive.

Finally we turned into my street. The driver got a good tip, for which he did not thank me.

'Too many crazies in this town,' he mumbled as he drove off. After he had brushed off the dog hairs, he would go on break. And he would vote for the 'Swiss Peasants' Party' at the next elections. His colleagues had told him they were going to get the city calmed down at last.

Miriam Cahn

Miriam Cahn was born in 1949 in Basel. She studied graphic arts in Basel and Paris and has received prizes and stipends from the cities of Berlin, Geneva, London, and Frankfurt, as well as the Käthe Kollwitz Prize of the Akademie der Künste in Berlin. She has shown her work at galleries across Switzerland and in Austria, France, Germany, England, Holland, and Bosnia, among other places. Cahn has also published in *Lettre Internationale* and *du* magazine and has designed many catalogs for museums throughout Europe. 'WHAT REGARDS ME' unites several of Cahn's regular themes, including the role of sex and gender in art and the plight of refugees in the 'postwar' world. Mixing memories of her own life as a Swiss Jew between Basel and Berlin with visions of soldiers in Sarajevo, on the Persian Gulf, and fighting the Spanish Civil War, Cahn develops a series of meditations on *Guernica* and on the role of Picasso in her artistic coming-to-consciousness that becomes a commentary not only on the weary, war-filled progress of our century, but also on being a female artist with primarily male role models. The text was part of a performance at the Picasso exhibit at Vienna's House of Twentieth-Century Art in 1994. The text, rattled off agitatedly by Cahn, was interrupted by 'Short Pieces,' in which the artist clattered, bowed, and ground away on a wooden object.

Miriam Cahn

soldiers
(men)
little carts
suitcases
water buckets
wood
sarajevo
weepers
women
picasso

WHAT REGARDS ME

for years i've seen soldiers soldiers watching me from out of the
television first in the gulf war much earlier still before i had a
television i saw fewer soldiers above all in the newspaper but above
all since i got a television soldiers watch me from out of the television and the most conspicuous of all were the soldiers in the
falklands war warriors you could hardly see more conspicuous still
were the soldiers in the gulf war warriors you could hardly see like
in a promotional film because there was a prohibition against it a
prohibition against showing soldiers at work or only at work when
they were doing their work at machines at electronic machines that
they didn't show doing the work of killing but rather as they were
pushing a button as they were steering giant machines yet you
didn't see the result although the camera was mounted on the
projectile you saw the result only from the projectile's point of view
that is only from the machine's eye view not from the point of view
of the person of the soldier who of course was not only blowing up
buildings with this projectile but persons too.

actually I first saw soldiers consciously or soldiers watched me
from out of the television when this yugoslavian war broke out
when young rambos soldiers who look like sylvester stallone from
the film were proudly declaring that they got rewards if from the
ring of hills around sarajevo from the mountains of sarajevo they
shot at people in sarajevo and that the smaller the target to be shot
the higher the higher the reward a child a dog a cat even got you a
bigger reward than a grown person.

these rambos watched me from out of my television exactly like in a
film a rambo or a schwarzenegger or a terminator not only the
expression on these young faces was interesting but rather it was
men after all it was men after all it was men after all but rather the
insignias that is the clothing that set these rambo-types apart the
sweat-rag the sportily knotted handkerchief around the head this
head with a headband that today sets the head of a soldier apart for
me of a white soldier of a western soldier or a middle-european
soldier a soldier a man who is running absolutely wild.

these soldiers are for me today at the moment now one of the
images of a man one of the images that regard me and that I as
artist regard me as artist that I as artist that i try to represent that i
try that I try to represent.

these soldiers watched me as i was looking at guernica conveyed
carried transported to madrid secured behind bulletproof glass
framed by soldiers two to the right and left of guernica they were
probably two policemen from the guardia civil but i think they have
the same outfits as the fascist militia picasso so hated i was looking
at guernica the horse the electric light bulb the light bulb and the
screaming women the gray of the picture the black and white of the
picture and these two soldiers were staring back into the room in
their function as overseers they were staring at the spectators both
men and women who were in their turn staring at the picture that
had in the end a political purpose insofar as picasso had painted it
because the city of guernica had been bombed by fascists with the
help of the national socialists but the two soldiers who were watching over this picture the condition for whose return for whose
return picasso had made the cessation of fascism in spain the condition and the picture returned to spain after his death that's what i
think anyway after the death of franco so these two young soldiers

were staring at me the two men still in the old uniform of the
guardia civil and that made for an absurd situation.

i saw guernica when it was still at the museum of modern art it was
just hanging there just like that there it hung there just as it was a
picture that i actually it was a picture on which i the lightbulb and
the horse the horse reminds me that i only ever drew horses when
i was young they were my favorite subject it was a picture that
showed something i don't believe you can show that is weeping
women it was a picture that reminded me that the horse was my
favorite animal when i was young like for so many young girls the
horse that i really rode like for so many young girls the horse that i
would rather stroke touch currycomb than ride and above all i
would rather gaze at it the horse was a riddle to me the horse was
uncanny and when i see this lightbulb with this horse on the guernica picture it is uncannier still.

as a child i planned an entire car i planned it all in my head and
carried it out the next day in cardboard it was really more of a cart
made of tape and cardboard it actually got made which was rare
since already as a child i was very quick and impatient this cart was
my invention it was my own invention because the previous night
before going to sleep i thought down to the last detail how you had
to build such a cart so that it really looked like a cart on television
during this yugoslavian war they regard me from the television
from the television on television i see carts vehicles of all kinds the
water buckets wood suitcases booty and above all necessities they
are carrying the people in sarajevo or in other occupied places that
they have to drag since there are no usable means of transport any
longer because there is hardly anything there anymore i often watch
it every evening every evening i see these carts have to think of that
cart the one i invented and that actually wasn't really invented at all
but rather a cart a thing with wheels a vehicle is a survival a survival
object just like the water bucket is a survival object a modern survival object made of plastic which when i see it in the shop i find
pretty ugly and at the same time i have by now developed a love for it
it is a survival object just as remarkably wood is a survival object
although i know of course that with wood one can heat i never
made the connection that a whole city cuts down its trees because
there is no other fuel to hand because the fuel the wood is still only

wood not a tree in the garden a tree on the avenue i lived in an avenue every time i went outdoors there were these trees at the back the gardens sounds more idyllic than it was these trees these trees when i came back from berlin in january february in that too early spring basel farther south than berlin in that early spring these trees made me draw plants in the spring spring plants in the summer summer plants in the autumn autumn plants in the winter kneeling on the ground cowering blindly or rather with closed eyes i felt an inclination to these plants and i drew these plants with closed eyes in chalk.

during this period the exhibit 'picasso braque' was in basel the period of these two painters' collaboration braque painted drew many many trees plants picasso almost none it seems perhaps it's not true he seems to know fewer plants he knows fewer plants no feeling for plants or not much but the few plants the few trees in this exhibit overwhelmed me the few plants the few trees were the essence of plant were plant-essential were tree-essential were through his way of painting far more plantlike than through the rather intellectual way braque had with the brush quickly bored picasso stopped with plants again picasso was always for me someone who drew animals and people above all painted them or however he did animals and persons animals and women animals and women and men animals women men animals women men and perhaps animals women men children in a shared space from the bed over his atelier arena all the way to the sea and because when i was a child as many children do logically enough i liked animals best i liked the animals of picasso best too although i found them uncanny but they corresponded to my observations in the zoo next to where we lived and where if you looked carefully enough the animals looked back the animals were actually very uncanny above all the hyena whose smell sometimes penetrated all the way to our house the hyena had this lopsided gait when it walked the owl the white owl the snow owl which lived in a little old house the owl before which i would stand for long moments waiting until it finally turned its head opened its big eyes and looked at me as if it knew more than i did the owl scared me just the same way.

when i think of sarajevo i think of the luggage the suitcases not only of the cart I think too of these streams of refugees these streams of people that i saw especially at the beginning on television or in pictures strangely enough dragging old suitcases with them bundles as if they came from the second world war or i saw the second world war and although they are people like me although they are people like us here in basel or in zurich or in vienna strangely few of them were wearing these new backpacks that we all have after all those of us who live near mountains and sarajevo in the mountains too but rather they had again as if nothing else were possible when one was fleeing bundles old suitcases if they were lucky carts sleds bikes where they could load everything on if not they carry the strangest sacks then they carry sacks tied together and what they have on their heads too what they have for clothing but perhaps that i was looking in the wrong way is peculiar insofar as it was wool so-called old materials as if there had never been firms there like 'patagonia' or 'jack wolfskin' or 'the north face' as if there had never been such firms there producing that NASA-material we all need for the mountains or for sports and that the people in sarajevo tuzla and so on must certainly have needed when they played sports but perhaps these refugees were mostly farmers and poorer people who don't have these clothes which keep you warm in a practical fashion and which are above all easy wash-and-wear remarkable too the old backpacks and in any case it seemed as if the idea of a refugee meant people who had to flee suddenly and that the whole world over they must look the same whether in africa or in india or in china in tibet whether in vietnam or in south america and well now in europe again refugees look the same the whole world over bent over they drag themselves along the camera looks at their eyes their face and the face looks back in an empty exhausted way and looks in at me in my room.

to me sarajevo is the same to me sarajevo is another quality has another quality than the wars that preceded it i've always been preoccupied with wars naturally jewish perhaps also female and although entirely born in switzerland i grew up in the consciousness that there was this possibility that people start wars that people humans men above all suddenly out of the blue start wars start shooting at other people start bashing other people and the others perhaps in that case we have to flee the yugoslavian war and its sign sarajevo has this quality a new one a new quality has for me something new because it involves people who are like us it isn't so far away it is very near it is very near despite the fact that i have never been there it is very near it is too near although it seems cynical if things that are farther away wars that are farther away are less important but it is hypocritical to think untrue that there are no differences inexact it is a big difference whether a war takes place in europe or somewhere else despite the so-called global village it just isn't so that all the pictures that regard me from the television are becoming alike it just isn't so it is clear to me that pictures from somalia of those thin completely emaciated people that those pictures all the same despite their horror despite the dying people are further removed from me although they are electronically speaking as near as pictures from sarajevo.

i can imagine the same effect when the so-called civil war in spain began although there was no television and no electronics although there was no so-called global village it must have had a similar effect on intellectuals as this yugoslavian war must have for us intellectuals and politically minded people today it must have had it must have had as this yugoslavian war must have for us especially sarajevo as a symbol exactly as guernica was as a symbol of guilt of failure therefore the will to want to do something against it among the leaders as each and every one of us personally is able picasso was not a politician a political artist in the sense that he ideologically adopted illustrated indicted but he is a political artist in my sense because he is a very simple artist because he sees the things that are going on around him and paints them it's that simple exactly that simple and at the same time what one sees around one is of course so overwhelming is to its last detail so much that one develops the same speed as picasso who went every day into his studio and painted like a crazy man at top speed and drew that is the essence of drawing insane speed painted insanely fast sculpted insanely fast this was because he simply wanted to show what he saw around him and that was so overwhelming an everyday part of it was the information from his spain about atrocities in the so-called civil war no civil war rather a rehearsal of fascist thought of fascist thought and the military action of the fascists a rehearsal in which the nonfascist part the european part that was nonfascist failed miserably because it dismissed this rehearsal as a civil war i

can imagine that that war was a shock for many people that's why
so many found that they too had to act by going there and engaging
themselves in the brigades against the fascists and fighting others
who stayed home because they felt incapable of fighting like me for
example i would have stayed home but they still sought ways to
comment upon this horror this war or to represent it guernica
belongs for me in this camp as a commentary on this war no more
no less.

remarkable about guernica and not just guernica is picasso's attempt to draw or paint weeping women wailing shrieking weeping
women that is in fact weeping women it is these women who regard
me even today from the television still the women who weep today
are differently dressed they have a cloth over their heads when they
weep when they carry their son their husband their brother their relatives to the grave a cloth over their heads but these women's gestures are exactly the same as those of picasso's weeping women
except picasso's weeping women wear elegant little hats those man-
tilla things those embroidered spanish cloths with lace light cloths
lacy handkerchiefs they crumple with their fingers with their hands
so they are very elegantly dressed which you cannot say about the
women who regard me today from the television they are wrapped
in meager fabrics wrapped like peasants like muslims or just simply
like poor people while these spanish ladies are very elegant the little
hat is equal in value to the wailing and that astonished me it is the
weeping itself that picasso wanted to represent I think and still the
little hats are equally important it was important to picasso that the
little hat was as important as the hand and the little kerchief and the
eyes and the tears a passionate picture for weeping women of weeping women.

i saw these weeping women in the exhibit 'picasso after guernica' in
berlin during one of the climaxes of the war in yugoslavia everyday
pictures were displayed commented upon they looked at me from
the television torture concentration camps rape of women and girls
of women carrying their relatives to the grave who bore that expression of picasso's weeping women on their faces actually on the one
hand these pictures looked at me from the television on the other i
saw photographs in the newspapers that followed me around and
from which I then tried to create series by making drawn copies of

these photographs in part also from memory and part of this work
was my drawing of a postcard of these weeping women of picasso's
because i was sure that it was the precise counterpart of this situation of this european situation of this disgrace once again.

as a child i was always looking in books my parents had this book
'face of fame' with photographs of famous men and women there
were a few women but mostly men of course especially artists and
picasso there was a picture of picasso in which he wore a hat and
had turned up his coat collar you could see only his eyes of course
i wanted to become like all these people it's quite clear already at
that early age i wanted to be an artist of course i never dreamed
that there could be a difference between female and male artists i
wanted to be an artist i wanted like picasso i thought that was the
most wonderful the greatest this life every day to go regularly into
the atelier to do something paint something build something as i
had planned the little cart the night before and the next day had
built it and i was very pleased with my little cart my mother was very
pleased with my little cart everyone was always very pleased when i
did something like this and so i wanted early on to be an artist like
picasso was because he looked so good in his striped t-shirts besides he lived in the south on the beach by the sea.

i got this information from photographs not from pictures from
photographs which i swallowed greedily i thought as an artist one
had to live this way picasso the ur-picture these photographs which
have such a merry aura because there are always women children
animals in them too a southern a beautiful life which i wanted to
live as an adult and even though throughout this period my models
were changing daily there endured these three picasso giacometti
munch munch the idol of my puberty this dismal mood these
youthful women this unspeakably fluent drama and above all the
shadows behind the subjects the sick and the dead lying in bed
screaming looking at me melting away on an LSD-trip giacometti
the region the bergell the mayor of the village in which we spent
each winter who had gone to school with giacometti i knew everything quite precisely and also see the look of that beautiful man
almost more beautiful than picasso i wanted to become like giacometti because he had an atelier in the mountains lived in the big
city and always every day he went over to his atelier and all of

these pieces of information were in turn confirmed by means of photographs these photographs regarded me through this regard i wanted to become like these men for a long time i did not know the difference between women and men i wished for every child that it would not have to make this distinction only when i was twenty-three or thereabouts did i really actually notice that i cannot become like picasso like giacometti like munch i will lead another life i will live another life as i have already lived otherwise up to this point because i am a woman and because women live another life than men.

this realization was a shock one however that never handicapped me on the contrary this anger became my motor my machine a new world opened up i was lucky in the seventies many women my age thought this way somewhat older female artists thought this way and acted worked in new media video performance thought worked like me with the body out of rage anger female body unknown as an instrument never used as an instrument an active seismograph working directly with the instrument of the body an absolute nov-elty new realizations my newland mixing with my old childish wis-dom becomes my own mingled mixed up that was what i wanted to do i wanted to work with my whole body move with space with time in space in time and at the same time not forget everything i had already done everything i had already wanted everything i had al-ready wanted to become everyone i had already wanted to be i wanted to become picasso i wanted to become myself i wanted to become picasso and myself i wanted to be as good as picasso i wanted to go every day like picasso into my atelier and paint draw build and still i knew that this old image of the artist is over dated classic with a house a wife children café discussions a visit to the brothel circumstances of life that i would never have nor would i want them no wife no whore no house no children rather some-thing new where the woman the artist the woman working acting is the middle point i myself i myself a working acting artist then i must also break with this mythos of the artist that i had so loved consign my past to history but i have seen what i have seen what regarded me i have seen.

Stina Werenfels

Stina Werenfels was born in 1964 in Basel. She studied pharmacology, French, and philosophy before working as a scriptwriter and journalist. She began to make short films at the Graduate School of Film and Television of the Tisch School of the Arts in New York. Back in Switzerland, she assisted Richard Dindo in the making of his documentary *Grüningers Fall* (1997), on the problems faced by Jews attempting to enter Switzerland during the Holocaust, and produced her own feature on the topic, the English-language comedy *Pastry, Pain & Politics* (1998), here very slightly abbreviated. In the characters of the American tourists Fritz and Ellen Weintraub and the Palestinian nurse Hayat Khalili, Werenfels skillfully intertwines Jewish past and Jewish present to make some succinct remarks on the politics of asylum. She has since contributed the episode 'Making of a Jew' to the group documentary *ID Swiss* (1999), a study of Swiss multiculturalism. Werenfels's contribution, among the disparate and diverse accounts of other hybridities in that collectively directed film, both reaffirms the importance of Jewishness for the history of Swiss heterogeneity and challenges the assumed pre-eminence of that particular ethnicity, an assumption based upon its link to the Holocaust, the sheer volume of whose archival documentation threatens to block out all other attempts at historical reconstruction.

Stina Werenfels

Pastry, Pain & Politics

Title Sequence – Exterior Day

A Swissair plane floating over the Alps. We hear the announcement of the flight attendant.

FLIGHT ATTENDANT (*off*): Ladies and Gentlemen. We will be landing in Zurich in a couple of minutes. Please put your seat back into an upright position and make sure your seatbelt is fastened. The weather in Zurich is clear with temperatures rising above 30 degrees Celsius. Please note that for customs procedures. . . .

ELLEN (*off*): Fritzleben! Where is my passport? I can't find my passport.

WEINTRAUB (*off*): I have it, I have it. I have both of them. Relax!

ELLEN (*off*): Why did you take it? I always have to have it. You know that.

WEINTRAUB (*off*): Okay, all right! But relax now, Chaiele.

1. Hotel Veranda – Exterior Day

A panorama of high mountains in the background. In the foreground on a veranda, flocks of elderly guests around coffee tables, protected from the sun by hats and umbrellas. It's hard to find any free seats. At one table FRITZ WEINTRAUB *and his wife* ELLEN, *both in their seventies. Two seats at their table are not taken. Fritz is apparently suffering from the heat whereas Ellen, in spite of the temperature, is wearing long sleeves. She doesn't look happy. They are having tea.*

WEINTRAUB: Mmh, this is air you can breathe! Nu? (*To Ellen*) Just think of New York!

Ellen remains silent. On the table, we see her video camera. At the far end of the veranda, OTTO *and* LOUISE VON ZITZEWITZ, *a German couple, are searching for seats.*

LOUISE (*in German staccato*): Ach ist das aber voll, Otto! [Oh, it's so crowded, Otto!]

WEINTRAUB: This is what Paradise is about!

LOUISE (*steering them toward the Weintraubs's table*): Aber, nein, da! Guck, Otto! [But no, look there, Otto!]

WEINTRAUB: Nu? Chaiele, what are you fussing again? After all, I didn't shlep you to Germany.

LOUISE (*behind Ellen*): Ist hier noch frei? [Are these seats taken?]

Ellen turns around, startled, as Fritz makes an inviting sign. Otto and Louise sit down. Ellen moves her camera closer. Louise and Otto greet Fritz and Ellen with a polite smile. Meanwhile, a WAITER *sets down an enormous piece of Black Forest cake in front of the Weintraubs.*

OTTO (*to waiter*): Zwei Stück vom selben. [Two of the same.] (*Introducing himself and Louise*) Zitzewitz.

LOUISE: Von Zitzewitz.

WEINTRAUB (*about to dig into his cake*): Oh, forgive me. Weintraub. Ellen and Fritz. We are the Weintraubs.

OTTO: Nice to meet you.

ELLEN: Mein Gott Fritz, you can't eat that.

Ellen pulls the cake away from Weintraub. As she reaches out for the plate, her sleeve moves up. We catch a glimpse of a tattooed number.

WEINTRAUB: Why?

ELLEN: Did you take your pills?

WEINTRAUB (*munching*): Ah, I don't need any pills! Where are my pills?

Weintraub is apparently suffering from shortness of breath. He fusses around to find his pills. Otto and Louise are watching them.

LOUISE (*smiles*): Schmeckt's nicht? [You don't like it?]

Ellen gives her a suspicious look.

WEINTRAUB: It's good, it's terrific.

The Zitzewitzes laugh as they get their cake. Otto tastes his piece.

OTTO (*German accent*): I think the original Schwarzwälder we only get in Germany. It has something—it's—Louise! What is it?

WEINTRAUB: No. Yours is too rich, too sweet. You people make it too heavy. You Germans cook too thick. It's like your highways: there's so many of them. All day long Ein-fart with Aus-fart: Auto-ban! Too much. Like you people can't have a little war. It's gonna be total war: World War! (*Otto and Louise look up irritatedly.*) You can't just get rid of one Jew, you gotta kill them all! (*Otto and Louise have stopped chewing.*) But Swiss pastry is perfect, just like the country. It's perfectly balanced out! It works beautifully. That's why there's never a war!

ELLEN (*to herself*): Yes, bring the gold in, keep the Jews out.

WEINTRAUB: My wife always wants to go to Israel. I say, Chaiele, we're going, but first we gonna stop over in Switzerland. See Switzerland and die! That's the ticket, right?

LOUISE: Oh, Israel! We had a wonderful time there, didn't we, Otto?

Ellen gives Louise a scrutinizing look.

WEINTRAUB: No, no, too hot. And too many Arabs.

The waiter pushes the dessert trolley by.

WEINTRAUB (*pointing at a cake with whipped cream on top*): Ah, the Matterhorn! That's my favorite. Waiter, bring it to me.

OTTO: Aren't there Arabs in the States?

WEINTRAUB: Well, there's no Arabs in Switzerland! And the heat is bad for me. My heart can't stand it. Personally, I think my wife is trying to kill me!

The waiter arrives with the Matterhorn dessert.

ELLEN (off): Fritzleben, this is going to kill you!

WEINTRAUB (breathes heavily): Don't be silly, Chaiele.

ELLEN: Fritzleben, are you all right?

We hear the sounds of falling dishes and see the waiter's startled face. The Zitzewitzes jump up to help.

2. Hospital Room – Interior Night

WIPE *of a trolley carrying hospital utensils, revealing Ellen in a corner of a hospital room with two beds. In the left bed is* KURZ, *a man in his fifties, all wired up and asleep. To his right is Weintraub, breathing heavily. He's taped to several infusions. Ellen observes the scene very worriedly. A beautiful dark-haired nurse,* HAYAT, *stands with the trolley beside his bed and takes notes.*

WEINTRAUB: Yeah, yeah. Measles, chicken pox, hernia. I've seen them all! You actually should congratulate me I made it this far.

HAYAT (foreign accent): Glasses?

WEINTRAUB: Chaiele, where are my glasses? Give me my glasses! I wanna see her face.

Ellen gets his glasses out of her purse and hands them to Hayat, smiling worriedly. Hayat smiles back. Then she hands the glasses to Weintraub. Weintraub only now sees how worried Ellen looks.

WEINTRAUB: Chaiele, don't worry, the doctors are famous here. Didn't Onassis die in a Swiss hospital?

ELLEN (starts sobbing): No, that was in Paris.

Otto and Louise stick their heads through the door.

LOUISE: Is there anything else we can do?

Hayat gives her a sign to leave.

LOUISE: Das tut uns ja so leid, Frau Weintraub. [We are so sorry, Mrs. Weintraub.]

They leave.

WEINTRAUB (takes a closer look at Hayat): Now look at this. Isn't this a beautiful face!

HAYAT: Dentures?

WEINTRAUB: Dentures, bypass, pacemaker. . . . I've got all the improvements! (Looks around curiously and now focuses on Kurz.) Hello? Hello! (He reaches for his cane and bangs on Kurz's bed.) Hello, what's your name?

Kurz wakes up, lifts his head, and looks at Weintraub in a gaze. He then turns around and falls asleep again. Hayat approaches Weintraub with a syringe. He looks at her.

WEINTRAUB: What's your name?

HAYAT: Hayat.

WEINTRAUB: Hayat! What does it mean?

HAYAT (feeling for his vein): Life.

WEINTRAUB: What language? (Looks at his arm.) Listen, you gotta go deep for my veins. They're really hidden down in there. But I tell you what. You're such a nice girl, I give you two extra tries. So? Where are you from?

HAYAT (finished with injection): I'm a Palestinian.

WEINTRAUB (pulling his arm away): That's nice. (Pause.) A Pale-what? Wait a minute. My god. Chaiele, give me a phone! Go get the manager! Didn't you hear?

ELLEN: Fritzleben, don't get excited. It's dangerous!

WEINTRAUB: She's the one that's dangerous! Will you go get someone!

HAYAT: I don't think your heart appreciates that kind of excitement.

WEINTRAUB: What excitement? I guarantee you, you're not going to give me this shot!

HAYAT (applying a bandage): I'm finished anyway. (Approaches Ellen.) This will put him to sleep. (Walks toward the door, turns around. To Ellen.) And tomorrow? Tell him to calm down.

Weintraub almost dozes off. Kurz turns around and their eyes meet. Weintraub is keeping his eyes open with great effort.

WEINTRAUB: Fritz Weintraub. Who are you?

KURZ (*in Swiss German*): Au! Mis Bei! [Ow! My leg!]

WEINTRAUB: Mister Misbeih, I'm sure glad you're here. Because should I wake up three o'clock in the morning and find out I'm dead, I want somebody to tell.

3. Hospital – Nurses' Wardrobe/Coffee Corner – Interior Day

Hayat opens her wardrobe cupboard. Its inner side shows a photograph of a large Palestinian family. She takes out a brand-new white apron and slips into it.

HEIDI (*off*): Morge. [Morning.]

HAYAT (*greeting Heidi, a tall red-haired nurse, who then leaves*): Morge. [Morning.]

4. Hospital Room – Interior Day

Hayat enters the room with two trays and puts them on Kurz's and Weintraub's tables. In a chair in the corner, Ellen has spent the night. Hayat visibly disapproves.

KURZ: Schwöschter, ich han' Hunger. [Nurse, I'm hungry.]

HAYAT: Das ist ein gutes Zeichen. [That's a good sign.] What about you, Mister Weintraub? (*Weintraub doesn't answer.*)

KURZ: Was, jetzt müemmer änglisch rede? [What? Now we have to speak English?]

WEINTRAUB (*waiting until Hayat has left the room: to Kurz*): Hello Mr. Misbeih, remember me? Fritz Weintraub.

KURZ (*eating breakfast, looking occasionally at Weintraub*): Sorry, ich kann kein englisch. [Sorry, I don't speak English.]

WEINTRAUB: I don't speak any German, but I'll give it a shot in Yiddish. (*Looks at his breakfast.*) Nu mir hobn noch a tug. Plitzm wert schwer ze kempfn. [So we've got another day ahead of us. Suddenly it's hard to struggle on.]

KURZ (*looking at him, munching*): Si, was reded Sie da für en Dialäkt? [Hey. What dialect do you speak?]

Hayat enters the room and delivers medication to each of the patients. Then she exits the room. Weintraub is following her with his eyes.

WEINTRAUB (*to Kurz*): Ich red nit met ihr. Ich gleb ihr nit. [I'm not talking to her. I don't trust her.]

Ellen has watched Hayat from her corner. She now jumps up and they examine the pills.

WEINTRAUB: I'm not taking them! What do you think?

ELLEN (*whispering*): I don't know. We'll ask the Professor.

WEINTRAUB: Ah, where's the damn Professor anyway!

HAYAT (*entering, to Ellen*): The Professor visits soon. You have to leave now.

ELLEN: I'm staying with my husband.

HAYAT: You are not allowed to stay.

They stare at each other. Then Hayat firmly steers Ellen out.

5. Hospital Hallway – Interior Day

Ellen sits in the hallway, her purse on her lap. A patient is rolled by from the OR. She gets up and walks up and down, passing some posters. She stops to look at one depicting the Alps.

6. Hospital – Nurses' Coffee Corner – Interior Day

Hayat pours water into her mint tea. A little cassette deck plays modern Arabic music. Hayat is smoking. HEIDI appears.

HEIDI: Du! Dä Chef isch scho da! [Hey, the boss is already here!]

Hayat hastily checks her face in the mirror, puts a strand of hair back into her bun, and dashes out of the room.

7. Hospital Room – Interior Day

Hayat slips into a room in which the PROFESSOR *and his entourage of assistants stand, gathered around Kurz's bed. The Professor turns to Weintraub, whispering to his assistants.*

WEINTRAUB: Weintraub, Fritz Weintraub. Hi.

The Professor reluctantly shakes Weintraub's hand and continues, his assistants hanging on his every word. Hayat notices Ellen entering the room and gives her a sign to leave.

ELLEN *(harshly)*: What's the matter?

Hayat gives her a sign to keep quiet.

WEINTRAUB: And this is— *(He looks around.)* Chaiele?! Where are you? Say hello to this topnotch Professor!

PROFESSOR *(shaking Ellen's hand disinterestedly)*: Nice to meet you. *(Swiss accent.)*

He wants to leave. Ellen stops him.

ELLEN *(off)*: Professor, was ist mit meinem Mann? Er wird doch wieder gesund? [Professor, what's wrong with my husband? He will get well again, won't he?]

PROFESSOR: Ähm, Frau. . . .

HAYAT *(whispering)*: Weintraub.

PROFESSOR: Er wird sich erholen, er muss aber noch eine Weile liegen, sein Herz— [He'll recover, but he's still got to rest for a while, his heart—]

WEINTRAUB: Okay doc, let's talk business; we've got a few problems here.

They all turn to Weintraub again. The Professor visibly disapproves of Weintraub. He walks with his entourage toward the door.

WEINTRAUB: Number one, we've got this terrorist nurse here. I want a nice Swiss one.

The Professor gives Hayat a sign to follow him. They all leave the room.

WEINTRAUB (*off*): Wait, I also need a TV in my room and a phone! I have to call my son!

8. Hallway – Interior Day

Hayat has forgotten to close the door properly. The Professor takes a look at Hayat's name tag.

PROFESSOR (*hissing*): Fräulein— (*Attempts to pronounce her name.*) Halten Sie mir bei der Chefvisite gefälligst die Familie vom Leibe! [Miss— Keep the family away from me during rounds!]

HAYAT: Professor, ich kann diesen Patienten nicht pflegen. [I can't take care of this patient.]

PROFESSOR (*barking*): Wieso nicht? [Why not?]

HAYAT: Er hasst mich—er ist ein Zionist. [He hates me—he's a Zionist.]

PROFESSOR: Wenn ich Juden behandle, können Sie das auch, Fräulein! [If I treat Jews, you can too.]

The Professor wants to walk off.

HAYAT: Khalili. Hayat Khalili.

PROFESSOR (*mockingly*): Auf meinem Pult liegt glaub' ich noch ein Papier, Fräulein. . . . Khalili! Müemmer nüd no euses Arbetsverhält-nis verlängere? Und ihri Ufenthaltsbewilligung lauft doch au in 2 Monet ab, oder? [There's a form on my desk, Miss Khalili. Am I right that you're still on probation? And that you need to renew your residence permit in 2 months?]

Hayat stares after the Professor walking down the hallway. Then she turns her head and notices Ellen, who's observed their argument through the crack in the door. Their eyes meet. Ellen closes the door.

9. Hospital Cafeteria – Interior Day

It's raining. Ellen and Louise at a table, Louise in a travel outfit. On the table we see two large tickets featuring a waterfall. Ellen chews forlornly on some bread.

ELLEN *(sniffing)*: And now? What are we? Stuck!

LOUISE: Eben! Ach Gottchen. Aber umso mehr! Nutzen sie die Gelegenheit doch aus! [Right. Oh, dear. But why not just take advantage of being here?] *(Pushes the tickets closer to Ellen.)*

LOUISE: Die Rheinfälle können Otto und ich sowieso nicht zurückgeben. Is' doch Schade, nich'? [And you know, the Rhinefalls, we can't give them back. What a shame!]

Ellen hesitates, then picks up one ticket and looks at it suspiciously.

ELLEN *(in thought)*: Rheinfälle. . . .

LOUISE *(insistently)*: Ja! Das wär' wie—ja, sagen wir die Niagarafälle bei Ihnen. Oder so ungefähr' jedenfalls. [That would be like— yes, let's say like your Niagara Falls!]

ELLEN *(looking at the bread)*: Die Semmeln hier kann man auch nicht essen. In Bielefeld bei— [You can't eat this bread here. In Bielefeld at—]

LOUISE: 'Knigge?'

ELLEN: Ja, 'Knigge!'

LOUISE: Gibt's immer noch! [It still exists!]

ELLEN *(considering again)*: Aber mein Mann. . . . [But my husband. . . .]

10. Hospital Room – Interior Evening

At Weintraub's bedside a phone has been installed. Hayat is neatly exchanging the sheets of Weintraub's bed without disturbing him. Weintraub is reading the paper. Kurz is dozing.

WEINTRAUB *(to Hayat)*: I don't like your boss!

HAYAT (*giving him a soft slap on his leg*): What?

WEINTRAUB (*obediently turning over*): Your boss!

HAYAT: The Professor?

WEINTRAUB: No, this Arafat!

Weintraub accidentally knocks a glass to the floor. Hayat bends to clean the mess. Weintraub mumbles an apology as he sees how she's cut herself.

WEINTRAUB: Oh, is this blood?

HAYAT: What did you expect, water?

The phone rings. Weintraub picks it up.

WEINTRAUB: Hello! Eliott? (*To Kurz.*) Mein zin. [My son.]

At the sink, Hayat throws away the broken glass. Louise and Ellen open the door. Louise carries a large bouquet of flowers and waves with them.

LOUISE (*German staccato*): Tach Herr Weintraub! [Hello Mister Weintraub!]

Kurz starts in his bed. Weintraub looks up.

WEINTRAUB (*into phone*): The stormtroopers are here. (*To Ellen.*) It's our son, it's Eliott.

ELLEN: Eliott!

Ellen grabs the receiver. Weintraub smiles meaningfully at Kurz.

LOUISE (*to Hayat*): Können wir dann noch 'ne Vase haben? [And could we have a vase?]

Hayat leaves the room. Louise approaches to hand over the flowers.

WEINTRAUB: Chaiele, he's won a prize. Ask him for what!

ELLEN (*into phone*): For what? The play about the nymphomaniac pastry maker!

WEINTRAUB (*grumpily*): Is she Jewish?

Louise hands the enormous bouquet to Weintraub.

ELLEN (*into phone*): Jewish? (*To Weintraub.*) Orthodox!

WEINTRAUB (*shouting from behind the flowers*): Thank God. Tell him to forget about his *verkackte* plays. Better he should give us some grandchildren!

Hayat enters with a vase.

ELLEN (*into phone*): Eliott, look! Someone invited me to see the Swiss Niagara Falls.

Ellen waves two tickets in the air. Weintraub looks at them.

WEINTRAUB: Why don't you wait until we get out of this joint. We'll do some traveling!

Hayat glances at the tickets and frees Weintraub from the flowers.

WEINTRAUB (*turning to Hayat*): You've seen it all, right?

HAYAT: No.

WEINTRAUB: What do you mean? You live here in Paradise and you haven't seen any of it?

HAYAT: I have no money to travel.

WEINTRAUB: Come on, you must make at least 150 bucks a day!

HAYAT: 120—francs.

WEINTRAUB: So? You only travel first class?

HAYAT: I send the money to my family.

WEINTRAUB: To what?

HAYAT: To my family in the still occupied territories.

WEINTRAUB (*bursting out*): Ah, thank God! To Gaza!

HAYAT: Bethlehem.

ELLEN (*on phone*): What? (*Looks at Weintraub.*) Eliott says I should go now.

Weintraub doesn't listen to Ellen. He is still looking at Hayat, who puts the flowers into the vase.

ELLEN: Eliott says I should go now.

WEINTRAUB (flabbergasted): But Chaiele, you'd be lost without me!

LOUISE: No, no, no, your wife won't be lost. This is a travel with a Führer—äh—in. (Searches embarrassedly for the English word.) A guide!

WEINTRAUB (giving Louise an upset look): But Chaiele. . . .

Through the phone receiver we hear Eliott talking intensely.

LOUISE (incensed): Aber Herr Weintraub, jetzt gönnen Sie ihrer Frau doch mal was! [Mr. Weintraub, allow her some enjoyment for once!]

ELLEN: Eliott says I should find a companion and go. But I don't want to leave you alone.

WEINTRAUB (grumbling): No, no. You go. Have a good time. Just bring me something.

HAYAT: I'm done for the day. Good night.

WEINTRAUB: Another 120 bucks to Gaza. Gut' nacht.

11. Nurses' Coffee Corner – Interior Evening

Hayat's changing into her street clothes. Heidi enters the room and puts something down on the desk. As Hayat slips into her jacket, she notices that Heidi has put down a large ticket featuring the Rhinefalls. Heidi notices Hayat's look.

HEIDI: Wotsch es? [Want it?]

Hayat doesn't answer.

12. Bus – Parking Lot – Interior Day

The bus is cramped. Ellen in full tourist gear. In one hand she holds her newspaper. On her knees is her video camera. To her right there is an empty seat. The bus starts up and is about to leave.

GUIDE: Welcome, ladies and gentlemen, to our exciting trip to the Rhinefalls. . . .

TOURIST with stiff neck (shouting): Wait! Someone's late!

The bus stops again. Ellen notices Hayat running across the parking lot to the bus. Ellen doesn't understand. But then, abruptly, she piles her luggage onto the empty seat beside her. Then she opens her newspaper and hides, just as Hayat climbs onto the bus. As Hayat passes her, she notices Ellen's head behind the paper, which features a photograph of a bombed bus, its headlines saying: Bus bombing: Arab terrorists suspected! *Hayat takes the seat diagonally behind Ellen, across the gangway, and opens up her newspaper. The bus takes off without the women noticing.*

GUIDE: From the Rhinefalls, as you all know, we will take a brief jaunt over the border to the Black Forest, where you will have the chance to select from a vast selection of famous cuckoo clocks. . . .

Ellen peeks over her shoulder at Hayat, who now hides behind her Arabic paper showing the same bombed bus, but with a different headline: Israelis undermining peace process! *Ellen and Hayat's eyes meet. Hayat greets Ellen with a nod.*

GUIDE: The Rhine is born in Switzerland. Near Schaffhausen, it forms. . . .

13. Rhine Falls – Exterior Day

A flock of tourists stands and stares at the waterfalls.

GUIDE: . . . the most important waterfall in Europe. . . .

14. Bus – Interior Day

ZOOM BACK WITH HIGH 8 VIDEO CAMERA: Ellen has not moved from her seat. Instead, she is filming the falls through the bus window.

15. Bus – Interior Day

The bus is driving again. Ellen is filming through the window.

GUIDE: We are now approaching the Black Forest. In order to cross the border, please keep your passports handy.

ELLEN (*lowering her camera*): The border? (*Louder, taps tourist with the stiff neck on the shoulder.*) Which border? (*Louder.*) Which border?

TOURIST WITH THE STIFF NECK: Germany.

Hayat looks up.

ELLEN: I didn't know we were going to cross the border! I don't want to cross the border!

Hayat becomes very nervous herself. Ellen's hands are clinging to the front seat. The other tourists turn their heads and stare. The GUIDE *approaches her.*

ELLEN: Stop the bus! Stop the bus!

GUIDE: What's wrong?

ELLEN: It's enough! I don't want to cross the border! I want to get off!

Ellen starts squeezing herself down the gangway. Hayat observes the scene uneasily.

GUIDE: It's forbidden. Besides that, our tour description very clearly says we are going to the Black Forest which, as we all know, is not part of Switzerland but—

HAYAT: I'm not allowed to cross the border.

15A. Bus – Interior Day

ELLEN (*shouting*): I didn't buy the tickets!

The bus approaches the Swiss-German frontier. The CUSTOMS OFFICER *gives the* BUS DRIVER *a sign. The bus zooms through.*

HAYAT: I don't have papers. I need a visa!

ELLEN (*in a state of panic, speaking over Hayat*): I didn't know!

HAYAT (*looking at Ellen*): Stop the bus!

The bus speeds up and enters a freeway.

GUIDE: I won't. First she *doesn't* want to step off the bus, now suddenly she *does* want to step off the bus. (*To herself.*) Mir sind en organisierti Busreis, Gopferteli! [This is an organized bus trip, for crying out loud!]

HAYAT: Can't you see? Stop the bus.

GUIDE: It's against the law. I'm responsible. . . .

HAYAT (her mind racing): I'm a Palestinian. And I know how to stop a bus.

Shot of the tourist with the stiff neck staring at Hayat, then at the front page of the paper; he hides behind the seat.

16. Freeway – Exterior Day

The bus stops with squealing tires. Ellen and Hayat get off. They are in the middle of nowhere: nothing but cars racing by noisily.

17. Embankment – Exterior Day

Hayat is climbing up a steep embankment followed by Ellen, who refuses Hayat's hand for help. Background noise of a cargo train. Ellen turns around and sees it, then reluctantly follows Hayat.

18. Freeway – Exterior Day

They continue alongside the freeway.

ELLEN: I told Fritzleben I didn't want to come here!

HAYAT: I think if we follow this freeway first and then turn right into the forest we'll avoid the customs.

ELLEN (staring horrified into the forest): The forest? I can't, I can't. . . . Swiss customs. . . . (She loses control and starts sobbing.)

HAYAT (trying to hear what she is saying): What?

ELLEN (sobbing): Deported . . . back to Germany! . . . to the camps. . . .

HAYAT: Look, we cannot cry now.

ELLEN (*sobbing*): I told Fritzleben I wanted to go straight to Israel!

HAYAT (*shouting*): Ah, Israel? That solves all our problems now! (*Pause.*) What business do you have in Palestine?

Hayat walks off. Ellen stops sobbing.

ELLEN (*not sure if she has understood Hayat correctly*): What? (*Shouting.*) I was in Auschwitz . . . do you understand? We have the right!

Hayat stops and approaches her again. The two are now shouting into each other's faces. Cars are howling by in the background.

HAYAT: I don't give a damn about your Holocaust! Another excuse to take away our land!

ELLEN (*showing her arm to Hayat*): What is this, Hollywood?

Hayat looks at it, then walks off again. Ellen is shouting after her.

ELLEN: You just hate Jews! All Arabs hate Jews! You want to kill us all!

HAYAT: Oh yes? That's why I treat your nasty husband, hm?

Hayat approaches Ellen again. In the background we see a field with large bales of straw.

HAYAT: What do you know! Tell me about the Arabs you know so well!

ELLEN: You can't trust them! Everybody knows that! You turn your back on them and they stab you!

HAYAT: All right, let's see! Go ahead! And who killed Rabin? And who killed my brother? And who tortures us. . . .

From the distance we hear the sirens of a police car approaching. The women are too absorbed to pay attention.

ELLEN: And who blows up innocent little children?

HAYAT: Am I a monster?

ELLEN: Am I?

The sirens have come very close and the women now also hear a dog barking. They both look around, terrified.

FEMALE VOICE (*off*): Stehen bleiben, Zoll! [Stay where you are, customs!]

Hayat is slammed up against a customs police car where Ellen stands already, also with her hands up. A GERMAN CUSTOMS POLICEWOMAN *finishes searching Ellen and now starts searching Hayat's pockets. She finds her wallet. As she opens it, papers slip out and fall to the ground at Ellen's feet: a photo of a young Palestinian man in a rebellious pose. Ellen stares. Meanwhile the police woman unfolds a paper she has found in Hayat's pockets.*

CUSTOMS POLICEWOMAN: Ich hab' die Palästinenserin. [I got the Palestinian.]

Ellen suddenly covers the photo with her foot. Now the policewoman turns to Ellen.

CUSTOMS POLICEWOMAN (*southern German accent*): Who is she?

ELLEN: My husband's nurse.

The customs man and woman look at each other, stupefied.

19. Patrol vw – Interior Day

The two women are seated in the back of the car. Behind them, in a cage, two German shepherd dogs are breathing down their necks. Ellen is still clinging to her passport. A long silence.

ELLEN: Fritzleben is not nasty.

HAYAT: Yes he is.

ELLEN: No he's not.

HAYAT: Yes he is!

There is a pause. The policeman is following their argument in the rear view mirror.

ELLEN: He might act now and then a little unpleasantly. But he is not nasty. . . . Sometimes maybe.

HAYAT (*deliberately staring in the other direction out the window*): Teach him better. Once a man treated me like that, so I left him.

ELLEN *(pulling out the photo)*: This man?

Hayat grabs the photo and very carefully puts it back into her purse.

ELLEN: Who is he?

HAYAT: My brother.

Sounds of radio: the policeman picks it up.

POLICEMAN: Was? Also die sind harmlos. Völlig harmlos. Wir bringen sie zurück. Was? Oh, irgendein Familienstreit, oder so. [What? They're completely harmless. We're taking them back. What? Oh, some sort of family argument.]

20. Black Forest Town – Interior Day

We see a tourist shop selling cuckoo clocks. The patrol vw passes by.

21. Patrol vw – Interior Day

Through the window, Ellen has discovered the tourist shop. She looks back and taps on the policeman's shoulder, pointing into the direction of the shop.

ELLEN: Excuse me, would you mind?

22. Hospital Room – Interior Day

Weintraub lies in bed staring at the ceiling, lost in thought. Kurz is happily working on the crossword section of the papers. Heidi enters and starts preparing an injection.

KURZ: Weinreb! Boxer! Berühmter Boxer mit M? [Weinreb, what's a famous boxer starting with an M?]

WEINTRAUB *(to Heidi, administering the shot)*: That's a pretty good drilling job you're doing there! *(Grumpily, to Kurz.)* Okay, met M. [Okay, with an M.] Max . . . *(he thinks)* Mohammed Ali!

Kurz zealously fills in. Weintraub looks at Heidi.

KURZ: Ja, das gooht, Max Schmeling wär' nüd gange. [Yes, that works. Max Schmeling wouldn't have fit.]

WEINTRAUB: Where's Hayat?

HEIDI: Why? Isn't she on the bus with your wife?

Weintraub doesn't understand.

WEINTRAUB: Hayat? With my wife?

Heidi leaves the room.

KURZ: Weinreb. Ägyptischer Politiker, Mit T am Schluss. [Egyptian politician. Ends with T.]

WEINTRAUB: Sadat. —Ich ken net gloibn as zei zennen arois gegangen zusammen. [Sadat. —I can't believe they went off together.]

KURZ: Ich hett mini Frau sowieso nie gah lah. Pack us em Nahe Oschte, sind doch alli gliich, Jude und Araber! Da, Vogel mit B? [I would have never let my wife go. Real scum those Arabs. Not a bit better than the Jews. So, bird with B?]

Weintraub sits up, staring at him.

KURZ: Mit B? (Pause.) He, Weinreb! (Only now looks up.)

WEINTRAUB: My name is Wein-traub. Fritz Wein-traub. Got it? It's not Weingold, Weinstein, or Weinstock. It's Weintraub! And I am a Jew!!

Kurz stares at him without understanding his anger.

WEINTRAUB: A yid!

KURZ (mixed up): Oh, das tuet mir aber leid, Herr Wein—äh. . . . [Oh, I'm terribly sorry, Mr. Wein—ehm. . . .]

WEINTRAUB (shouting): Heidi! Heidi!

HEIDI: Was isch? [What is it?]

WEINTRAUB: Get me out of this room!

HEIDI (Swiss accent): What's wrong with it?

WEINTRAUB (*pointing to Kurz*): This guy is an anti-Semite!

HEIDI (*shutting the door*): Mister Weintraub, I thought it was something important.

23. Patrol VW – Interior Day

Ellen and Hayat are still sitting in the rear of the VW. But now Ellen is proudly holding a cuckoo clock on her lap.

ELLEN: Isn't it great?

HAYAT (*uneasy*): You think Fritzleben will like it?

ELLEN: Why not?

24. Street – Exterior Day

The women look out of the window; they notice at the same time a street sign saying SCHWEIZER ZOLL *(Swiss customs).*

25. Patrol VW – Interior Day

The police car stops at the German customs. The man and the woman get out, and through the windshield we can see them walk up to their colleagues from German customs. Dead silence in the rear of the car. Only the dogs can be heard.

HAYAT: I could lose everything now. My job, my permit.

ELLEN (*looking at her*): Why?

HAYAT: Because I wasn't allowed to exit Switzerland. I'm not allowed to enter again.

ELLEN: Why?

HAYAT (*aggravated*): Because I have no passport. . . .

Now Ellen pulls out her passport.

HAYAT: What's your problem?

ELLEN (still looking very distressed): Don't you understand? I was here before and they sent me back.

26. German Customs – Exterior Day

The man and the woman open the door of the vw. Ellen and Hayat get out, yet both remain completely paralyzed.

HAYAT: Let's go.

Hayat takes Ellen's arm. Together they walk toward the German custom inspector's booth. The two officers look at them curiously. In silence they approach the Swiss customs booth.

27. Swiss Customs Booth – Exterior Day

A car slows down, and through the window a hand holds out the Swiss passport: red with a white cross. THE SWISS CUSTOMS OFFICER waves it through.

SWISS CUSTOMS OFFICER: Jawohl, isch guet! Danke. [Yes indeed, fine, thanks.]

In the background the two women approach.

28. Swiss Customs Booth – Interior Day

A mirror allows the officer to control the traffic from Germany. In the same booth, his COLLEAGUE eats a sandwich. The customs officer sees Hayat and Ellen approaching. He stands up.

29. Swiss Customs Booth – Exterior Day

They have reached the booth. Ellen pulls her passport out and waves it at the booth.

SWISS CUSTOMS OFFICER (off): Danke, jawohl. (Pause.) Ja und s'Fräulein? [Thanks, yes indeed. And the young lady?]

The customs officer steps out of the booth.

HAYAT: Oh no.

They freeze. Ellen gathers herself. Covertly, she hands over her passport to Hayat, who now turns around and sticks it in the air. The customs officer walks back into the booth. We hear him laugh.

30. Swiss Customs – Exterior Day

Hayat and Ellen have reached Switzerland. They exhale and stand for a moment in silence. Suddenly, Ellen rids herself of her bag and video camera and hands them over to Hayat. Then Ellen runs off back across the Swiss and German borders, past the officers looking at her, scratching their heads. Then they swing over to Hayat: she's dealing with Ellen's luggage and discovers that the camera is still running. She's pointing the camera toward Ellen.

31. Hospital Curb – Exterior Night

Hayat and Ellen get out of the car. (The taxi drives off.) Ellen walks straight up to a yellow garbage bin and dumps in the cuckoo clock. Hayat looks at her questioningly.

ELLEN (upset): Okay, okay! It's ugly!

Hayat looks at her. Both smile exhaustedly.

HAYAT: Good night, Mrs. Weintraub. (She walks off.)

ELLEN: Good night. (She looks after her.) See you tomorrow!

32. Hospital Room – Interior Night

The door flies open. Ellen enters the room and goes to Weintraub. Weintraub is sitting on his bed in his underwear, awkwardly trying to get into his socks.

ELLEN: Fritzleben! I'm back!

Ellen swings the camera onto his lap. Kurz sits up in his bed.

WEINTRAUB (*grumpily*): I'm checking myself out! My wife leaves me behind with an anti-Semite. And not only does she go off with a Palestinian, but she takes away my nurse!

Ellen looks questioningly at Kurz, who turns his head away.

ELLEN (*a little bit guiltily*): Come, Fritzleben. It's late, we can check out tomorrow.

Then she tenderly helps him move back into his bed and puts the video camera on his lap.

ELLEN: Don't you wanna see the pictures I took in Switzerland?

She presses the play button.

Cut to high 8: Weird shots of feet, wheels, etc., with the voices of two women shouting at one another. In the background heavy car noise.

ELLEN (*off*): I told Fritzleben I didn't want to come here.

ELLEN: Oh, no, not this— Later!

She presses the fast forward button and releases it.

HAYAT (*off*): What business do you have in Palestine!

Weintraub is confused, but Ellen presses the button again. Now Weintraub's attention is caught by what he sees on the screen:

Cut to high 8: Ellen in the distance under the sign 'DEUTSCHLAND' where she turns around and runs back toward the camera in Switzerland. Coming closer, she notices Hayat filming her. She waves into the camera.

ELLEN: Fritzleben! Look!

She turns back to 'DEUTSCHLAND' where she turns again, running toward HAYAT, waving into the camera. The camera wipes over the CUSTOM OFFICERS scratching their heads. Ellen runs into an extreme close-up of the camera and stands still, breathing heavily.

ELLEN: I did it. I did it!

WEINTRAUB (*smiling as he watches Ellen's footage*): Chaiele, you did it!

Weintraub reaches out to Ellen. They embrace happily. Ellen looks very happy and proud of herself. Then Weintraub turns back to the camera. Ellen is still laughing into the camera triumphantly. Then she thinks for a moment, and raises her eyeline above the camera. Her eyes meet there with Hayat's.

ELLEN: We did it.

We see Ellen's arm reaching for the camera, which now swings around and frames Hayat and Ellen in an extreme close-up. Hayat and Ellen smile.

Weintraub stares at this image. Then he presses the rewind button.

33. Hospital Room – Interior Day

Ellen is packing up Weintraub's stuff. Weintraub sits on his bed half dressed with the camera on his lap. He looks distressed.

HAYAT (off): . . . that's why I treat your nasty husband? (Rewind.) . . . your nasty husband?

HEIDI (sticking in her head): So, sind sie immer nonig parat! [So, you're still not ready!]

WEINTRAUB (turning around): Where's Hayat? I gotta talk to her!

HEIDI: It's her day off.

34. Hospital Curb – Exterior Day

The stuffed trunk of a cab. Ellen stands with the DRIVER in front of the trunk. Weintraub approaches, hears ticking, hesitates.

ELLEN (to driver): No, no. This won't fit. Turn it around. Thank you.

WEINTRAUB: Wait, I can hear ticking!

ELLEN (off): Get in! (Pause.) It can't be!

WEINTRAUB: I'm telling you!

Weintraub takes some steps in the direction of the garbage can. The driver looks as if he feels sorry for Ellen.

DRIVER (to Ellen): Does your husband have a hearing problem?

ELLEN (insulted): My husband can hear perfectly fine, thank you!

A JANITOR who's been spraying the hospital roses follows their conversation.

WEINTRAUB (off): Chaiele, are you deaf?!

ELLEN: Get in the car!

Ellen slams the door. Weintraub reluctantly follows her. The taxi pulls off. The janitor now approaches the garbage can. He hears ticking.

35. Taxi/Street with Hospital Curb – Interior Day

The Weintraubs in the moving taxi. Fritzleben is thinking hard. Sirens of a police car. The taxi lets it pass. Ellen turns her head and looks after it.

36. Hospital Curb – Exterior Day

The janitor and a SECURITY MAN. They are listening carefully. Close up of a garbage bin. A SECOND SECURITY MAN joins them. Distinct ticking can be heard.

37. Taxi/Some Street – Interior Day

WEINTRAUB (still thinking hard): Ah, I'm not nasty. (Silence.) Do you think I'm nasty?

Weintraub would like to wipe away this thought. He makes a gesture with his hand.

WEINTRAUB: I think she liked me.

It seems very important that this thought be true.

38. Hospital Curb – Exterior Day

High security around the garbage can. A MAN in special gear approaches the garbage can. We hear ticking. Just as the man wants to reach into the can the cuckoo sticks his head out, announcing two o'clock.

Acknowledgments

All translations are by Rafaël Newman unless otherwise specified.

Daniel Ganzfried, excerpts from *Der Absender* (Zurich: Rotpunktverlag, 1995). Used by permission of the author.

Rose Choron, 'Swiss Transit,' reprinted from *Family Stories: Travels beyond the Shtetel* (Malibu CA: Pangloss Press, 1988). Used by permission of the author.

Jean-Luc Benoziglio, excerpt from *Le Feu au lac* (Paris: Editions du Seuil, 1998). Copyright © Editions du Seuil, 1998.

Yvonne Léger, excerpts from *Eljascha* (Zurich: Pendo Verlag, 1990). Used by permission of the author.

Charles Lewinsky, excerpts from *Hitler auf dem Rütli* (Zurich: Unionsverlag, 1984). Used by permission of the publisher. Translation of the line quoted from Schiller's *Wilhelm Tell* by William F. Wertz, Jr.

Roman Buxbaum, 'Träume,' from *Blei* (Oberehrendingen and Ostrava: Ostravské tiskárny, 1999). Used by permission of the author.

Marta Rubinstein, 'Der Schneider,' from *Der Schneider Vier Erzählungen* (Zurich: edition eden, 1990). Used by permission of the author.

Luc Bondy, 'Elsa *oder* Wo war ich?' from *Wo war ich?* (Zurich: Ammann Verlag, 1998). Copyright © 1998 by Ammann Verlag, Zurich, Switzerland.

Gabriele Markus, selected poems from *Unverzichtbar* (Zurich: Pendo Verlag, 1986) and *Ohr am Boden* (Frauenfeld: Verlag im Waldgut, 1997). Used by permission of the author.

Sylviane Roche, excerpts from *Le Temps des cerises* (Orbe: Bernard Campiche, 1998). Used by permission of Bernard Campiche Editeur.

Sergueï Hazanov, excerpts from *Lettres russes* (Vevey: Editions de l'Aire, 1997). Used by permission of the author.

Amsel, 'In the Tower.' Used by permission of the author. Translation of the line from the Brothers' Grimm 'Rumpelstilzchen' by Robert Godwin-Jones.

Shelley Kästner, 'Antisemitismus oder die Lust, gemein zu sein' (1997). Used by permission of the author.

Michael Guggenheimer, 'Adler,' from Personal (St. Gallen: Typotron, 1999). Used by permission of the author.

Regine Mehmann Schafer, 'Trefe und Kascher' (1998). Used by permission of the author.

Marianne Weissberg, excerpt from 'Männerjagd, oder Lili und die Schmocks.' Used by permission of the author.

Miriam Cahn, 'WAS MICH ANSCHAUT,' from du: Die Zeitschrift der Kultur, no. 9 (September 1998); originally published as 'Guernica, Sarajevo.' Used by permission of the author.

Stina Werenfels, Pastry, Pain & Politics (1998); screenplay of the film of the same name. Used by permission of the author.